RETURN TO ODESSA

by

HAROLD N. WIENS

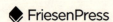 FriesenPress

Suite 300 - 990 Fort St
Victoria, BC, V8V 3K2
Canada

www.friesenpress.com

ISBN
978-1-4602-8252-6 (Hardcover)
978-1-4602-8253-3 (Paperback)
978-1-4602-8254-0 (eBook)

1. HISTORY, CANADA, POST-CONFEDERATION (1867 TO PRESENT)

Distributed to the trade by The Ingram Book Company

To Diana, my love, who encouraged me to persevere with this project
and patiently listened to book sections read over, and over, and over.

To my daughter Juliana and my son and daughter-in-law
Michael and Brooke, who offered advice and support.

To Braxton and Alexa, my darling grandchildren, who will receive their
inheritance once they have read this book in its entirety at least once.

Table of Contents

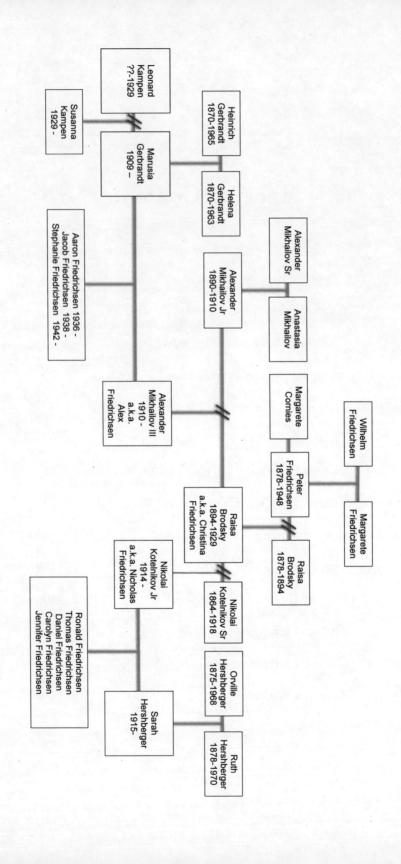

Chapter 1
Harwood – 1965

THE SUN'S RAYS WERE BEGINNING TO PIERCE THROUGH THE DENSE atmosphere of the late afternoon sky, clearing away the incessant rain that seemed to have gone on forever. Had the earth slipped off its axis? Did the torrential rains of the last few weeks indicate a shift in weather patterns? Or, were the dire warnings by television preachers predicting an imminent end to the world coming true? These were thoughts that flashed through the minds of the mourners who plodded along through the saturated Manitoba gumbo, away from the comforts of the Harwood Mennonite Church and toward the desolation of the adjacent cemetery. This is where life, at least the earthly part, came to an end. This is where the journey of Heinrich Gerbrandt reached its conclusion, and this is where his body of ninety-five years would be laid to rest.

The condition of the poorly maintained pathway that led from the church to the gravesite added to the grief of the bereaved congregants. Wet mucky clay clung to their feet as they slogged along across slippery, partially concealed rocks, while thick clumps of freshly mown wet grass soaked their feet. But the pallbearers bearing the body of Reverend Gerbrandt from the hearse to the grave, faced an even greater challenge. Their task, to maintain secure footing over the slick and uneven terrain while carrying the heavy oak casket was both concerning and daunting.

Once the last of the mourners had arrived at the freshly dug grave and crowded in under a hastily-erected shelter, they heard the young preacher raise his voice and read from the Gospel of John:

Let not your heart be troubled: ye believe in God, believe also in me. In my Father's house are many mansions: if it were not so, I would have told you. I go to prepare a place for you. And if I go and prepare a place for you, I will come again, and receive you unto myself; that where I am, there ye may be also.

The poignant message of this rarely heard passage stood out to the older generation now confronted by the reality of their own impending end. The young people, whose lives were still largely before them and who would no doubt live forever, heard only words. Following the reading of scripture, the preacher offered a short prayer petitioning the Creator to accept the soul of the old man into His care and provide comfort to those who mourned. As the people sang the hymn, "It is well with my soul," the body of the old patriarch was gently lowered into the earth to rest once again beside his recently departed wife. Then the people committed the old man to the grave and followed the same muddy route back to the church.

***

The death of Heinrich Gerbrandt was deeply felt by the people of Harwood, the town where he had lived. They venerated this old saint and feared they would miss his influence upon their community. No one should have been surprised at his passing, but is anyone ever prepared for the death of an esteemed leader? On the day of his funeral, they showed their deep respect by closing their businesses and interrupting their daily activities, ignoring, at least for an afternoon, the work ethic that had made them prosperous.

Harwood was home to ambitious people who embraced hard work as a way of life. They prided themselves on the "Progressive, Forward-looking Community" they had built. At least this is what the town council had boldly painted onto the welcome signs that greeted visitors who entered the village. The sight of paved roads, new houses, and prosperous businesses with huge signs advertising fertilizer, farm equipment, and new machinery confidently backed up this claim. Harwood was a town clearly on the move, at least economically.

The condition of the cemetery, however, suggested something quite different. These same visitors, who would see Harwood as a progressive forward-looking community, would also notice that the local people spent little time looking back. Tall grass and unruly weeds grew between the gravestones, and the fence enclosing the churchyard needed a coat of paint. The bushes and trees that once surrounded the place had been cut down to allow farm machinery to plant crops as close to the fence as possible. Consequently, the biting wind that greeted the mourners encountered little resistance from the surrounding landscape as it howled through the churchyard unimpeded. Chilled to the bone, the grieving congregants drew coats, sweaters, and hoods tightly against their bodies and wondered aloud why nature had so little warmth to offer. Was this not the beginning rather than the end of autumn? Why did it feel so cold? Was this not September rather than the end of November?

Perhaps nostalgia had clouded their memories, or perhaps the people had forgotten the cycle of contrasting seasons that descend upon the prairies each year. Did they need to be reminded that summer was fading and autumn, as the prelude to winter, was merely the dress rehearsal for the severe cold that would soon settle in upon them? Perhaps the cruel wind had been sent to remind them that their world would soon be frozen solid and they had better savour the last few days of warmth. Why did it take prairie people all summer to fully appreciate the season's last few beautiful days?

And yet, the calendar clearly stated the opposite. It was the harvest season – the most rewarding time of year for those who lived on the land. Farmers had impatiently kicked the tires of their combines for several weeks and checked the fields each day to see if the grain was turning colour. Families, anxious to beat the frost, were picking ripe vegetables from their gardens, covering tomatoes on chilly nights, and separating forkfuls of potatoes and other root vegetables from the rich earth. Everyone, especially children, savoured the smells that emanated from steaming farmhouse kitchens as fruits and vegetables were preserved, jams and jellies cooked, and beets, cucumbers, and watermelon slices pickled and stored for winter. Mothers secretly looked forward to a few hours of quiet as children sent off to school no longer required make-work projects to keep them out of trouble.

Autumn was also the season to appreciate nature's wonderful array of beauty before winter turned everything white. Flowers that had survived the early frost were much more brilliant, or so it seemed, and who could deny the splendour of leaves that now displayed every shade of colour from bright yellow to deep orange. The Canada geese added a whisper of sadness to this autumn spectacle as they congregated along swollen streams, rehearsed short practice flights, and then, as they had done for thousands of years, flew south along ancient migratory routes. Their flight, in amazing configurations of V's, enhanced nature's awe-inspiring beauty.

This year, however, the autumn season had lost its lustre. Heavy rains had robbed the summer of much of its heat. Early frost had stripped the flowers of their beauty, and the harsh, cold winds had prematurely blown the colourful leaves off the trees. Farmers were anxious to harvest what little they could find. Days of drizzle had blocked the warm sunshine, so vital for maturing crops, and had weighted down the immature grain stocks, forcing them to buckle under the burden of excessive moisture. The strong prairie winds that followed pushed the grain heads into the mud. Not only Harwood, but also other large parts of the Manitoba grain belt lay under water. Creeks had turned into rivers, fields into swamps, the large swathers and combines sat idle, and the geese were long gone.

The few recent days of sunshine had lifted the people's spirits, but even a funeral, sad as it was, provided only temporary relief from the intense worry faced by farmers, especially those who were mortgaged to the hilt. Surely the sky would cloud over in sympathy with those who grieved the death of the old patriarch, but ironically, just the opposite was true. The clearing sky was revealing yet another of nature's many twists.

***

The distance from the church to the cemetery, where the body of Heinrich Gerbrandt was carried, was only a few hundred yards, but the rain that turned the rich black dirt into mud had slowed the procession of mourners to a laborious, exhausting crawl. From many a footstep, one heard the sucking sound of a boot being pulled from the mire. One young mourner compared this to the sound made by cows hooves when forced to plod through thick, wet manure once the muck around the barn door got too deep.

The worn tires of the old Cadillac hearse that bore the coffin from the church to the cemetery squished and slid both forwards and sideways. Behind the hearse, two stylish vehicles transported the family of the old man. The first was an early version of a Hummer, an impressive vehicle, capable of clawing its way through any muddy surface Harwood had to offer. The second, a European suv of some sort, probably imported from Germany or Sweden and every bit as pretentious as the first, was equally indifferent to Manitoba mud. The luxurious vehicles clearly upstaged the old Cadillac as they boldly asserted the fact that the family members who rode inside were people of means. Years of hard work and a generous measure of good fortune had established their economic position and allowed them to crawl out from under the burden of their humble beginnings. They, at least in their own minds, had crossed the social divide from poverty to affluence and now deserved as much status as that of any other citizen of the area.

Not only were the members of the extended Gerbrandt family rich, they were also healthy and in reasonably good physical shape. All could afford decent boots to keep their feet clean and dry, and all were capable of trudging through mud along with the other mourners. Yet, they preferred the comforts of riding in luxurious vehicles. They were not attempting to pull rank on their friends and neighbours – at least not this time. And in their defence, the old hearse with its bald tires could easily have become stuck in mud, and the expensive vehicles with their four-wheel drive transmissions and two hundred dollar tires would be there to pull the hearse back to solid ground, or so the young boys reasoned. Some people wondered aloud why young Aaron Friedrichsen, the grandson who owned everything, could not have dug a little deeper into his bank account and laid the asphalt a bit closer to the cemetery. Now he would never get all the mud out from under the fenders of his expensive Hummer.

The family grieved deeply, especially the grandchildren. They had little experience with death and even less with the passing of an immediate family member, let alone a beloved grandfather. In their minds, *Opa* Gerbrandt had been with them forever. He and his wife Helena had lived in this area since coming to Canada in 1929, settling in Harwood, Manitoba, a tiny prairie town forty miles northwest of Brandon. Their recently widowed daughter Marusia, and her six-month-old baby, Suzanna, had travelled with them from Russia. Marusia had lost her husband, Leonard Kampen, to typhus a few months after their marriage, leaving her pregnant and penniless. Her older sister and husband, Elizabeth and Peter Suderman, had arrived in Canada a year earlier and had established a life for themselves in Winnipeg. Other members of the Gerbrandt family, however, had been scattered by the events of the Russian Revolution and the First World War, and all contact with them had been lost.

Heinrich Gerbrandt had died in the local nursing home where he lived alone since losing his wife Helena in 1963. Although old age and ill health robbed him of his sharp wit and clear mind, his physical presence, even in a weakened state, still provided strength and stability to many. What a shock to the family members when early morning telephone calls confirmed the dreaded news that their father and grandfather had passed away during the night. Only now, as they carried him to his final resting place, were they coming to terms with the fact that he, one of the last of his generation, was gone and that with him, an era had passed.

Everyone remembered Reverend Gerbrandt as a strong, kind and gentle man – someone who throughout his life had been a loving parent to his daughters, their husbands and their children. He gave sensible leadership to the Harwood Mennonite community that was continually threatening to divide itself over silly issues or minor religious differences, but all too frequently, disagreements based on power and status as determined by houses, cars, machinery, and especially land.

Heinrich Gerbrandt was a learned man and a good theologian, mainly self-taught, yet also a practically-minded and sensitive pastor. His leadership provided the necessary cohesion to keep various generational interests "singing off the same page," as his son-in-law Alex Friedrichsen liked to say. His sermons found the balance between head and heart, mind and emotion, and he always succeeded in saying something worthwhile.

Unfortunately, the planning for Heinrich Gerbrandt's funeral was anything but an indication of the good sense he had so admirably demonstrated. The service threatened to become a somewhat chaotic affair, eclectic at best, hastily pieced together with elements from various worship styles and practices all competing for relevance and a little more elbow room. Someone needed to step up, take leadership, and demonstrate the qualities that Heinrich had so capably shown. Old Reverend Gerbrandt, now lying in the coffin, should have officiated at his own funeral. He would have restored peace and order to the surrounding confusion. He had preached many a sermon at funerals and memorial services, always finding the right words to bring comfort to the mourners in an atmosphere of dignity and decorum. But now, he was gone.

"It's only natural," declared Alex Friedrichsen, "that a funeral service worthy of Heinrich Gerbrandt should be conducted by Wilhelm Bergman." Wilhelm, or Will, or Willy, as Alex and his brother Nicholas called him, was a local farmer and close friend of the family. Willy had attended Bible College and had been mentored by Heinrich in pastoral responsibilities. He was very capable of leading a meaningful and dignified service. As far as Alex was concerned, Willy should have been the heir apparent to succeed Heinrich Gerbrandt as leader of the congregation, but this was an opinion he had learned to suppress and keep to himself.

Marusia, Alex's wife and Heinrich's youngest daughter, was of a different mindset. She had immediately vetoed her husband's suggestion. "It's only right," she stated, "that young Pastor Randy should be asked to conduct my father's funeral service."

Pastor Randy – he had a last name but no one ever used it – had recently arrived in Harwood as the newly-installed lead pastor of the Harwood Mennonite Church. He was still finding his way among the parishioners, the sheep that were threatening to scatter. According to some quiet murmuring, he needed to gain the respect and understanding of the older congregants. Perhaps by asking Pastor Randy to conduct her father's funeral service, Marusia, as member of the church pastoral search committee, could reaffirm the decision to call Randy "Whatshisname" as pastor, and thereby soften the negative comments made by her husband and several of his close friends regarding this decision.

"Pastor Randy is a sincere and intelligent person," she emphatically stated, "with no one to mentor him."

"Or perhaps no one good enough to mentor him," Alex would interject.

"He is trying to make his way as best he can," Marusia affirmed.

With the ink on Pastor Randy's seminary degree barely dry, this prophet of the future blew in with an abundance of suggestions for change. He knew exactly what was needed in Harwood and what was wrong with the Mennonite church, and he intended to inject life into this old fossil. He started with worship, "upbeat worship" as he liked to say, along with upbeat music, and the introduction of lively, more popular worship styles that he thought would attract younger people. He hoped to knock the stuffiness out of the church and lead the congregation in worshiping God as He hoped to be worshipped: with optimism, exuberance, and joy. And, according to the Bergman brothers, "Tinged with a little phoniness and loudness in the extreme."

Under Pastor Randy's leadership, the Harwood Mennonite Church was clearly charting new territory, especially with a more modern approach to liturgy or "unliturgy" as some claimed. Johnny Bergman, Willy's brother and another close friend of the family, claimed that quiet reflective worship must have been taught at seminary on the day that Pastor Randy had cut class. Apparently the wax from Johnny's ears, along with respect for Pastor Randy's methods, was blown away by all the amplified music. This kind of talk made Marusia very angry.

At some level, Pastor Randy was probably relieved that old Heinrich Gerbrandt was gone, for now he could freely implement his ideas and methods. This was clearly shown in his plans for Heinrich's funeral. During the service, Pastor Randy read the appropriate scripture passages and offered a short homily based on 1 Thessalonians, Chapter 4:

> *For since we believe that Jesus died and rose again, even so, through Jesus, God will bring with him those who have fallen asleep ... For the Lord himself will descend from heaven with a cry of command, with the voice of an archangel, and with the sound of the trumpet of God. And the dead in Christ will rise first. Then we who are alive, who are left, will be caught up together with them in the clouds to meet the Lord in the air, and so we will always be with the Lord.*

In his most officious voice, Pastor Randy extolled the joys of heaven in contrast to the pain and suffering Heinrich Gerbrandt had experienced here on earth.

Pain and suffering, thought Johnny Bergman. *He would have starved to death had his son-in-law, Alex, not been such a good farmer.*

The pastor's young wife, a singer-songwriter of Christian music, sang her recent composition entitled, "He Has Made Me Forever Glad," during which Julie Friedrichsen rocked back and forth from one foot to the other with her arms raised heavenward. Her arms would have honoured her husband's grandfather's memory even more had she been able to raise them higher, but the constraints of the high hemline on her new dress prevented her from fully expressing the worshipful feelings she carried in her heart. The old quartet of Alex and Nicholas Friedrichsen, along with Johnny and Willy Bergman, sang, "*Ich weiss einen Strom,*" followed by a set of worship music performed by a newly-formed praise band accompanied by amplified guitars, amplified drums, and amplified microphones. Before the service began, young Pastor Randy asked the quartet if they cared to join the praise band for the final number to which they, in perfect unison, emphatically said, "No."

Actually, Alex Friedrichsen was heard to utter the words, "Hell, no," to his friends in the quartet. This was only the third time that Nicholas had ever heard his older brother swear in church. The first time occurred during a biting November wind when Alex whacked his thumb with the hammer while nailing loose shingles to the church roof. His second inappropriate utterance slipped out during the wedding ceremony of his son, Aaron, as bride and daughter-in-law, Julie, promised to love, honour, and obey in her marriage vows. Actually, those were not really swear words spoken on that occasion, and his utterance of "bullshit" never fully came out, as it was rudely interrupted by a blow to his rib cage from his wife's exquisitely covered left elbow.

As expected, the funeral service was full. The young men sported jackets and shirts with ties while the girls all wore dresses or skirts. Someone suggested that people had dressed for the occasion out of respect to old Reverend Gerbrandt. "It is good that God is not dead," quipped Wilhelm Bergman. "Otherwise, they would have to dress this way every Sunday."

The first vehicle behind the hearse carried Alex and Marusia Friedrichsen, or Maria, as her friends called her. Stephanie, their youngest daughter who had come home from New York to see *Opa* one last time, rode with them. Earlier that week, when she arrived at the terminal of the Brandon airport, she was greeted by the dreaded news that he had died during the night. *Opa* had never understood why his youngest grandchild, his sweet little Stephie, had to go to New York to study voice, and why it was important for her to become an opera singer, a profession about which he knew nothing. But he supported her dream. He was deeply moved by her singing and would weep profusely whenever she sang an old German hymn, even though her diction had been cleansed of all Russian Mennonite dialect. Also riding in the first vehicle were Elizabeth and Peter Suderman of Winnipeg, Rev. Gerbrandt's eldest daughter and son-in-law. Their children, Robert and Helena, had also travelled a long way to be at the funeral and now shared the very back seat of the vehicle with Cousin Stephanie.

The last vehicle in the funeral procession was a new, fully-loaded, European-built SUV owned and operated by grandson Aaron Frederickson, who also owned the John Deere dealership, the GM dealership, and most of the good farmland in and around Harwood. Aaron, the wealthiest man in the area, simply could not hide the evidence of success that followed him, nor did he try very hard, according to several local critics who experienced the occasional pang of jealousy toward him whenever he drove by in a new car. Actually, Aaron was a decent young man, very kind and very generous, who could not escape the fact that every venture of his would make him a little more money.

His young wife Julie, however, was much more adept at dealing with her husband's wealth. She knew exactly how and where to spend money to prop up the family image of success even though it really didn't need propping up. She wore designer dresses, Italian shoes, and make-up that cost a small fortune. She flew to New York to shop at Macy's and even Saks Fifth Avenue, while looking in on her young sister-in-law Stephanie, a student at Julliard. Her active social calendar hadn't yet allowed her to find a suitable time to have babies.

Julie exacted very high standards upon those around her. She understood what personal qualities were required to cultivate high society and took it upon herself to help mold the farm families of Harwood into socially acceptable citizens. She spent time volunteering for recognizable charities and doled out Friedrichsen wealth to causes that would make her look good. Her husband, Aaron, had a business degree from somewhere and certainly put into practice all the principles of acquiring wealth he had learned at university.

Susanna, Marusia's eldest child, and her husband, Dr. George Miller, occupied the middle seat of the SUV. In the back seat sat Jacob, Aaron's younger brother, all alone. Jacob's name was actually James or Jimmie to his friends, but he took on the name Jacob to honour some distant relative, and quite possibly to woo the Jewish vote. Jacob was a rising star in the political world. He was smart, articulate, and possessed a drive he had inherited from his father, Alex Friedrichsen. He played up the fact that his surname was Scandinavian, even though this connection to this ancestry could be debated, and depending upon where he spoke, he would make reference to the fact that his given name was Jewish. This was true. Actually, his maternal grandmother was Jewish, and the fact that his paternal great-grandfather was a pre-Bolshevik Russian industrialist was also true. Nor did he ever try to clarify the rumour that his maternal great-grandmother was a Russian aristocrat who could trace her family lineage to the last czar.

Jacob was perfectly suited to a life in politics. He could be Russian to the Russians, German to the Germans, and Jewish to the Jews. The fact that Jacob could speak a little Russian, Ukrainian, German, and some French, helped to back up these claims. He constantly tossed Yiddish words and Mennonite Low German phrases into his speech, even if at times he confused the two. Some who knew him accused him of insincerity and claimed that his character traits mirrored those of another Jacob, the one in the Old Testament with whom he shared, at least in part, a common ancestry.

Behind Jacob's back, they called him "tricky Jimmie," and claimed that his favorite colour was plaid. In reality, he was well suited to run for the Liberal Party as most of his political views were somewhat left of centre, yet because of his youth, those views were not completely calcified. Many of his sharpest critics were prairie rednecks who were angry over the fact that their opinions did not carry as much weight as his. His older brother, Aaron, saw to it that Jacob, at the very least, paid lip service to the principles of free enterprise.

Jacob had been chosen to deliver the eulogy at his grandfather's funeral. The tears he shed amidst several emotional interruptions were real. He loved *Opa*, admired him greatly, and tried to follow in the footsteps of faith that *Opa* had modeled for him. Many of his convictions were still being formed, but he took his Christian faith seriously and his membership in the Harwood Mennonite Church with its many Liberal voters was not to be trifled with, according to his critics.

Following the committal service, all three vehicles backed out of the mud without difficulty and transported the occupants onto the newly-paved asphalt parking lot donated by Friedrichsen Enterprises. From here, the family walked comfortably into the church basement for a short reception. Susanna, or Susie, grieved deeply as she held Marusia's arm and reassured her mother that she was not alone. Marusia Friedrichsen, on the other hand, was quite philosophical about her father's death. She had lost her mother several years earlier and felt some relief that Mother and Father were now together, no longer suffering the indignities of old age and senility in the local nursing home. She and her sister Elizabeth were now the older generation, but she had not yet fully comprehended the implications of this generational shift. Susie and her mother were very close. Susie was pregnant, but this welcomed joy was tempered by the fact that she and her husband would soon be returning to their home in Toronto and this was simply too far away for both her and her mother.

Marusia's other daughter, Stephanie, had totally run out of tears as she clung to her mother's other arm. She would have gladly sung for *Opa* anytime and anywhere, but at his funeral she could not even squeeze out a thin white sound. Someone had suggested that in *Opa's* memory, they play a tape recording of Stephanie's singing at the service, but the only recording Stephanie had on hand and would allow to be heard in public was her performance of the second "Queen of the Night" aria from Mozart's *Magic Flute* where the character threatens the revenge of hell upon a disobedient daughter unless she stabs to death her mother's enemy – hardly the stuff for *Opa's* funeral, and certainly not appropriate for a service in a Mennonite church. Stephanie's other hot recording was the aria, "Glitter and be Gay," from Bernstein's *Candide*. This aria would certainly have been appropriate for celebrating sister-in-law Julie's life, but Julie was alive and well and was heard railing against the fact that her new Gucci boots had mud on them, blaming her husband Aaron for driving so stupidly. So, it was decided that this recording of Stephanie's singing should also not be played on this occasion.

Marusia felt alone. Her parents were gone. Her eldest daughter, Susanna, would be returning to her home in Toronto. Jacob, her younger son, had hopes to win the seat in the local riding during the next federal election and then he would move to Ottawa, probably forever. Always the politician, he shook the hand of every mourner of voting age and even addressed the undertaker's assistant in every language he knew before finally realizing that the unresponsive lad was deaf. Stephanie was determined to sing opera, preferably in Europe, and Aaron, although very rich and very much a Harwood resident, was married to Julie, who just might put her aging parents-in-law into a nursing home should they begin to show signs of vulnerability.

Alex, Marusia's husband, was aware of his wife's concerns and shared her anxieties. Before the reception had drawn to a close, he accompanied his brother Nicholas out of the church, away from the clanging of dishes and bumping of chairs, across the newly-paved parking lot they had donated, towards a park bench located at the farthest corner of the churchyard.

This old, familiar bench, alone and forgotten, was a metaphor for Alex's feelings on this day. Like him, the bench had arrived in Harwood quite by accident, young and strong. It had mistakenly been unloaded off a truck that was delivering building materials to the church site during the major renovation of 1936. New at that time and unpainted, the bench was probably destined to become a centrepiece for an upscale schoolyard or community park in a neighbouring town. No one knew who owned the bench, and as the church people were basically honest folk, they decided to leave it near the road, hopefully to be seen and claimed by its rightful owner. But no one ever came, and each year the bench was moved farther back from the road until it became the honoured centrepiece of the church's modest front yard landscaping scheme.

Over time, the harsh Manitoba climate had taken the life out of the bench, and before long, the unpainted wood became weather-beaten, warped, and cracked beyond repair. Each year, as more flowers claimed space near the front of the church, and especially once the new rock garden had been created, the bench was deemed expendable and was moved to the farthest corner of the yard awaiting its final disposal. The ultimate indignity occurred one Halloween night when several local boys sprayed it with purple paint and defaced the once elegantly shaped boards with crookedly carved pink hearts filled with arrows and initials. Like Alex, the bench that had once been new, strong, and valued by the local people, now faced an uncertain future.

Through the years, this old bench became the community earpiece. It had eavesdropped upon many conversations ranging from marriage proposals – some accepted, some not – to counselling sessions for self-righteous Sunday School teachers and disobedient youths to exchange their views on "acting in a Christian way." Now it was about to hear Alexander Friedrichsen spill his innermost thoughts and anxieties to his brother Nicholas.

"Do you realize how many years have gone by since we first arrived in Harwood? Where has the time gone?"

Nicholas remained quiet waiting for his brother to reload.

Alex continued, "Neither of us intended to stay, yet somehow we never got around to leaving."

Nicholas offered an understanding nod.

"Do you ever think back to those first few nights when we slept in Gerbrandt's barn, when we had nothing to eat and desperately wanted to return to Russia?" Alex asked.

"I didn't know you ever wanted to go back," interrupted Nicholas.

"You were just a kid. I had to put up a strong front for you."

Of course Nicholas remembered. "And how old were you?" he interjected. But he sensed that Alex was winding up for one of his emotional monologues, so he decided to keep quiet and let his brother get it all out.

"We were younger then, not smart enough to be concerned. Yet, not even Isbrand Riessen could get to us."

"We were looked after," Nicholas said.

"I know, I know! This bench looks like me," confessed Alex as he started up again. "I was once young, strong and respected…"

The cracks in the bench's frame and splinters in the wood mirrored the emotional aches and pains the Friedrichsen brothers had experienced throughout their lives. These adversities were undeniably revealed in the deep lines that many years of living had carved into their faces. Nicholas clearly saw that the death of old Heinrich had hit Alex harder than he cared to admit. Perhaps, for the first time in his life, Alex, Heinrich's son-in-law, had stopped to search inside himself for something he was not sure of finding. In his life, Alex had managed his emotions through busyness and driving ambition, fearing the unknown consequences that might overwhelm him should his deepest anxieties and insecurities ever see the light of day. If he once slowed down, he might have to face the wounds he and Nicholas had encountered during their stolen childhood, and possibly deal with the pain that their late mother, who was barely sixteen years old when Alex was born, had been forced to endure. These were issues that simmered below the surface of his consciousness, and issues he instinctively avoided.

From Nicholas's perspective, Alex was having another of the many self-doubting moments that had dogged him his entire life. In baseball terms, Alex was always behind in the count. He was the batter who went to the plate with two strikes against him. Nicholas understood such feelings all too well. He, too, had survived a painful childhood, and also continued to deal with feelings of insecurity and worst of all, these feelings could turn to moments of deep, dark depression. There were also paths in his past along which he was afraid to walk.

The bench had been kinder to Nicholas and today it helped lighten his mood. He was able to see things from a more realistic perspective. This is the place where his wife Sarah had accepted his marriage proposal, and where on several occasions Heinrich Gerbrandt had helped Nicholas address the demons of his past and work through memories of ugly childhood events in Russia that he simply could not face alone.

It seemed only fitting that the feelings that had simmered inside the brothers for such a long time should be addressed so near the church. This is where Heinrich Gerbrandt had helped them work through their struggles with insecurity and rejection. The church was where they had finally found a home – a refuge – but not without struggle. It was a place where healing began. Would all this disappear now that Heinrich Gerbrandt was gone? Harwood was a small community with only two churches, and it was very difficult to be a part of anything unless one was a part of a church community. But it was ironic that the Friedrichsen brothers had to fight so hard to gain acceptance by people of a Christian church, especially by a Mennonite church that preached peace. From the pulpit, they had heard sermons based on Ephesians 2: 8–9 where Paul states, *"For by grace are ye saved through faith; and that not of yourselves: it is the gift of God: Not of works, lest any man should boast."* The members of the congregation accepted this gift of grace for themselves, but had not always extended it to the Friedrichsen brothers. They had been saved by their own efforts, and not by grace ... or so it seemed.

***

In 1929, as teenagers, the brothers had escaped Russia by joining a group of Mennonites who had found refuge in Canada with the help of the Mennonite Central Committee and the Canadian Pacific Railway. The brothers had travelled with this group, passing themselves off as Mennonites, but rather than being accepted as Mennonites, they were held at a distance and viewed with suspicion. They had entered Canada carrying illegally obtained documents, and they had bribed their way out of Russia with stolen jewelry. Unfortunately, such stories do get around. Furthermore, the brothers' bloodlines were anything but pure. Their maternal grandmother was Jewish and their fathers were Russian. As was the custom in early Manitoba, settlers of similar ethnic and cultural backgrounds would group together into villages, and it was not easy for people of different origins to be accepted by those living in these tight-knit communities. Even the name Friedrichsen – actually their mother's maiden name – was not typically Russian Mennonite. Then there was the matter of their association with Nestor Makhno, the anarchist and ruthless terrorist who had sadistically brutalized the Mennonite villages in Ukraine. As teenagers, the boys, when threatened by starvation, had indeed ridden along with the Makhno bands into Mennonite villages and eaten food taken from the intimidated and terrorized people.

In their favour, there were those in Harwood who had heard of the boys' mother and were familiar with the reputation she had won for herself before her untimely death. This helped to stave off complete ostracism. The brothers had both married women who came from socially acceptable families and this association had certainly raised their standing in the community. Perhaps an even greater asset for gaining acceptance into the Harwood Mennonite Church was the brothers' ability to sing. This was a talent they had inherited from their mother, who had sung to them as babies, sung with them as children, and had helped them develop the ability to sing in harmony. From the mixed and confused gene pool that made up the Friedrichsen boys, there emerged two unusually beautiful tenor voices, and very few choirs on the face of the earth ever have enough quality tenors.

Singing was a gift that even poor people, like their mother, could enjoy. In church, she could sing along with the congregation and feel a part of the larger group. Beautiful singing has been known to touch many a heart, heal many a soul, and forgive many a sin, and so it was with the people of the Harwood Mennonite Church. Reverend Heinrich Gerbrandt was known to call upon the brothers, usually Nicholas, to sing a particularly fitting hymn following a successful sermon, and the Brandon Oratorio Choir did its best to recruit the brothers for larger choral programs.

It is a credit to old Heinrich Gerbrandt, the man whom the brothers now deeply mourned, that they had achieved acceptance in the church community. He had encouraged them to follow their mother's wishes and be baptized as adults based upon their confession of faith. At their baptism, Reverend Gerbrandt offered a public apology to the brothers on behalf of the congregation.

"We have not acted toward you in the Christian way. We have not shown you acceptance. Our love to you has had too many conditions. We apologize to you and ask for your forgiveness." All the people present on that occasion rose to their feet in agreement with this confession.

The people from the Harwood Mennonite Church had eventually become the brothers' support group where problems had been confronted and tough decisions made. The church also became the social centre where they had spent many hours attending services and enjoyable musical events. Would this now change with the death of Heinrich Gerbrandt?

Alex Friedrichsen was beginning to realize that with this death, everyone had suddenly moved up a generation. The daughters and their husbands had become the old people charged with providing leadership, their
children were now entering the prime of life and would need to act more
responsibly, and soon another group of babies would become the spoiled
little tykes that his children had been to *Oma* and *Opa*.

Alex's wife, Marusia, was a wonderful support. Through the years, she
had fallen into step with him. Not that she was a wallflower – far from
it – but the two of them had developed common values and learned to
think alike. Between them, they had good personal qualities, but they
needed a person, a strong source of stability to balance their ambition and
require them to stop and reflect, to ask if what they were and what they
had become, and is what they wished to be. Heinrich Gerbrandt, his old
father-in-law, had been that person and Alex knew that he would miss him.
Together they had arrived in Canada with nothing, together they built up
the farm and several businesses, and together they supported a number of
community organizations. Now Alex felt the entire burden of maintaining
family, church, and community descending upon him and Marusia. With
Heinrich gone, there was one less person to challenge Alex's ambitions, and
one less person to temper his driving energy, and one less person to force
him to stop and reflect. Alex instinctively knew that this was something he
would deeply miss.

When he heard that Heinrich, his father-in-law and mentor, had died,
Alexander broke down and wept for the whole family. He wept for step-
daughter Susie and her husband, George, who would be off to Toronto
and not be seen for some time. He wept for young Stephanie who was
returning to New York with his brand new Chargex credit card, and for
Jacob who was glad-handing his way to Winnipeg and back, hoping to win
enough votes to send him on to Ottawa. He still had Aaron living nearby
in Harwood, and Julie, oh yes, Julie.

***

"What will happen to Marusia and me when we cannot do it anymore?" Alex wondered aloud. "Julie belongs to this service club that's behind a plan to construct a new retirement centre in Brandon. Once she and Aaron have consolidated our holdings, will she shuffle us off to this nursing home?"

Nicholas rarely gave his older brother advice, and so it was on this occasion. By remaining quiet, he allowed Alex to work through his anxieties and concerns. Yet younger brother Nicholas was never far away, and in his own quiet way, offered support and encouragement. He needed to reflect upon his own future with Sarah, his wife. He, too, was the father of a first generation of overly ambitious Canadian kids.

Chapter 2
Raisa – 1894

ON A COLD, RAINY AFTERNOON IN APRIL 1894, A TINY UNIMPORTANT little creature fought her way into this world and with her first feeble cries, announced to the people of Blumenau that she had arrived. Her birth was unplanned, her arrival premature, and her presence, although unwanted, had now become a fact of reality. All day long, the midwives struggled to help the physically immature teenager deliver her first baby. Finally, by late afternoon, after many hours of intense labour, a tiny infant was delivered – the smallest baby anyone there had ever seen. She opened her eyes, took her first few breaths, and squeaked out the news that she was alive and well, and here to stay. No one could foretell the influence this small, defenceless little being would have on the world around her.

***

Blumenau, where the birth took place, was itself a tiny, insignificant village barely large enough to deserve a name, yet small enough for everyone to be aware of each other's activities, and certainly small enough to take note of every new baby. As one of the last villages to be established in the area, Blumenau had been built along the northern edge of the Molotschna Colony and located about eighty kilometres south of the city of Aleksandrovsk. The few residents who lived here built their house-barns along both sides of the only street and bought their supplies at the village's only general store. Blumenau had one school where all the children were educated and one church where all the villagers worshipped. Consequently, the people knew each other very well. Most had emigrated from West Prussia and had lived together and intermarried for several generations. They were very much the same – they dressed the same, looked the same, and thought the same. By 1894, the village of Blumenau had simply not been in existence long enough to develop much diversity in thinking, and certainly not large enough to tolerate any situation that didn't conform to its established customs and values.

The Molotschna Colony, of which Blumenau was a part, consisted of fifty-seven villages, all larger than Blumenau. The colony had developed on a tract of land about 1,750 square kilometres in size and was populated by Mennonite people who had been invited by Catherine the Great to emigrate here from West Prussia. The Imperial government had hoped to populate this area and develop the rich agricultural soil of south central Ukraine before the Turks could return to claim the land from which they had been driven. The Molotschna River, a pretentious little creek that flowed from Tokmak to Melitopol and on to the Sea of Azov, defined the western boundary of the Molotschna Colony. The Molotschna River was said to be so narrow that it had only one bank, yet this bank became a significant dividing line between the lifestyles and values of the Mennonites of the Molotschna Colony and those of their neighbours who lived on the western side of the river.

Several kilometres east of Blumenau was the town of Tokmak, not nearly as large nor as important as the city of Aleksandrovsk, but nevertheless, larger and more significant than many of the surrounding Mennonite villages. Tokmak had grown into a thriving little centre of commerce, offering goods and services to the people in the surrounding area. There were merchants, machinery dealers, and tradespeople who could build or repair most anything. There was also a bustling market where people from surrounding villages came to sell their goods: chickens, eggs, produce from their gardens, homemade crafts, and articles of clothing.

Every Friday morning, young Peter Friedrichsen, a resident of Blumenau and the eldest child of Wilhelm and Margarete Friedrichsen, would load his cart with produce harvested from the family garden and drive his horse to the market in Tokmak, a distance he covered in an hour or so. The extra income generated by Peter's modest enterprise, as his proud parents pointed out, helped the family financially. From their perspective, their teenage son was becoming a mature young man, developing proper values and a serious work ethic. But from Peter's point of view, this weekly trip to Tokmak became an excuse to escape the confines of the tiny village of Blumenau where his family, and far too many of his relatives, lived. Most teenage boys would consider it a punishment to get up this early on any morning, but not Peter. He considered this weekly excursion a wonderful opportunity to spread his wings, develop his independence, and rub shoulders with people who were anything but Mennonite.

A Jewish family by the name of Brodsky who lived across the Molotschna River on the nearby Franko estate also came to the market every Friday. Their attractive display of colourful flowers and fresh vegetables always attracted many shoppers. Peter, an astute young businessman, soon realized that if he were to locate his stand next to the Brodsky display, he would catch the attention of more buyers and thereby improve his own sales. The Brodsky family had a pretty teenage daughter, Raisa, and this may have been another reason why Peter took such an active interest in the goods they were selling.

Initially, Peter was too bashful to start up a conversation with strangers, but slowly he overcame the Mennonite shyness he had inherited from his parents. He soon began to seek opportunities to speak to the Brodsky girl, all the while pretending to be totally engaged in the activity of pitching his potatoes and carrots to potential buyers. Whenever the young girl's mother was busy bargaining with customers, and whenever the girl's younger siblings were off running around with other children, Peter would seize the opportunity to speak to her. These initial moments of innocent chatter became more frequent and soon developed into longer, more personal, conversations, yet always subdued, at least when Raisa's mother was near.

Peter was definitely attracted to Raisa and sought opportunities to get to know her a little better. By late fall, after most of the produce had been harvested from the garden and after most of the flowers were now frozen, Peter still found it worthwhile to dig up a few root vegetables and make the journey to Tokmak. For her part, Raisa, the young Jewish girl, continued to encourage her mother to also bring whatever she could find to peddle at her stand, even after summer had all but gone. Peter's parents were unconcerned, even pleased, by the activities of their mature teenage son who so willingly drove back and forth to the market every Friday.

The Brodsky family, with whom Peter was becoming acquainted, had taken up residence in the Tokmak area, but not by choice. Along with other Jewish people, they had suffered severe discrimination, even harassment apparently condoned by the czar's police, thus forcing them to leave Odessa, the place where they had lived for many generations. Their trek in search of a more peaceful home took them east, away from Odessa, and then north along the Dnieper River. Along the way, some families became discouraged by still greater hardships and returned to Odessa. Others dropped away and stayed behind when they felt they had found a place with acceptable living conditions. Eventually, a remnant of fewer than thirty refugees who continued their trek north came into contact with a benevolent landowner named Franko whose estate was a mere six kilometres west of the town of Tokmak. Here, they found temporary accommodation that included extremely modest living quarters consisting of several huts, a dilapidated old barn, but a decent-sized garden plot. They settled here, at least for the short term, and attempted to eke out a living from the meagre resources the situation allowed for them. The Brodsky family intended to eventually continue north along the Dnieper River and meet up with an aunt and her family who lived somewhere near Kiev.

Among the newly-arrived Jewish residents on the Franko estate, lived a very good blacksmith, a man who could build and repair most everything, especially wagons, buggies, and horse-drawn farm implements. In a casual conversation with Peter, Raisa Brodsky praised the work of this versatile blacksmith, an uncle of hers, and recommended him very highly. When she mentioned that his makeshift shop was located just behind the communal barn and next to the house where her family lived, the services of this handyman took on a whole new meaning for Peter. He considered this to be an invitation to visit Raisa.

Peter brought the reputation of this handy blacksmith to the attention of his father. He convinced him to allow Peter to take the family buggy to the Franko estate so the axle could be properly straightened to prevent the left front wheel from continually breaking loose – a simple problem that no one in Blumenau could repair successfully. A few days later, with his father's permission, Peter drove the horse and buggy to the Franko settlement and met the blacksmith. Within a few hours, the axle was straightened and the loose wheel properly repaired. Upon returning to Blumenau, Peter's father was delighted at the high quality of the work. Peter immediately saw a golden opportunity to visit Raisa more often, and of course, provide additional business for the poor underemployed blacksmith. During the next few months, Peter located every item in Blumenau that needed repair and volunteered to take these to the handyman on the Franko estate. The longer and more complicated the repair, the more time he could spend with Raisa. The Mennonites in Blumenau, all reasonably well off were happy to pay someone to have their equipment fixed and returned, especially at such a modest price. Peter often received a small tip for his efforts and generous praise for the time he had been required to spend away from Blumenau.

The telltale signs of a budding relationship between Peter and Raisa were there, but both the Brodsky and the Friedrichsen families failed to recognize the attraction the teenagers were developing for each other. On trips to the Franco estate while Peter waited for the repairs to be done, he would spend as much time with Raisa as she was free to take. Together, they would tour the garden and the fields and walk through the estate owned by the well-intentioned landlord. Everyone was happy. The blacksmith saw his business expand, the farmers of Blumenau saw their equipment repaired and improved, and Peter and Raisa saw their relationship blossom. Often, her younger siblings would tag along behind them, but the resourceful Raisa knew how to send them away searching for berries, chasing butterflies, or simply finding colourful stones that probably did not exist. This gave her more time to be alone with Peter.

And then it happened. Somehow people discovered that Raisa Brodsky was pregnant. Both families, along with the people from both communities, were dumbstruck with paralyzing fear of what the consequences of this scandal could mean for them. Obviously a wedding needed to be hastily arranged, but where, in what cultural context, and within whose religious observances? As the parents' anxieties jumped from one fear to the next, the question of who would look after these children, soon to be joined by a baby. The people in the transient Jewish community were landless and extremely poor. Such poverty leaves people in a very weak bargaining position. The Mennonites, on the other hand, were economically better off. Like their Jewish neighbours, the Mennonites knew of no precedent for dealing with such an unimaginable scandal. It is a credit to both families that, in spite of the difficult predicament in which these two teenagers found themselves, they would not abandon the young couple, and at some level, both future grandmothers looked forward to cuddling a newborn grandchild.

Various scenarios for dealing with the situation were considered, but none led to a solution. No one could satisfactorily address the objections posed by either side. Raisa's parents were vehemently opposed to a wedding in a Christian church, and the Friedrichsen family could not accept a Jewish wedding. So, for a time the situation was at a stalemate. The Friedrichsen family, who took advantage of their position of being better off financially and their belief that the man in the relationship should make all the important decisions, finally resolved this dilemma. They decided that the couple would marry and live in Blumenau, and the Friedrichsen family would care for them, at least initially. The Mennonite preachers were of little help. One person even cautioned that the "baby's soul would be in peril" unless a wedding was performed in a Mennonite church by a Mennonite preacher.

The Friedrichsen family found a small room in the back of their house to shield the teenage couple from the disparaging gossip that had become the main topic of conversation of every resident busybody. Peter found some local work and contributed to the family income while his mother managed to care for her pregnant teenage daughter-in-law. Over time,

Mother Friedrichsen grew rather fond of Raisa. But the pregnancy was a difficult one. Many days the poor girl felt too ill to get out of bed. She longed to be home with her own mother and family whom she desperately missed. Raisa was also worried that her people might be uprooted and driven away from their present location simply because they were Jewish, as had happened so often before. She did not want to lose contact with them. Her mother and siblings managed to travel to Blumenau once or twice to see her, but they were simply in no position to help the young couple financially. Raisa's father had abandoned his daughter. By doing so, he felt he could rebuild the family honour, restore the family reputation, and thereby protect the future of his other children.

The elders of the Blumenau Mennonite church arranged religious instruction for Raisa to prepare their new convert for baptism. But before this could be considered, the young couple had to appear before the church – very well attended upon this occasion – to confess their grievous sin and receive forgiveness from God and from the people. Once this was accomplished, Raisa was baptized and taken into the membership of the church. Shortly thereafter, she and Peter were married.

Raisa's pregnancy continued to go badly. Every midwife in the village and beyond was consulted, and every remedy known to the women of the Blumenau area was considered, but all to no avail. Perhaps the girl was simply too small and too frail to endure a pregnancy. Perhaps God was raining down His punishment upon her. At about the seventh month of her pregnancy, Raisa began to experience abdominal pains that steadily grew worse. Again the midwives were consulted, and yet again, no useful information came forward. Her symptoms continued, became more severe, and several days later she went into premature labour.

Raisa gave birth to the tiniest baby anyone had ever seen. The little newborn, although very weak and very much underweight, managed to emit a few feeble squeaks, bringing relief to the midwife and delight to Grandmother Friedrichsen. On the day of her birth, shortly before sundown, this little baby was forced to bid farewell to her mother as Raisa lapsed into a coma and died. She had simply given too much strength and too much blood, as she passed along everything she had to her precious little infant.

The death of their teenage daughter was a horrible shock to the Brodsky family. The entire family, including Raisa's father, came to Blumenau for the funeral. Although no Brodsky entered the Mennonite church for the funeral service, they all stood alongside the Friedrichsen family at the graveside and watched their daughter's depleted body lowered into the ground. The grandmothers hugged each other, sobbing and cuddling the tiny baby. Peter insisted that his daughter be named Raisa after her mother, and so she was.

***

The people of Blumenau set aside their prejudice, at least for a time, and came together to provide the necessities of life to keep the little baby alive. Little Raisa began to respond to the love and care shown to her, taking in nourishment, and beginning to grow and gain strength. Peter's mother accepted the baby as her own, and for the first few years of her life baby Raisa always had enough of everything. She was smaller than the other children her age, but appeared to be just as strong and just as healthy.

Socially, however, Raisa experienced difficulty. Perhaps it was her premature birth that contributed to her smaller stature, or perhaps her timid nature that caused her to withdraw from boisterous play, because Raisa simply found it difficult to make friends and fit in with other children. Also, as early as elementary school, nasty bits of gossip – tiny insidious cells of malice – began to circulate and these kept her in her place. Some people whispered that she looked different from other children, but to any discerning eye, any differences in appearance between her and the people of Blumenau would have been seen as similarities with members of the Rosenfeld and Strauss families who also shared Jewish and Mennonite roots. Children picked up the gossip from their elders and related it to Raisa in even more cruel and direct ways than adults could.

As Raisa became older, members of the Friedrichsen family, and Peter in particular, also began to feel discrimination directed toward them by the self-righteous people of Blumenau. One day, after Raisa had been to school for a year or two, the taunting children on the school yard told Raisa that her mother had been pregnant before she was married, and that her "brother," Peter, was actually her real father. These ignorant bullies continued to cast stones, cruelly declaring her not to be a true Mennonite like the other children, claiming that God had judged her mother by allowing her to die as punishment for the grievous sin she had committed by becoming pregnant out of wedlock. Raisa ran home crying because the girls at recess had told her, among other things, that her mother was not her real mother. This was the first time the family explained to Raisa who her parents were. She appeared to accept the truth rather easily, at least on the surface, but in reality, this little bit of perceived deception created seeds of insecurity that grew into larger problems during her teenage years.

She began to withdraw into a shell. She refused to go to school, refused to go to church, and refused social contact of any sort with people outside her family. She wanted to become a Brodsky and find her mother's people who certainly must be kinder and less cruel than these schoolyard Christians. But by now she was also old enough to realize that years had brought about change and people had moved on. While she was growing up, Raisa had fewer and fewer visits from her Grandmother Brodsky. The family had other children to look after, and poverty, that uninvited guest, remained its constant companion. Perhaps she no longer belonged with the Brodsky family, and quite possibly she no longer belonged anywhere.

***

Wilhelm Friedrichsen, her grandfather or "Father" as she had always called him, came to realize that life in the tiny village of Blumenau where everyone knew everything about everyone was not good for his family, especially not for Peter nor for little Raisa. Even Peter referred to her as his little sister rather than his daughter. Peter was only sixteen years older than

Raisa and in the minds of new friends and neighbours this might not be seen as a problem, but in Blumenau everyone knew the facts.

Wilhelm Friedrichsen had lived in Blumenau his whole life. He was a miller by trade who had learned to operate and repair the mechanical workings of a flour mill. He was particularly adept at installing the new engines that powered the mills and made wind power obsolete. As a land-less Mennonite in Blumenau, he was destined to work for a wage and stand by while the landowners who grew the wheat and the mill owners who ground the flour became rich. As a wage earner, he brought home enough income to keep his family fed, but not much more. The employment he had found in the tiny village of Blumenau seemed secure, but the village was simply too small to deal with the scandal his son had brought down upon the family. Fortunately, his work experience and technical skills were in demand, and this might help him find employment elsewhere so his family could start over. So Wilhelm decided to move. He contacted a cousin in Rosenthal, a town in the Chortitza Colony some eighty kilometres away, to inquire about employment opportunities in the area. Fortunately, within several weeks suitable employment was found. Wilhelm uprooted his family from Blumenau and moved to Rosenthal where the prospect of a good job, and hopefully better relations with neighbours, would be possible.

Not long after the family had settled into their new home, it became clear that the move from Blumenau to Rosenthal, although a change in location, was not a solution to the family's problems. The reasons that had driven them away from Blumenau had unfortunately followed them to Rosenthal. Raisa's grandparents, usually referred to as her parents, thought that by changing her name to Christina – a more Mennonite sounding name – she would be seen as a typical Mennonite girl living in a typical Russian Mennonite village. The situation was not helped by Raisa, who upon occasion would refer to herself as Raisa Brodsky. However changing her name from Raisa Brodsky to Christina Friedrichsen did little to solve Raisa's problems. She still felt alone and isolated.

The burden of scandal that had been thrust upon her from the moment of birth still weighed heavily upon her tiny shoulders. She also felt guilty over the fact that her mother had died while giving her life. Why was this so? Why did she have to live, and why did her mother have to die? Did her mother not want to live? Was death a conscious choice on her mother's part – a way out of the shame and embarrassment she must have felt? Raisa, or Christina, or whatever name she now chose to live by, seemingly had lost her place in the world – a world where not knowing who you were or where you belonged were sufficient reasons for a little girl to fall between the cracks. The move to Rosenthal, although a huge adjustment to everyone, had failed to create the opportunity for the family to start over.

Peter, Raisa's father, or brother as he preferred to be called, continued to drift out of her life. He had grown into a decent, mature young man and had done well at school. The family saw his education as a potential rise in social standing – not merely for him, but for the whole family. This could be a way of polishing their tarnished image. In order to allow Peter to receive an education, the family scraped together what they could to help him finance his studies at the *Halbstadt Kommerzschule*. For a poor family with modest means, a son's education was considered a questionable luxury. However from his family's perspective, their eldest child and only son's education would benefit everyone, and hopefully improve the chances for his younger sisters to marry well.

Unfortunately, the family's investment did not pay off quite as handsomely as his parents had hoped. While in Halbstadt, Peter began to court a girl from a wealthy and respected family. If this relationship was to flourish and if a marriage was to take place, it would be necessary to raise his family's profile, or at least expunge the family reputation of any sense of scandal such as the one that Peter had brought down upon them. Although the Friedrichsen family lived a fair distance from Halbstadt, news along the Mennonite gossip lines travelled quickly. To ward off any threat to Peter's courtship, Raisa, now known as Christina, officially became Peter's younger sister rather than his daughter. For Peter's sake, the grandparents and the other children now insisted upon this sanitized narrative, reasoning that no one would get hurt if the facts were rearranged somewhat and tidied up just a little. The only sacrifice was the memory of Raisa's birth mother.

The courtship of Peter Friedrichsen and Margarete Cornies led to a marriage with a Christian ceremony in the Mennonite Church in Halbstadt and a lavish celebration following. Christina felt hurt, shunned, and pushed aside, all because of a scandalous birth over which she had absolutely no control. Eventually, when the truth of Peter's first marriage did leak out, Christina felt even worse. Students at school began to ask her about her "brother Peter."

Raisa had simply had enough. Her grandmother could see the depressive weight drag the young girl down. She worried that Raisa was reaching her breaking point. But in reality, there never was an identifiable breaking point, no outburst. Raisa just slowly drifted into isolation, accompanied by dreadful anxiety and fear at having to attend school, church activities, or any social events outside the house. She hated Margarete, her stepmother, or sister-in-law, and saw in her the person who was attempting to erase the memory of her own mother, who had been just a young girl who bled to death giving Raisa life. *Oma* Friedrichsen was at a loss to know what to do.

***

No one had anything to say to Raisa. Even if their intentions had been better, they would still not have known what to say or what to do. In the absence of any sound advice, Raisa began to search inside herself for a solution, for some plan, for something that would allow her to escape the current situation that had pushed her to the periphery of social acceptance. Peter Friedrichsen, her father, had drifted out of her life. Along with his new wife, Margarete Cornies, they made little attempt to maintain any contact with Raisa. How should she address them? Should she call Margarete "Mother," perhaps "Stepmother?" Would this allow her to be noticed? The ensuing confusion made her feel even more alone.

One day, she announced to *Oma* Friedrichsen that she wanted to go live with her Grandmother Brodsky. This shocking announcement seemed to come out of nowhere and left the Friedrichsen family, especially *Oma*, speechless. Was such a hurtful request even possible, and yet, what could they say? They realized that revising the details of Raisa's birth to benefit the family had contributed to Raisa's isolation and depression and for this they felt guilty. They loved their little Raisa. They loved her enough to conclude that they could not stand in the way of her legitimate request to seek a better life, even if it meant leaving home to go live with her mother's family. But, as reasonable as such a request might seem, was it even possible? Did anyone know how to locate Grandmother Brodsky? There was a rumour that the few Jewish families who had lived in the Tokmak area had moved on, and everyone assumed that the Brodsky family had travelled north to Kiev to reconnect with their relatives, but the Brodsky family failed to leave a forwarding address. This hurt Raisa even more.

One day, a possible solution to Raisa's predicament appeared in the form of a dirty and well-travelled letter. It had been sent from Kiev to Blumenau. Before finding its way to Rosenthal, it had been forwarded to the addresses of other Friedrichsen families who also lived in the Molotschna Colony. The ink on the address had been smudged and a corner of the envelope had been torn away, but inside Raisa found a letter with a few lines giving her hope that she could alter the course of her life. The letter was from Grandma Brodsky and clearly stated that her grandmother loved her and missed her very much. There were details of the Brodsky family and their neighbours whom Raisa knew, who had once lived near Tokmak on the Franko estate. Grandma wished her well and said she longed to see her. Sadly, the return address on the envelope was smudged beyond recognition.

Raisa's spirits soared as she read the letter. A flame of hope for a better life that had almost been extinguished was rekindled in her as the possibility of reconnecting with this grandmother became real. She realized she had not been forgotten – there were others who still loved her. In the spirit of youthful optimism, Raisa made a plan. She would travel to Kiev, a place she had never visited. There she would seek information from people whom she did not know and try to connect with the Brodsky family, who may or may not still be in Kiev. This plan filled *Oma* Friedrichsen with anxiety and despair. She quickly pointed out to Raisa the dangers of this ill-conceived idea and went on to explain to her the remote possibility that such a strategy, even under the most favourable conditions, could ever succeed. Raisa's determination to see this through wore on the family. Her constant questions slowly led them to realize that some gesture toward Raisa's aspirations needed to be made. They at least had to meet her part way and attempt to satisfy her curiosity. How could they deny the hope and the joyful optimism that the young girl was desperately clinging to?

Oma Friedrichsen very reluctantly agreed to a compromise as she and Raisa hammered out the details of a new plan. A friend of hers, a distant relative living in Kiev named Frieda Rempel, with whom *Oma* maintained contact, might take in Raisa for a week or so. *Oma* wrote a letter and received a quick reply, confirming the hope that this friend would be happy to meet Raisa at the train station and take her home with her. Raisa could live with the Rempel family for a short time while she searched for Grandma Brodsky, and thereby satisfy her almost futile desire to find her. *Oma* hoped that after a week or so in Kiev, after Raisa had exhausted all possibilities of reconnecting with her Brodsky relatives, she would return home and realize that life in Rosenthal with the Friedrichsen family was not all that bad.

A week or so later, Raisa packed a suitcase with clothing, toiletries, and lunch supplies of buns, sausage, and fruit, as well as a little emergency money sewn into her garments. On the morning of her departure, *Oma* and *Opa* Friedrichsen, along with their two older daughters, accompanied Raisa to the Rosenthal train station where she boarded a train to Aleksandrovsk. She was given many warnings of how to avoid potential dangers, numerous instructions on where to go in Aleksandrovsk, and advice on how to purchase a ticket to Kiev once she had arrived in Aleksandrovsk. Raisa showed little feeling as she said goodbye. Perhaps the early hour of the day had not yet awakened her emotions or perhaps the relief at seeing no one who might bully her provided consolation. *Oma* cried and *Opa* restated his warnings on how to avoid unpleasant eventualities, but sadly, Peter and his new wife who were home for a few days, chose to stay in bed that morning.

Raisa's excitement and exhilaration at being free caused her to abandon all common sense and make a decision that would radically alter the course of her life. While she was standing in line at the wicket in the Aleksandrovsk train station waiting to purchase a ticket to Kiev, Raisa impulsively changed her mind. Instead of travelling north to Kiev as planned, she purchased a ticket to Odessa and boarded a train travelling south in the opposite direction. She recalled that Grandmother Brodsky occasionally mentioned to her that the family had deep roots in Odessa. At one time, the extended Brodsky family had been rich and very well connected. To the naïve fifteen-year-old girl, this information led her to believe that she would find a wealthy Brodsky on every street corner and somehow they would welcome her with open arms. Surely, some relative would help Raisa locate her grandmother. But what Grandmother Brodsky had failed to tell young Raisa was the sad reality that the Brodsky family and their relatives had been stripped of their wealth and influence simply because they were Jewish, and most, if not all the family, had fled the city.

A week or so later, two letters arrived at the Friedrichsen home in Rosenthal, fortunately on the same day. One letter sent by Frieda Rempel from Kiev informed them that Raisa had not been on the train from Aleksandrovsk. The Rempel family in Kiev had met every train from Aleksandrovsk for several days and had finally assumed that the plan for meeting Raisa had changed. The second letter, written by Raisa and sent from Odessa, informed them that she was safe and now living in this city. This letter gave very few details.

***

The express train steamed along the main line at a dizzying speed travelling south along the Dneiper River before turning west toward Odessa. On board, Raisa watched in amazement as villages, trees, fields and beautiful countryside flashed past her window. By early afternoon, the train reached the outskirts of Odessa and shortly thereafter rolled up to the city's main terminal building. Raisa was impressed. Through the train windows, she saw buildings that were much taller than any she had ever seen, and beautiful wide streets lined with trees. There was so much to see and no one to share it with. Her first encounter with the general bustle of the city stirred up further feelings of exhilaration. Being in Odessa and away from Rosenthal filled her with excitement – she was free.

"*Hier ist was los,*" she whispered to herself. Loosely translated this means, "Here things are happening." Raisa stepped off the train onto the platform, picked up her suitcase, took off her coat and confidently walked out onto a main street away from the train terminal. To follow along with other pedestrians became her way of finding her bearings. While moving she could decide upon a further course of action. Teenagers tend to live only in the moment and Raisa was no exception to this rule. She entrusted her guardian angel with the huge responsibility of looking after her and keeping her safe. To watch over a young fifteen-year-old girl adrift in a big city with no plans, not even for the night, with all her earthly possessions contained in the small suitcase she was carrying was a tall order even for the most competent, most caring guardian angel.

Wide-eyed and innocent the naive girl found herself on the Pushkinskaya, a street straight enough to see buildings many blocks ahead and wide enough for carriages to pass each other with ease. Raisa clutched her suitcase and instinctively continued to follow along, not knowing where people were going or where this street was taking them. She was amazed at the sights and sounds that not only impressed her but appeared to become more fascinating and more alluring as she walked along. She passed rows of tall trees interspersed with manicured shrubs, park benches and interesting fountains that seemed to invite little lost girls to keep on walking. Certainly nothing in Blumenau or Rosenthal could compare to these sights in any way.

Wide, clean sidewalks, free from debris and horse manure allowed pedestrians to move along to unknown destinations at a very quick pace. Along her walk, she noticed large pictures posted against the sides of the buildings depicting interesting scenes. One picture in particular fascinated her. It showed a large group of men sitting in an arranged order, dressed in black suits, and holding musical instruments. She recognized the violins and some of the brass instruments, but the larger violins that stood on the floor and the other strangely shaped wind instruments that men were blowing into suggested huge sounds that she imagined to be incredibly beautiful.

She was astounded to notice that the buildings were growing taller and more impressive as she walked along. *Could the tallest ones ever reach the clouds?* she thought. In the distance, one building in particular caught her eye. It was not the largest but even from several blocks away it stood out above the rest. She felt intimidated by its sheer size, yet at the same time, felt drawn toward it. This magnificent structure that she imagined to be so incredibly beautiful became still more impressive as she drew closer. Raisa wasted little time plotting a route that would take her directly towards this imposing edifice. She left the main boulevard and followed narrow streets and even narrower alleys, always keeping her new destination in view. At one point, her forward progress was abruptly blocked by a solid stone wall that appeared before her. Raisa quickly retraced her steps, located a path that led from the side around to the front of this barricade and past an open iron gate. As she peered inside, she was surprised to see an old cemetery and marvelled at the large impressive headstones. *A person would need to be very important to be buried here*, she thought.

The upper part of the stately structure that defined the skyline was now in clear view. Its size and grandeur was simply breathtaking. This was the most beautiful, most highly ornate building she had ever seen. *This must be what the buildings in heaven look like. Oma Friedrichsen always described heaven in such glorious terms.* Raisa however did not spend much time thinking about heaven. She still had too many earthly issues to deal with, forced upon her by her experiences in Rosenthal. As she drew closer, she marvelled at the massive façade that was held in place by huge columns. She was astounded by the number of exquisitely sculpted statues that were carefully positioned at various places all along the roof. Were these figures meant to honour very important people? The building wasn't even square or rectangular like other buildings she had seen – it was shaped like a horseshoe. Even the many windows and doors were ornately decorated. It was almost too much to take in. *Oma* Friedrichsen had always cautioned against too much decoration. It was an indication of pride, and according to *Oma*, God expected his followers to practice simplicity, and not pursue vainglory. Large pictures of dancers and singers in varieties of colourful costumes and interesting poses were posted along the front. What were the people depicted in these pictures doing? This piqued her curiosity even more. She would need to return here she told herself.

As she walked along the side of the horseshoe-shaped structure, Raisa heard singing from an open window behind some balcony on the upper floor. She heard a woman sing high notes that only she herself imagined anyone capable of singing. *How fulfilling it must be to sing as freely as one wished without being told to keep quiet,* Raisa thought. According to her restricted upbringing, people made sounds according to their status in the community. Some people were permitted to speak and sing as loudly as they wished, while others, obviously of lesser importance, were told to sing softly and not stand out. They should blend with the group, or even better, simply keep quiet.

Raisa strolled aimlessly through an adjoining park, reflecting upon the edifice in all its magnificence that had so impressed her. She passed an interesting fountain with statues of naked people positioned along the top. *Oh dear! What would Oma Friedrichsen say?* She stopped a moment to observe, and then began walking again. Soon she found herself on an even wider street, with shop windows displaying large and extravagant merchandise – things she had dreamt of, but never actually seen, and certainly not in such abundance. She saw elegant ladies dresses, fancy hats and entire counters full of ornate jewelry. Could women who covered themselves in these items please God? Again, she was reminded of what *Oma* Friedrichsen would say. The sights and sounds that overwhelmed her senses and gave her limitless energy also created an appetite for the lunch *Oma* had packed for her. Raisa selected a quiet park bench and sat down to eat a bun with some smoked sausage.

After a short rest, she resumed her brisk walk, moving directly toward the Richelieu monument and onto the Primorski Boulevard with its breathtaking view of the harbour. She waited a moment to watch a remnant of a military parade march past. She marvelled at the spectacle. There were elegantly dressed officers riding beautiful horses and foot soldiers dressed in smart uniforms marching in such straight lines with exact precision. The parade was now officially over, but a few people still stood along the street and cheered as the soldiers retreated back to their base. Two or three people threw flowers. Near the back of the disbanding crowd, she noticed young men who had gathered in small groups. Why were they so sullen and why were they speaking so quietly?

Raisa walked to what would be known in the twentieth century as the Potyomkin Steps, descended down to the water's edge, and strolled along the harbour front, admiring the marine life, the tall ships, and the fishing boats that were being attacked by hungry seagulls looking for scraps of fish. *Does bullying never end?* she thought. After an hour of strolling leisurely along the waterfront, she retraced her steps and returned to the city centre. Her wonder and amazement at all she had seen energized her, but it also clouded her judgement. She failed to notice that midday had long passed and the sun was beginning to set. Her only concern was the fact that she had not yet spotted any person who resembled a Brodsky. Slowly, it dawned on her that she did not even know what her Brodsky relatives looked like or how to contact them.

As evening approached, the exhilaration of her newfound independence – the feeling of freedom rather than restricted confinement – slowly wore off as the stark realization that she had nowhere to spend the night began to set in. Since arriving in Odessa, walking had been her only course of action. To see where her feet might take her had become her only purpose. If the guardian angel was attempting to tell her something, she had not recognized his voice, at least not until now.

As Raisa continued to walk away from the city centre, she noticed the opulence of downtown Odessa slowly giving way to more modest architecture. Tall buildings and wide streets were now replaced by rows of functional townhouses and unpretentious apartment buildings built along narrow streets. These residential buildings may have appeared inviting during the day, but now at dusk, the front doors were closed, windows were covered, and shutters were being drawn shut. Still, she continued to wander aimlessly, barely noticing that the sun was setting and day was turning to night. At some point during the evening as her sense of exhilaration and her limitless energy had neared its end, Raisa's feet finally came to a complete stop.

For the first time since arriving in Odessa, a sense of reality began to take over. All day, she had allowed her eyes and her feet to guide her, but now she had to call upon her ears to give her some point of orientation, some sense of direction for she had nowhere to go. Raisa listened for a sound … any sound. It was almost dark and for the first time since leaving home, a feeling of uneasiness began to descend upon her. She looked around and saw nothing familiar – nothing that reminded her of her home, of her grandmother, or of her bed. She tried hard to subdue an uncanny feeling of impending danger that now began to grow stronger as the last light of day all but disappeared.

In the darkness, she saw nothing. She heard nothing – not a moving carriage not even a barking dog. As she stood frozen to the ground, Raisa became afraid to breathe, fearing any sound she made might expose her to danger or interfere with the help that surely must arrive at any moment. Time now stood still. The silence was deafening. After what seemed like a long while, the frightful stillness around her was interrupted by a faint sound that only her heightened sense of hearing could possibly perceive. The sound did not add to her fear. It actually quieted her and calmed her heart. It was a reassuring sound – not a noise that in any way unnerved her. She wasn't sure what it could be, but something in her drew her toward this far-off sound, so she slowly began to walk toward the place it was coming from – a place her guardian angel was leading her to.

As she drew closer, Raisa thought she recognized a voice, then more voices. With renewed energy, she instinctively quickened her pace until she found herself standing before of a modest-sized building with a large, yet firmly closed, front door. From behind this door, she clearly heard voices – they were singing. Was this a familiar melody, perhaps a song sung by people whom she knew? Was this a gathering of Mennonites? Was she hearing a folksong that Grandma Brodsky had sung to her? Raisa listened for a moment, and then, drawing upon every ounce of courage she had she walked up to the door and knocked gently. There was no response.

She breathed deeply to quiet her fear, waited a second or two, and then knocked again. This time, just as the song finished, the door opened and an elderly man with an astonished yet kind expression greeted her and invited her to come in. As she entered the room, Raisa was surprised to see a group of about thirty people, strangers to her, packed tightly into a small space. The room was not overly decorated. It had plain white walls, one or two pictures, wooden chairs, and little else. The people stared at her. Who was this bewildered, plain-looking teenage girl who was adequately, but certainly not elegantly, dressed? Why was she clutching a suitcase?

Raisa did not know what to make of this unsolicited attention. Did these people know her? Had they heard that her Jewish mother had become pregnant before her wedding? Would they begin whispering about her to make her feel uncomfortable? Someone, possibly the guardian angel who had led her here, offered her a chair and invited her to sit down and sing along with the next song. Fortunately, Raisa recognized the melody and sang along heartily. Slowly, she began to feel more at ease with the situation as she realized she somehow had stumbled into a service of some religious group – a group that appeared to be welcoming her. After another song and a short time of sharing, there was a prayer and a benediction and the service ended. As the people rose to leave, Raisa looked at each one, hoping to see someone who might resemble a member of the extended Brodsky family. She recognized no one.

The leader of the service, along with a woman who appeared to be his wife, approached Raisa and asked her who she was, where she came from, and what drew her to find this group. Raisa's familiarity with one or two of the congregational songs had convinced them that she came from a Christian background, but why was a young girl out alone on the streets so late at night, with a suitcase in her hand? Her story, even the shortened version, brought gasps of surprise from the woman. She listened to Raisa and extended kindness by inviting her to spend the night with them.

Within a few minutes, the makeshift sanctuary was converted into living quarters for the couple and their three children. Raisa was offered a mat on the floor and a quilt with which to cover herself. Raisa finished the rest of the food her grandmother had packed for her and slept reasonably well. The next morning was Sunday and an even larger group squeezed into this living space that was again converted into a church sanctuary for the worship service. The people were friendly and asked questions about her family and her home, but when Raisa made inquiries about her relatives in Odessa, she became increasingly concerned that no one in the group had ever heard of anyone named Brodsky.

The people were kind and determined to help her. They took time with her, gave her food, listened to her story, and encouraged her to return home where concerned family members must be worried about her. Raisa's repeated and stubborn refusal to even consider such an idea made her newfound support group realize that a new plan was necessary – again an opportunity for her guardian angel to intervene. Some of the adults whispered aloud that perhaps a day or two in the real world was needed to convince this teenage girl to return home. Others agreed. To experience the more realistic side of living in Odessa, a city considered a paradise for the rich and famous, but a very hard place for those who were poor – even for those with modest means – would change her perspective on where to live. A person from the church group knew of someone at the Odessa army base who had some influence over the hiring of local workers. Perhaps a day or two of hard labour at some menial and ill-paid job would change her mind.

Jobs at the base for unskilled, non-military personnel consisted of keeping the barracks clean and functioning at a level to which rich young officers were accustomed. Local peasants, usually young boys and girls, were hired to look after certain of the army's tasks. These workers assisted cooks, cleaned barracks and stables, pressed uniforms, and did any number of menial chores for as little pay as the army could get away with. They were treated badly, yelled at, humiliated, and even beaten when something went wrong. But because many young people needed employment – any type of employment just to survive – the workers felt lucky just to have a job. This is the place where Raisa was expected to work, at least for a day or so, until she could be convinced to return to her family. But no one knew the extent of this young girl's determination and stubborn fortitude, and the lengths to which she would go to avoid returning to Rosenthal.

The next day, Raisa was escorted to the base and introduced to the person in charge of hiring. After a short interview, she was offered temporary employment. Raisa was elated. She saw no dark clouds, no danger. She revelled in her independence, trusted her self-reliance, and eagerly accepted the job without asking details of her employment. Freedom and independence were all she saw. Hard work did not scare her. Raisa was finally free of the lifelong verbal harassment and sideways glances from the people of Blumenau and Rosenthal.

The temporary job provided food, mainly leftovers once the military personal had eaten their fill, as well as a bed. It was actually a smelly, discoloured mattress laid across a poorly constructed wooden frame located in a large room shared by other female army base employees. According to the other girls, the pay, if it came on time, consisted of a handful of kopeks each week. The tasks were difficult and menial, and sexual harassment or worse could be expected at any time from military personnel. Survival depended on resilience, and above all, reliance on one's guardian angel. Raisa took the job and determined to make the most of it. She considered herself fortunate to have found work. More importantly, she was finally free, as she kept reminding herself – free from abuse, and free from the rigid conventions that life with the Mennonites of Rosenthal had imposed upon her.

***

Raisa corresponded with *Oma* Friedrichsen, but in her letters she focused on the benefits of her new job and downplayed the actual working and living conditions. She was clearly on the bottom rung of the ladder as far as supervisors and other girls were concerned, and this revealed itself in the tasks she was assigned.

She was small, physically immature, and spoke with a strange accent, yet somehow Raisa managed to get by and took everything directed toward her in stride. Because she was quiet and shy, Raisa survived the unwanted attention of soldiers, officers, and male workers. Several times she made enquiries about people by the name of Brodsky who may have lived in the area. The reactions to her queries were such that she soon realized Jewish people were no longer welcomed here, so she chose to be known only by the name of Christina Friedrichsen.

Chapter 3
Alexander Mikhailov, Jr. – 1906

AT THE BEGINNING OF THE TWENTIETH CENTURY, THE IMPERIAL Russian army was still contending with systemic problems. Technological advances were not keeping pace with the improvements made by Russia's potential rivals, army personnel were poorly trained and even more poorly assigned, and generally morale was low. If anyone doubted the extent of Russia's problems, they just needed to examine the career of junior officer Alexander Mikhailov, and wonder at his rapid rise through the ranks. Here was a young man sent to the army by a wealthy influential father who hoped that the military would recreate his son in his own image, or at the very least, make a man out of him, which in father's mind were one and the same. No one could doubt Alexander's physical maturity or his intelligence. He even had technical and mechanical skills that he could call upon, but Alexander simply had no interest in the army or in anything remotely connected to the military.

Alexander Mikhailov, Jr., the young officer in question, was his mother's son. His career interests, passed down from her, lay in the arts: opera, theatre, even ballet. Unfortunately, all these areas were not considered of value for the future laid out for him by his father. Young Alexander's first career choice had always been to sing opera professionally. Possibly this career path was a little over ambitious, but if this dream could not be realized, then perhaps his second choice could be pursued – to direct opera, even ballet, anything as long as it involved the theatre. In 1906, these were laudable career choices for young people, mainly women, but entirely unsuitable for a young man being groomed to manage the Mikhailov industrial complex.

Anastasia Mikhailov, Alexander's mother, was a stylish, good-looking woman born into wealth and entitlement. She was well connected to the hated Russian Aristocracy, which the less fortunate people were beginning to resent. There was even a rumour that her family and the Romanovs had common ancestral roots that, according to some, could easily be traced. Anastasia's interests had nothing to do with industry, steel, coal, weapon manufacturing, or the like. She never interfered nor showed the slightest interest in any of her husband's business undertakings. Consequently, she knew very little about what he did. Her background, education, and experience were all in the arts – activities she understood well and supported generously with her money and time. The composer Rachmaninoff and the great Russian bass, Feodor Chaliapin, had been guests in the Mikhailov home, and whatever they or others in their position may have thought of her husband's opinions regarding music or theatre, his financial support was more than enough to keep them quiet. His money and her energy created a powerful force that no artist could afford to ignore. As a privileged woman, Anastasia had never worked – at least not what common people would define as work – and perhaps this also had an influence upon her son. A love for theatre and the arts, and leisure in general, is what she passed along to him.

Her husband, Alexander Mikhailov, Sr., was cut from a different cloth. He had not been born into wealth nor position. Everything he acquired had been attained through energy, hard work, and a measure of good fortune. As a self-made man, he presided over a large industrial complex with factories that supplied the Russian army with tanks, armaments, and guns. In conversations with friends, he liked to refer to Henry Ford, the gifted American innovator with whom he had contact and to whom he compared himself. Alexander's principal strength lay in his ability to hire talent and inspire those with whom he worked to be inventive, pursue creative ideas, and make whatever they were working at just a little bit better. Some ideas by his employees may have been beyond the scope of reality, but other ideas, if successful, were handsomely rewarded with lucrative government contracts.

Alexander, a natural leader, surrounded himself with ambitious technical school graduates, some of whom had been his school buddies from his time in Moscow. Fortunately for him, Alexander also stumbled upon a brilliant economist whom he hired to help organize the business end of his factories – always along principles of free enterprise rather than the ill-conceived economic theories espoused by Marx and Engels. In addition to wealth, Alexander also had connections extending all the way up to the czar. Anastasia had introduced him to several of her rich, influential uncles who were anxious to invest their rubles in anything that would increase their wealth. His wife's contacts helped Alexander break into high society. His wealth and influence, however, were not merely the result of connections. Although no one ever disputed this advantage, Alexander was also an intelligent businessman, as well as an extraordinarily gifted engineer and inventor. Russian industry was ready for such a person.

At the Mikhailov factories in Tsaritsyn, huge machines hummed day after day as the tall chimneys of the giant smelters belched out rich, black smoke. The newly-founded steel that poured from the ovens created new, very mobile tanks with high-caliber, high-velocity guns capable of blowing the Japanese to bits, or any other armies that might attempt to humiliate the czar's forces. The Japanese embarrassment of the Imperial Russian Army in 1905 still hung thickly in the air and festered in the minds of many. This needed to be avenged, or at the very least, prevented from ever happening again. The perceived need for modern, efficient armaments became a terrific boon to the fledgling Russian industry, making entrepreneurs and factory owners such as Alexander Mikhailov very rich. The czar and his military advisors saw to it that sufficient resources and raw materials flowed in the direction of innovators, especially munitions manufacturers who could produce weaponry for the army to keep up with technological advances made by Russia's potential enemies: Japan, England, and France.

Alexander and his staff were on the constant lookout for new technological advances. The fact that warfare on horseback was obsolete suited them just fine. New weapons were on the drawing board – everything from heavy artillery to hand grenades to field communications equipment. Motorized vehicles to compete with those being built in Europe and United State were being developed, and the new flying machines they were hearing about were also under consideration. The early Russian tank program probably would have been scrapped had Alexander Mikhailov not managed to reconstruct the track assembly to allow the tanks to function with greater mobility and better maneuverability, even in sub-zero temperatures. He also found a way to mount heavier 75 mm guns that he manufactured onto these moving beasts. With his help, the army could now dispense its carnage more efficiently and over a wider range of territory. Because these military products functioned so well, senior officers revered the weapons and machinery supplied by Mikhailov's factories. Consequently, he was awarded more lucrative military contracts.

Alexander Mikhailov firmly believed that a modernized and fully-mechanized Imperial Russian Army could again establish national authority and would right itself under the leadership of Czar Nicholas II, thereby allowing the Russia of the past to go on forever. According to Alexander's reasoning, if the wealthy were allowed the freedom to develop national resources, then they would become the economic engine to create more wealth, and thus provide opportunities for the poor to improve their standard of living. He was sure that revolution and war could be averted. Unfortunately, he did not pay proper heed to the Bolsheviks, and had not even heard of Lenin.

The opposing interests and talents of Anastasia and Alexander Mikhailov clashed in the life of their eldest child and only son, Alexander, Jr. Even at a young age, it was obvious that the interests and abilities he had inherited from his mother held the upper hand over the influence his father tried to pass along to him. To correct this imbalance, the young lad's interests in the theatre were put on hold, and upon his father's insistence, at the age of sixteen, young Alexander was enrolled in the prestigious Moscow Technical School to begin preparing for the role of heir apparent to the Mikhailov business empire. Everything was paid for: tuition, clothes, living accommodation, spending money, and even a car. All young Alexander needed was provided for him. This new lifestyle suited him very well. He found the experience of being a student living in Moscow, and especially being away from his father's pressure, to be stimulating and thoroughly enjoyable. Yet, while other students chose to complete assignments and prepare for examinations, he used every opportunity to slip away to the theatre and indulge his passion, namely opera. Consequently, by the end of the first term, the poor academic report sent home forced his father to visit the school to determine what was going wrong.

"This can be remedied," stated the school director as he sugar-coated young Alexander's academic achievement, trying desperately to keep the donations from Mikhailov industries flowing into the Technical School budget. But what could not be hidden from reality was the fact that young Alexander had no interest in becoming an engineer, and had possibly less aptitude for technical or mechanical things than originally thought. He was a good singer, a decent tenor, but he failed to realize that the Mikhailov factories did not need an opera tenor, regardless of how many Italian arias he could sing.

"Enroll him in the Military Academy," advised the director. "There, he will develop leadership qualities." Under his breath, he meant hard-nosed discipline that a year or two in the army would teach him. "Thereafter, Alexander can return to complete his education here at the Technical School. Then he will be ready to take up his rightful place as leader in the Mikhailov empire."

Alexander's father, a practical man, saw merit in this plan. Since Russia was not at war, he reasoned that his son would be safe, and besides, a Mikhailov in the army would help keep the lucrative contracts flowing his way. Once the army had succeeded in making a man out of his boy, he would take him back into the family businesses and young Alexander would become useful. Upon his father's suggestion or insistence, depending upon one's perspective, Alexander enrolled in the Military Academy. This course of study was more practical, less theoretical, and suited him much better. He was now a year older and his work habits had matured exponentially. Consequently, he did reasonably well, even in the academic disciplines. Furthermore, any prospects of developing a brilliant military career were in no way impeded by his father's influence.

***

Above all, young Alexander was no fool. With his father's rubles clearing the way, he rose rapidly through the ranks. In reality, however, he was even less of a soldier than he was an engineer. He hated the military and chafed under the many humiliations soldiers and even young officers were forced to endure. Were his superiors not the same incompetent officers who had messed up so badly in the 1905 conflict with Japan? What was he expected to learn from them? Furthermore, young Alexander possessed few of the hard-nosed character traits required of rising young officers. As a drill sergeant, he would much rather have taught singing to the young recruits, rather than try to harden these boys into crack fighting machines.

Nevertheless, discipline was the new mantra preached by high-ranking army officers and everyone, including Alexander, was expected to buy into this. Discipline, the vital character trait needed to be hammered into lazy cowards for them to become effective soldiers if another abysmal showing by the Imperial Russian Army was to be avoided. But what was not being addressed was the suitability, even competency, of officers at all levels, many of whom owed their commissions to wealth and influence, rather than intelligence and courage. These officers would likely fare no better in actual battle situations than their predecessors had in the 1905 conflict. According to widespread gossip, the Russian Imperial Guards had not carried their weight in the war with Japan. Consequently, poorly trained volunteers – cannon fodder – had waged much of the battle.

This was the army into which young Alexander had enlisted, and this was the army in which he rapidly rose through the ranks. Whenever the name Mikhailov was recognized during roll call or incidental contact with a superior officer was made, the strict rules of army discipline would be slightly compromised in his favour. This suited Alexander just fine. Thus, he survived. Alexander really did not fit in with other officers who, in his view, fell into two groups. On the one hand, there were the overachievers, the rank pullers, those who would kiss ass, and rat on each other at the drop of a hat if it were to their advantage. The other group – many like him – had been sent to the military to grow up or simply get away from parents. These tended to be slothful drunks-in-training, lacking ambition. His social skills and natural abilities allowed Alexander at least to get by, but inwardly he was hurting.

***

Alexander's lot in life began to improve when a small contingent of the Imperial Army, to which he had been commissioned, was reassigned to Odessa. He loved this city and knew it well – a city that held happy memories for him. The Mikhailov family owned a dacha along the Black Sea, and each summer they came to this area to escape the industrial stench their factories in Tsaritsyn were producing. Odessa was not merely a beautiful city, but also a significant cultural centre with libraries, museums, and above all, a lovely opera house boasting a full season of opera, ballet, and drama productions. Alexander's mother, Anastasia, was related to the concertmaster of the opera orchestra and her money encouraged local cultural endeavours.

From the military perspective, battalions sent to various parts of Russia had orders to reform and restructure the Imperial Army to address the problems that had led to defeat at the hands of the Japanese in 1905. In truth, however, the Imperial Russian Army was still an old boys club, led by the same officers who had performed so badly in the Russo-Japanese war. A second reason for the battalion to which Alexander was assigned to be sent to Odessa was to establish a military presence in the area and protect the wealthy Russians who owned summer properties there. Not that a war was imminent, but groups of Ukrainian nationals were starting to make noise, and if these discontented nationalists ever joined forces and became organized under Bolshevik or Menshevik leadership, there could be serious trouble.

Chapter 4
Christina and Alexander – 1909

RAISA, NOW KNOWN AS CHRISTINA FRIEDRICHSEN, HAD SETTLED INTO her new job at the Russian army base. She had drifted from her home in Rosenthal to Odessa and fallen in with common labourers, embracing a daily routine of hard work, poor food, little sleep, and boredom. On Sundays, she occasionally attended the tiny house church she had stumbled upon on her first day in Odessa, but these people also had lives and problems that kept them occupied throughout the week.

On warm evenings, after assigned duties had been completed and if they still had enough energy, the young workers with whom Christina associated would gather informally at city parks, even street corners, and entertain themselves with singing, storytelling, and a variety of folk dances. Ironically, these poor workers found a *joie de vivre* in their mind-numbing monotonous existence, while the officers, whose standard of living was vastly higher than theirs, contended with hours of meaningless boredom. Officers who chose not to habitually drink themselves into oblivion became aware of the free entertainment provided by these workers, and on long evenings would cautiously approach the action, always at an appropriate distance, to listen and take in these joyful activities. If the singing and dancing was particularly good, they might toss a few coins in the direction of the performers.

In this strange environment of working long hours at menial jobs, living in poor conditions, and singing together with her coworkers, Christina found her place. For the first time in her life, she felt valued and appreciated for what she could do, rather than judged or criticized for what she could not do. This group of ragtag street performers had one or two people who were reasonably proficient on stringed instruments – guitar, mandolin, and bandura – as well as several who played the harmonica. Christina remembered some guitar chords taught to her by *Oma* Friedrichsen, so she accompanied herself while singing folk tunes she had learned from somewhere in her past. Christina loved these sessions. Singing was something she enjoyed immensely. It provided some relief from the stresses of life. Singing allowed her to feel good about herself, feel worthwhile, and escape into a different world – a world without prejudice or rejection. In Rosenthal, even this activity had at times been marred by criticism and disapproval, but here her singing was appreciated, even encouraged. Now she could sing as freely and loudly as she wished. Fortunately for Christina, the genes she inherited from her Friedrichsen and Brodsky relatives combined to give her a beautifully natural singing voice. Her tone was clear, well supported, resonant, and free from major technical faults. As a result, she could sing higher, lower, softer, and louder than anyone her age. Even when she sang very softly, her tone was still vibrant and resonant enough to carry very well, and when she chose, even within a given note, she could increase the volume to a sizeable forte or decrease it to a whisper without any loss of breath support or tonal beauty. Her talent was just waiting to be discovered.

In Rosenthal, whenever the children sang, Christina's voice was always heard above the others even when she thought she was singing softly. Choir leaders would ask her to blend in with other singers. "You must, at all times, hear the voice next to you," they would instruct. But whenever there was a note a little too high for other singers, or a passage too difficult for other young voices, they would cut her loose and allow her to carry the choir through these challenging passages. This, of course, created problems with several budding prima donnas. On the one hand, Christina was not worthy to be included in their inner circle, yet on the other hand, she made them look rather inadequate where singing was concerned.

In Odessa, the problems she had experienced in Rosenthal were soon forgotten. Here her talent was valued, even encouraged, by coworkers who enjoyed listening to her sing almost as much as she enjoyed singing for them. Fellow workers would add harmony to her songs while others would improvise instrumental accompaniments as best they could. Before long, Christina's singing was backed up by a small band of singers and players.

***

At one of these impromptu street performances, the dashing young officer Alexander Mikhailov first heard Christina sing. His education and life experience had taught him to ignore these poor young peasant girls, who, according to him, were all the same. All were dressed poorly and all according to the views of privileged young officers had arrived at the station in life to which they were destined. But this young girl captured his attention. Here was someone who challenged his view that poor people had little worth. Musical talent was not the sole prerogative of the rich and famous as he had been led to believe. This young girl helped him to see peasants in a different light. Little did Alexander realize that meeting Christina would bring about a radical change to his life.

One Sunday night, when Alexander yet again found himself in a state of complete boredom, he strolled away from the barracks toward the centre of the city. The solitude and fresh evening air helped brighten his mood and allowed his imagination to float freely away from the infernal army life he so detested. Before long, he found himself at the City Garden, a beautiful park located along Preobrazhenskaya Street. As usual, he was lost in his thoughts and completely unaware of how far he had wandered. These walks allowed him to explore his dreams of returning to Tsaritsyn as a civilian, the city where his family and his father's wealth was located. As he approached the pavilion, the lovely centrepiece of the City Garden, he noticed a group of young people – peasant workers he assumed – singing, dancing, and laughing, clearly having more fun than he could ever remember.

His instinct and training told him to move on, but a melody caught his attention. He stopped and listened intently. Alexander recognized the song, a folk ditty that his mother had taught him. His nannies also knew the song and would, no doubt, have sung it much better than these poor street urchins ever could. As he listened memories of his childhood flooded back, he had to admit that the singing he was hearing was actually quite good, much better than he had expected. One voice clearly soared above the rest with a tone like something he might have heard at the Odessa Opera. Was this indeed the same soprano who had recently sung the leading role in *Rigoletto?* Surely not! Alexander was so starved for good entertainment – music, singing, any song or dance that could provide a diversion from his mind-numbing routine – perhaps he heard more than there actually was.

During the next few days, Alexander could not get this voice out of his mind. On quiet evenings, he began to seek out places where these impromptu performances might take place in hopes of hearing this singing again. He searched parks, street corners, and even alleys, always keeping his ears attuned to hear this special voice. His efforts were rewarded. Several weeks later, he again heard her sing and quickly identified the girl with the amazing voice. Her dress and looks certainly didn't capture his attention, for in his eyes she was as poorly clothed as the other peasant girls. It was not her size, for she was short and rather skinny, clearly no stranger to hunger. Alexander did notice that she had a pretty face, but when she opened her mouth to sing, everything else paled by comparison. He couldn't imagine how such an immature and undernourished frame could produce such a beautiful sound. Her broad vocal range, very difficult for many trained singers to achieve, appeared to be no problem for her. Also, she sang only in keys the four-stringed instruments could manage, and successfully negotiated the high notes with an ease that would create envy among the prima donnas he had known.

Unlike many streetwise peasant girls, Christina appeared to be oblivious to the attention, especially the sexual advances made by the louts who passed themselves off as officers. Perhaps it was her youthful appearance or perhaps the beauty of her singing that elicited nobler thoughts in the minds of these uncouth fools, for she appeared able to escape their unwanted attention. Alexander became a little possessive of her and annoyed with officers who tossed coins at her feet. Did they actually recognize her talent? Were they even interested in her singing, or was this merely another way of initiating unwanted advances toward poor underprivileged girls? Did they need to be reminded that for security reasons, soldiers were forbidden from fraternizing with locals? Regulations demanded that contact with the workers, especially girls, must be strictly avoided.

At first, Alexander maintained a safe distance and applauded politely whenever Christina sang, but soon he was drawn in toward her and became more animated in his expression of appreciation. When others sang, he listened quietly, but whenever this young girl sang, he moved in closer, and before long, he began shouting titles of songs he wished her to repeat. Christina did her best to avoid eye contact with this smartly dressed officer, yet she was totally aware of his presence, listening very attentively to hear the titles of songs he wished her to sing again. She was also aware of the rule that forbade soldiers, especially officers, from fraternizing with local girls. Any attempt to acknowledge an officer's presence could be interpreted as a security risk and that girl could immediately be banned from the army base.

Nevertheless, Christina and her coworkers could not help but notice the presence of this officer who kept appearing. Was it her imagination, or did he move in a little closer to her each time? One evening, after all the officers and most of the people had left, this officer walked up, brushed past her, and dropped a tiny pouch next to her guitar case. She picked it up, took it home, and to her surprise found that it contained money. Was this a trap? What was she to do? If someone had discovered the money, she could certainly have been accused of stealing. Fear kept her in her room for a few days as she sought a solution to this confusing dilemma. Her coworkers, however, begged her to come with them. She agreed, and again, there he was. Before Christina could reach for her guitar, the officer began requesting his favourite songs.

Christina did not know how to cool this unwanted attention. Not just a man, but a sharp-looking young officer – the first man who had ever taken notice of her – appeared to be paying her special interest. What did he want? Certainly her coworkers and other officers must also be aware of the situation. She no longer feared him, and something in her longed to know him better, but she knew full well that any friendship between a young officer and a lowly peasant worker was totally out of the question.

Christina continued to pass herself off as a Ukrainian girl. This, in her mind, was better than admitting to being either a Mennonite or a Jew. He, every inch an officer, appeared to be an aristocrat who had possibly attained his rank through wealth and position. Even in her wildest fantasies, Christina knew the social distance between them would rule out any relationship, even a casual acquaintance. This is where the budding friendship might have ended, and, depending on one's perspective, perhaps it should have.

Over time, the mutual attraction between Christina and Alexander continued to grow. At one of these street performances, Christina managed to fit a Mussorgsky melody into her repertoire of folk tunes. Again, she was rewarded with loud applause from the admiring officers. Alexander knew the melody well and felt certain her rendition of this song would enhance its popularity within the art song repertoire.

Her high notes are exquisite, thought Alexander. *How can such a small, undernourished frame sustain such gorgeous legato lines?* He realized that the opera prima donnas he knew from the musical events he attended must outweigh her by at least seventy-five pounds. Alexander continued to become less circumspect, less cautious, and began speaking to her directly, encouraging her with compliments and a few discreetly discarded coins. Perhaps in his mind, he had discovered the prima donna for the opera company he wanted to build with his father's wealth once he had escaped this stupid army life.

Christina began to acknowledge Alexander's attention, and before long, they exchanged words and subtle pleasantries. His words were soft and friendly – not the abrasive shouts and rude commands she had grown to expect from other officers. Alexander thought he noticed that she was paying more attention to her personal appearance, but he wondered how she could make herself look so attractive with the few clothing and make-up articles she had at her disposal. He, for that matter, took his own appearance and decorum to levels far greater than what the army demanded of him.

***

For the unmotivated army personnel, life at the base continued to drag on from one day to the next. Soldiers stuck in the same old routine, with boredom being the greatest challenge faced by soldiers and officers alike. Finding meaningful activities for everyone during peacetime became a senior officer's greatest concern. Drills and manoeuvres could only be done so many times before the drudgery of the incessant repetition became obvious, even to the dumbest soldier. Athletic endeavours and games also become redundant, even before every bat and ball had either been hit out of circulation or kicked to bits. Board games, especially chess, had long since exhausted the intellectual capacity of the majority of soldiers and officers. Yet without creative activities to keep soldiers occupied, they would drink too much, fight too much, and find far too many opportunities to get into trouble.

With the rapidly depleting list of meaningful activities almost at an end, some high-ranking officer made the suggestion that an evening of music for the troops should be organized. Such suggestions from superior officers were rarely ignored. It gave everyone, especially those who needed to spruce up their reputations, the opportunity to do something worthwhile in the eyes of their superiors and thereby enhance any future consideration for promotion. Alexander was well aware of this. He was delighted with the prospect of a change to his daily routine and excited by the opportunity to make music. He also welcomed the chance to raise his profile and polish the report that would surely be sent home to his father. Finally, he would be doing something he was good at, something at which he could excel.

Alexander was the first to volunteer. He gladly agreed to serve as impresario for such an event and immediately began to seek out and audition talent. Unfortunately, for this kind of endeavour, the musical aptitude among this group of soldiers was extremely thin. He found a few who played guitar, several who had some experience with stringed instruments, and one who played piano. But there was absolutely no one who could perform music at any acceptable level. Fortunately, Alexander received permission to draft musical talent from sources off the base. He immediately began to look for Christina, the peasant girl who sang folk tunes and Mussorgsky melodies so beautifully.

Finally, as the impresario of this event, he had an opportunity to officially meet the girl whose singing he so admired. Alexander found her and introduced himself to her, stating his request and offering to help her prepare several pieces for the evening of music being planned at the base. This event, in his runaway mind, would become her singing debut. Finally, now he could speak to her and find out more about her.

Their initial meeting was a little awkward. Christina was very shy, reticent about giving her name or sharing personal details about her life, but then Alexander also needed to be careful about offering too much personal information. His father had grown very rich supplying grenades and machine guns to the army seeking to modernize its weapons – weapons that could also be used to keep Ukrainian unrest in line. Stories to this effect had become associated with the Mikhailov name and appeared in local papers. Families of wealth and privilege who had ties to the aristocracy were beginning to attract unwanted attention.

Alexander requested, and was granted, the use of a small room with a useable piano as his practice facility. Christina was delighted to sing for him. It was a chance for her to escape work and indulge herself in the activity that she had so enjoyed since childhood. It also gave her a few hours away from kitchen and toilet cleaning detail to which she had recently been assigned. The first music lesson began with a few stretching and warm-up exercises that Christina most likely did not need and probably did not understand. Both young people were determined to make this session last as long as possible. Warm-ups were followed by a series of scales sung on various vowels at various pitches as suggested by Alexander. Christina imitated these with ease. Then the fun began. From somewhere within her body, or perhaps within her soul, the melody of the Mussorgsky song Alexander had heard her sing rang out with tone even more gorgeous than what he remembered. She sang the entire piece in a key too high for most singers to sustain, with vocal size and legato line that Alexander's singing teacher had hoped he would someday develop.

Alexander immediately joined her with accompaniment on the piano, filling in as many chords as his limited skills would allow. Following the song, the somewhat flustered "music teacher" immediately stepped away from the piano and suggested that his "student" imitate him as he began to demonstrate a number of vocal exercises he had learned from his singing teachers. Christina thought this was great fun and sang the many challenging exercises and vocalizations with such freedom and ease, and in such high keys, that this part of the lesson was soon declared unnecessary.

A week or so later, following a few more lessons, Alexander's first vocal student sang at her first public recital. The program was certainly not the cultural event of the season, but it did provide an entertaining diversion to keep soldiers occupied and out of trouble for at least a part of the evening. Christina, accompanied by Alexander's somewhat laboured piano playing, sang several folk melodies, two Mussorgsky songs, and was clearly the only real performer at the event. She was rewarded with thunderous and sincere applause.

Senior officers immediately saw value in these evenings of music and Alexander was allowed to continue his work with Christina. He would teach her songs and prepare her for additional appearances in their new-found recital series. Alexander also began training her voice as best he could. Actually, Christina needed more encouragement than training, and Alexander's admiration of her singing certainly provided this. She had a natural voice, a free voice capable of singing a wide range of notes in any dynamic and on any vowel. She flew through the exercises, sang coloratura passages with agility and clarity at breakneck speed. She could sustain the most beautiful legato lines on pieces written in a very high tessitura, yet meant to be sung in a very slow sostunuto character. And the fact that Alexander was allowed a private practice room for the frivolous activity of teaching singing to an army employee, a peasant girl, could only be attributed to the fact that his name was Mikhailov.

Fortunately for Alexander, his own star rose even higher during this time. His father had won the prestigious State Award for Outstanding Service to Russia for the high quality munitions that his factories were producing. Everyone knew that the czar, himself, had travelled to Tsaritsyn to personally present this award to Alexander Mikhailov, Sr., and also to get a closer look at the munitions factories. After this, his son, Alexander, Jr., could do no wrong.

Alexander's music sessions with Christina took place several times a week. They both enjoyed and valued this time, the most meaningful and fulfilling activity that either of them had recently experienced. Alexander had clearly fallen in love with her voice and her singing. One day he admitted to himself that he had indeed fallen in love with her. Oh, how he enjoyed gently pressing against her abdominal muscles while she sustained a high note, or standing behind her with his hands on her ribcage to see that her breath did not escape too quickly. He could never get enough of this exercise and found any number of excuses for repeating it over and over.

Alexander and Christina became close friends. Aside from these musical sessions, the strict code that forbade Imperial Army officers from fraternizing with local Ukrainian peasant girls was still very much in place. So any meeting between them beyond music lessons was carefully arranged and took place in secrecy. Alexander learned to deal with officers who could be bribed, or who were intimidated by the Mikhailov name, in order to keep their silence. Christina, who was afraid to reveal her real name to him, obviously did not fit in with the society girls who were invited to attend army sanctioned social events. She was uneducated. The little that she read was mainly in German. Alexander, on the other hand, was well educated and moved freely within the circles of high society. What drew them together was the physical attraction they now felt for each other, and of course, their love of singing.

Alexander considered contacting his mother's relative, the concertmaster of the Odessa Opera Orchestra, whom he knew as Uncle Viktor, to arrange for an audition with the best voice teacher in Odessa to evaluate Christina's incredible talent. To prepare Christina for this audition, he taught her songs and arias that he knew. She would sing these back to him, usually in a higher key with beautiful tone that would rival most anything he had heard in Moscow or St. Petersburg. Alexander preferred the more classical melodies, especially longer pieces from Russian operas. One piece was this melody by Tchaikovsky that he knew. It was the "Letter Scene" from Tchaikovsky's *Eugene Onegin,* sung by the character Tatyana.

Whether it was the poetry that stirred up feelings of love or the beautiful melody that tore at his heart, he could not say. He taught her the melody and, whenever they saw each other, she would sing it back to him. Once she had mastered this piece, Alexander taught Christina the music to the Rachmaninoff *Vocalise,* which she sang unaccompanied and always in the correct key. Most sopranos found the vocal line that ascended up to the C-sharp very challenging, but it was no problem for Christina. She sang it over and over, and just to tease him, would decrescendo on the highest note, holding it long enough for him to stop breathing.

Alexander had fallen hopelessly in love with Christina and her singing. This intense musical experience with her so invigorated him that some nights he just could not sleep. Before long, they freely declared their love for each other, and the social distance between them mattered less and less. He wanted to give Christina money to buy her a pretty dress and some good shoes, but unfortunately the army and his father kept him on meagre financial rations. He often brought her some treats and noticed how quickly she devoured them. From then on, whenever Alexander saw her, he would bring her a few morsels of food left over from his dinner.

Perhaps if his parents met her, they would feel the same way about Christina as he did. Summer was approaching and his family would soon be returning to Odessa for a lengthy vacation and a reunion with Uncle

Viktor and his family. Since being stationed in Odessa, Alexander had not spent much time with them. The army had tight restrictions regarding time spent off base and recently all his spare time was spent with Christina. Also, the recent rumblings among the local Ukrainian peasants had placed the military base on a higher state of alert. But young boys in love and away from home are hardly known for rational thinking. They fail to see any impending problems.

Alexander told Christina the story of Eugene Onegin, describing as best he could the lovely music Tchaikovsky had composed to this sad tale by Pushkin. He told the story of the "Letter Scene" where Tatyana, the leading soprano, confessed her love to young Onegin, the pompous ass who turned her down and went on to kill his friend Lensky in a duel. He later returned to marry Tatyana, who now was married to his old cousin, Gremin. Alexander had tears in his eyes as he described the lovely music, and wept openly when Christina sang it back to him in its entirety with incredible high notes.

One day Alexander asked her to dress in her best clothes as together they planned to go to the opera the following night. The plan may have worked except for the fact that Christina had nothing suitable to wear, and what she had would never hold up in comparison to the glittering gowns worn by other women attending the opera. The looks and glances directed at the couple as they approached the ticket counter were so intimidating that they gave up and slipped out the side door. They heard the "Letter Scene" from Tchaikovsky's opera by pressing their ears tightly against the partially opened stage door.

***

A few months later, in the cavernous St. Vladimir Orthodox Cathedral in Odessa, a short and slender figure walked slowly toward the altar. The dim light made it difficult to determine the age or gender of this figure, but as the person proceeded through the expansive nave, one could see the dress and the pretty face of a teenage girl. Had her hair been shorter or had she been wearing different clothes, her lean figure could easily have been mistaken for that of a boy, but as this young girl passed by, a slightly protruding abdomen could be seen under her ill-fitted gown. Well, not actually a gown, though from a distance the off-white material appeared new. A closer look revealed a somewhat worn dress that was pinned in a number of places, but still far too big. The picture now became clearer – she was indeed a very young girl, a bride, and she was clearly pregnant. In her hair, she wore an artistically woven wreath of locally grown flowers someone had kindly created for her. Waiting at the altar was the groom, a smart looking junior officer of the Imperial Russian Army dressed in a khaki tunic with embellished breast pockets, black piped cuffs, and highly polished metal buttons engraved with Russian Imperial eagles. Everything on the young man that could be polished was polished, and everything that needed to be well fitted was well fitted. Except for the fact that the officer's uniform clearly outclassed the ill-fitted bridal grown hanging loosely from the shoulders of the physically immature young girl, the bride and groom may have looked like a typical young couple.

The groom, Alexander Mikhailov, must have been well connected to achieve the rank of junior officer in the Imperial Army at the tender age of nineteen years. Christina, his bride, who was clearly younger than him, appeared to have the physical maturity of a fifteen-year-old. She certainly wasn't a blushing bride. Her thin, emaciated body did not have enough blood in its veins to even blush. The baby in her womb was claiming nutrients her body simply did not have and could not produce.

***

It was highly irregular for a young officer of the Imperial Army to marry while still on active duty. Permission from some high-ranking commander, who may have been bribed or inebriated, or both, must have been given to supersede the strict army regulations to allow such a marriage to go forward. Life for Alexander, the naïve and shielded young groom who had grown up under the protection of his family name, had always been a little easier. Consequently, he tended to live in the moment and not be overly concerned with the consequences of any of his actions.

Alexander was Orthodox, a practicing Christian. He attended services regularly and attempted to adhere strictly to the church's teachings and also the officer's moral code. When he realized that Christina was with child, Alexander chose not to compromise his values by abandoning his pregnant girlfriend. He quickly made the acquaintance of members of the clergy, including one young priest who felt honoured to be asked by Alexander to prepare Christina to receive the holy sacrament of baptism so that they could be married before God in an Orthodox cathedral. Because she felt little commitment to her own religious beliefs, she was certainly prepared to examine his.

The fact that Christina was expecting a baby was a poorly kept secret and even the priest chose not to ask too many questions. The church authorities had the impression that the parents of Alexander and Christina knew of the wedding and had given their blessings. No one had sought to verify this information, nor did anyone ask how old Christina was. The priest felt doubly honoured when asked to also perform the marriage ceremony of Alexander and Christina. He had visions of the church, if not the entire city of Odessa, being filled with the wealthy influential friends and relatives of Alexander Mikhailov. How totally surprised he was when so few people attended the marriage ceremony. The Mikhailov entourage, whom he expected to grace the church never arrived. Nor did the families of Alexander or Christina even know that this wedding was taking place. The hours spent by the young priest attending to wedding details and rehearsing his part in the service were lost on the handful of guests who attended the ceremony.

Alexander's superiors at the army base also knew little about recent events in his life. They were aware of the fact that he was off base more often than army regulations would allow, but they simply assumed he was taking care of business for his family's factories – the very factories that produced the grenades and explosives that helped them maintain a healthy respect among potential Ukrainian dissidents.

***

Try as he might, Alexander still had not developed a workable plan for introducing Christina to his parents. The speed at which events in his life were unfolding simply overwhelmed his youthful naive inexperience, thus preventing him from planning too far ahead. At the age of nineteen, his life seemed beyond control. His parents did not even know that he had a girlfriend, so how would they react to the news that he was married? And how would they deal with the information that they were about to become grandparents? The unthinkable had befallen him.

Alexander fully realized that the truth would eventually need to be told, and he accepted the fact that he was the one who needed to tell it. However, whenever he mustered up the courage to inform his parents, another piece of information would leak out and he would need to begin again to create a plausible narrative. His first problem was addressing the fact that the girl with whom he had fallen in love and now married was of Ukrainian peasant background. This was very serious. Tensions in the region between governing authorities and the local people, many of whom had been emancipated from serfdom only a few decades before, were on the rise. As displaced peasants, they were mistrustful of the Imperial Army. Furthermore, they were mistrustful of the czar, tired of the opulent lifestyle of the wealthy, and most of all, tired of their own poverty and starvation. The army's presence in Odessa made it difficult for them to voice their legitimate grievances.

That Christina was Ukrainian, an assumption on Alexander's part that she never attempted to correct was a fact he was prepared to live with. He knew she was intelligent, certainly as intelligent as he and although she admitted to having little formal education, she appeared to have the general knowledge of someone who read books. He had hoped to introduce her to his parents as a Russian girl whose family had fallen upon hard times and who needed to leave school prematurely. This account seemed plausible, and with a little tweaking, may have become credible. However, once Alexander discovered that Christina was pregnant, any plan to tell his parents was

completely derailed. He deeply loved Christina. He could not possibly live
without her and was prepared to risk being cut off from his family's wealth
in order to spend his life with her. His tour in the army was almost over
and Alexander felt confident that his father would provide some financial
support for his young family. If he were to stay in the Imperial Army, he
would likely be stationed goodness knows where – probably far away from
his wife and child. This would leave them to starve emotionally, perhaps
even physically. Surely his father would not allow this to happen.

The situation was difficult enough but when Christina shared more
details about her past, things got worse. Had it not been for the love for
his wife, Alexander might have considered a more drastic course of action
– worse than leaving her or possibly even worse than deserting the army.
She had introduced herself as Christina Friedrichsen of no fixed address
– when people are in love, are more details really necessary? But now,
Christina shared with him that her mother's name was Raisa Brodsky
and he now faced a far worse nightmare. She was a Jew, and not even a
full-blooded Jew, but a Jew with a Germanic father whose surname was
Friedrichsen. Jews were associated with the peasant unrest. Some had ties
to this new political movement known as Bolshevism, a movement his
father and all his wealthy business associates so vehemently opposed. And
to make matters worse, rumours throughout the officer's corps speculated,
even predicted, armed conflict with Germany. Had she taken her mother's
birth name, Christina would have been known as Raisa Brodsky. Alexander
was sure he had heard of a high-ranking official named Brodsky who had
ties with the Bolshevik movement.

Christina tried to calm his rising fear by explaining to him that her
name was more Scandinavian than German, and that her paternal grandparents were Mennonites, people of mainly Dutch extraction who believed
in peace. But Alexander heard only that she was Jewish and German, and
that she spoke German and some Yiddish, which explained to him why her
Russian was weak. Her father, whoever he was, did not believe in fighting
in the army, the very army for which the Mikhailov factories were producing munitions. This news was beyond comprehension. The realization that

Christina was a person with whom he should not even associate, and who would never be accepted by his army friends or by his family threatened to undo Alexander. The child she was carrying – his child – would be of Russian, Jewish, German, Dutch, Scandinavian, and whatever ancestry. How was this even possible? Though his heart was in turmoil Alexander knew that he deeply loved Christina and he loved the baby she was carrying.

Chapter 5
Christina – 1909

MARRIED LIFE FOR ALEXANDER AND CHRISTINA MIKHAILOV WAS QUITE unconventional, certainly not at all what newlyweds under normal circumstances would have expected. Russian society allowed recently married men in Alexander's position, born into wealth and social standing, to move into lavishly furnished quarters and be attended to by servants. At least this is the lifestyle he recalled from his childhood that his parents had enjoyed during their early years of marriage. Even the Mennonite girls in Rosenthal, whose parents were not nearly as wealthy as the Mikhailov family, could expect to begin married life with certain comforts and amenities as furnished by their families.

Alexander's marital status and comfort level were of little concern to his superior officers at the Imperial Russian Army base at Odessa. Military responsibilities were expected to be carried out to the full. Every night he was required to be in the officer's barracks and sleep in the bed to which he had been assigned. Unfortunately for him, people had noticed that the Mikhailov family had been conspicuously absent at his marriage ceremony and this fact adversely impacted his status and the number of entitlements he could now draw upon. In the minds of his jealous superiors, a perceived rift between father and son reduced Alexander's position to that of any other officer of his rank. One or two of his closest friends were aware of the situation with Christina, and fortunately for him, chose to keep the details to themselves. In his free time, Alexander would steal away from the base to spend time with his new wife in the tiny room he had found for her, but by the end of the evening he was expected to be back in his bed in the officer's quarters.

Once Christina realized that she was pregnant, she took the proactive step of leaving her job at the base before she could be fired. As she did not have many close ties with other workers, she did not find it difficult to leave. It felt good to vacate the louse-infected residence where she had lived, especially the stain covered mattress that she had slept upon, but now she was totally dependent upon Alexander for support. Life in the Russian culture at the time was tough on single girls in her condition, especially if they were suspected of being mistresses of army officers. She and Alexander kept the details of their relationship to themselves. Money was very tight. Alexander's father still believed that his son needed to learn proper financial management. Therefore any request for a larger allowance was promptly denied with the usual accompanying letter written by some secretary in his father's office extolling the virtues of living within one's means.

In spite of these awkward circumstances, Alexander and Christina managed to get by. They believed that their present living arrangement was only temporary. Soon Alexander's term in the Imperial Army would end, and he and his young family would return to Tsaritsyn where their standard of living would rise significantly. He would be a Mikhailov, a civilian, sitting in some stuffed chair with a cushy job in one of his father's factories. He and Christina would live in a comfortable apartment with a live-in nanny, and Christina could begin vocal training in preparation for a career in opera.

The Imperial Army had taught Alexander many things, but living in the real world was not one of them. He had learned to get along with superior officers by following orders and keeping requests for special favours to a minimum. But now, Christina's condition and that of their unborn baby deeply concerned him. Perhaps this was an indication that he was finally growing up and assuming responsibility for his actions. The landlord of the building where he had rented a modest room for Christina was not a charitable person. The man was unhappy at the prospect of housing an army officer's pregnant mistress in his building and hinted at terminating her rental agreement. He dismissed the marriage certificate that was presented to him as proof that Christina and Alexander were indeed married, believing it to be fake. At some point though, someone must have tipped him off to the fact that the unborn baby's grandfather was very wealthy, and he reasoned that if he were to treat Christina well, there might be a payoff for him at some point in the future. In spite of a tightly restricted budget, Alexander did his best to smuggle supplies to Christina. He found that he could obtain more nutritious food for her by bribing the cooks with money from his meagre allowance than by trying to purchase groceries in the markets of Odessa.

Life went on as best it could. Christina was unemployed, dealing with the boredom of being cooped up in her tiny room, staring at the same never-changing sights from her second storey window and waiting for the hours to drag by. She encouraged herself with the hope that conditions would soon improve. Fewer and fewer letters were exchanged between her and *Oma* Friedrichsen and she never mentioned any of the details regarding recent changes in her life. She reasoned that once Alexander was discharged from the army, their young family would travel to Rosenthal to introduce her new baby to the family members who still lived there and to friends, if such even existed. Alexander settled back into his army routine, checking off the days on a wall calendar until he could escape this boring, meaningless existence, scheming each day how best to inform his parents of his growing new family. Any change in his monotonous routine was a welcomed diversion for him.

Fortunately for Alexander, such a diversion was about to present itself. News reached the officers' corps that a directive sent to Odessa from the czar's inner circle in St. Petersburg strongly advised municipal leaders to plan public celebrations to commemorate the fifteenth anniversary of Czar Nicholas II's ascension to the Russian throne. The second part of this directive, also strongly worded, suggested that these celebrations take place on or near May 18, the czar's forty-first birthday. It was clear that the czar's advisors worried that the royal image that had been so badly tarnished

by the disastrous events of the 1905 war with Japan needed some reha-
bilitation, especially in the minds of the restless subjects. The Odessa civil
authorities took these suggestions very seriously and immediately began
planning public, very conspicuous celebrations. The Odessa contingent of
the Imperial Army also realized that such directives dared not be ignored
and also responded quickly. Within days, plans for a major military parade
to march through the streets of Odessa were laid out.

Intense preparations were immediately under way. Horses were
retrained and groomed, drills were rehearsed until they could be performed
flawlessly by even the dullest soldiers, and most importantly, the planned
parade route was cautiously scrutinized and repeatedly altered just to keep
security threats to a minimum. Armies had their own reasons for partici-
pating in these spit and polish events. Celebrations of this nature kept the
soldiers on their toes and allowed the senior officers to preen their egos
and reassure themselves of their own self-importance and indispensability.
This parade, however, had an additional agenda. The Imperial Russian
Army had taken notice of the growing unrest among poor and disenfran-
chised peasants in parts of Russia including Odessa and felt it was time to
remind the potential dissidents that the czar was still on the throne and in
complete control of every situation. The pomp and circumstance displayed
at this public event would be an implicit reminder that the army could
quickly, and with brutal force, put down any insurrection.

The day of the parade finally arrived. All the last minute preparations
were completed, down to the minutest detail. The weather was perfect.
Daffodils and crocuses were in full bloom, the May sun was warm and
inviting, and a gentle breeze blew in from the sea. Every detail of the parade
had been checked and rehearsed over and over. Even the highly trained
horses, groomed and well fed, had been prepared for every possible even-
tuality. The air crackled with excitement. Children needed to be restrained,
adults jostled for better viewing positions, and even the most cynically-
minded citizens of Odessa could barely contain their excitement as they
eagerly anticipated the arrival of this impressive spectacle.

At the head of the parade rode the political dignitaries, self-assured as always, all supporters of Czar Nicholas ii. Next came the army commanders, sitting tall in their saddles and oozing pomposity and pretension from every pore.

"So this is what they look like when they're not drunk," quipped Georgi Tschkoff, the young officer assigned to ride next to Alexander Mikhailov. Behind the commanders rode the junior officers, a little less glamorous and perhaps not as pretentious, but nevertheless far from displaying any sense of modesty. Somewhere down the line marched the foot soldiers. On this day, they carried live ammunition in their guns, prepared to ward off any attacks.

Possibly from bears or wolves, thought Alexander.

The route, finalized on the morning of the parade, was announced to only a few of the most senior commanders. The pedestrians who walked along Primorskaya Street that morning were pleasantly surprised to see the lines of soldiers and horses suddenly appear before them as the parade took shape in their part of the city. By the time the entourage had crossed the intersection at Odaria Street, full order had been established – the horses were under control and the soldiers were in exact formation. From here, the parade continued on in a southeasterly direction toward the Potyomkin Steps and on past the Richelieu monument where even the old marble statesman, according to several young officers, was seen to bow his head to the dignitaries who rode past. As the parade neared city centre it slowed down a little.

"We need more time to give the people every opportunity to be suitably impressed," quipped Georgi, as he flashed wide smiles at the girls who caught his attention.

Or be intimidated, thought Alex. He liked Georgi and laughed at his humour, but felt relieved that the security of the Imperial government was not in the hands of Georgi and others like him. Too many junior officers shared Georgi's frivolous attitude toward national security and this worried Alex. Soon Georgi would regain the status of a civilian and with his departure from the army, Russia would be just a little more secure.

The gentle breeze off the Black Sea worked its usual magic as it cooled the dignitaries who weighted themselves down with ceremonial dress and full regalia. It also calmed the nervous horses and helped relax the tense officers. The foot soldiers were allowed to sweat. All entrances to the parade route were quickly blocked to local traffic. Shops and schools had been closed for the day. The locals were expected to attend the event and demonstrate appropriate behaviour befitting the importance of the occasion, preferably by "directing wild cheers of admiration toward the senior officers," according to Georgi. But not everyone in Odessa was impressed. To the junior officers, the crowd seemed a little smaller than expected and rather subdued in its expression of admiration. The scarcity of noisy spontaneous cheers and fewer colourful bouquets of flowers tossed at the entourage by admiring spectators was noticed.

Once the parade passed Tamozhennaya Square, it turned south onto the wide Kanatnaya Street, slowly making its way toward Bol'shaya Arnautskaya Street. From here it turned west. As the procession crossed the elegant Pushkinskaya, Alexander took note of the beautiful trees and wide, clean sidewalks that had so impressed Christina on her initial arrival into the city. The lovely scene reminded him of his teenage wife whom he dearly loved and now missed. At Preobrazhenskaya Street, the route turned north and eventually connected again to Primorskaya.

"Almost there," whispered Alex to the rider beside him. "Soon we'll pass the City Garden and then be done with this silly spectacle." Alex looked forward to seeing the City Garden. This was a cheerful place that held happy memories for him. It was here that he first heard Christina sing and it was here he first spoke to her. Also, this is the place he and Christina would escape to on beautiful spring evenings. Together they would stroll arm in arm along the walkways, fearing the glances of no one, admiring the spring flowers and the tall oaks, and occasionally enjoying a minstrel or two. The City Park, especially the secluded bench near the pavilion, was a safe place – a happy place where he and Christina could forget their troubles and dream of the music careers they hoped to establish.

"You'll draw those stuffy self-possessed patrons out of their seats," Alex would say to Christina. "They will hear your high notes and forget that their once intimidating glances drove you out of the Opera House."

If those peacocks at the head of the line would only pick up the pace, he thought, *then perhaps there would be time to return to the park with Christina and enjoy the remainder of this beautiful spring evening.*

"Why don't you accidentally shoot your gun?" whispered his friend Georgi. "That will surely get their asses moving!"

The warm May sunshine had soothed the dignitaries into complacency. The senior officers, now convinced that the display of force had kept everyone in line, relaxed in their saddles. In the unhurried, midday heat, the horses began sweating, the commanders were perspiring, and the junior officers were doing their best to stay alert. The display of elegant force and tranquility on this pleasant afternoon had lulled them to sleep. Even Alexander, securely seated in his saddle, was barely awake. But, as they rode past the main entrance to the City Garden, the serenity of the afternoon was suddenly shattered.

"Have you lost your mind!?" screamed Georgi, as he instantly came to attention. His first reaction to a sudden blast near his head was to assume that Alex had somehow discharged his weapon. Georgi's horse reared up on its hind legs as he frantically hung on, trying to regain control of the beast. From the corner of his eye, Georgi saw Alex sitting on the ground firmly planted on the seat of his pants. Not many people took notice of this sudden noise that had caught the junior officers by surprise. Few realized that anything out of the ordinary had happened. Even the commanders at the head of the parade hardly flinched. From somewhere behind a tall oak tree in the City Park, a makeshift explosive device had been hurled toward the officers and had detonated. The ensuing blast caused several horses to bolt upright and throw two or three riders onto the ground. Nothing spiralled out of control, and the resulting confusion was quickly brought to order. A contingent of soldiers was immediately dispatched into the crowd to search for the perpetrator. A young man was arrested, the horses were calmed down, and the army, yet again, demonstrated its complete control over any potentially dangerous situation. Within minutes, order was restored and the parade continued on its way. An ambulance was dispatched from the rear of the parade to attend to several soldiers who required medical attention. Three officers were promptly given first aid. One appeared to be hurt more seriously and was immediately taken by ambulance to a hospital where important military personal received special medical attention. Unfortunately for this particular officer, a piece of metal had lodged in his neck, puncturing a carotid artery, and Alexander Mikhailov bled to death before he could reach the hospital.

Everyone hailed the attack a success. The dissidents claimed to have made a statement – the Bolshevik movement had now been officially introduced to the people of Odessa. The army also claimed success. They had quickly contained the situation, found and arrested a young student, a member of the Bolsheviks. A quick trial took place, and several days later, the student who freely admitted to tossing the makeshift grenade, was hanged by his neck until he was dead.

But for Christina, this event was anything but a success. Her devastation was indescribable. For several days after this incident, she waited patiently in her room and wondered anxiously why her husband, Alexander, did not come. She had heard that an incident had taken place along the parade route, but believed the news on the street that no one had been seriously injured. On the third day after his death, once Alexander had received full military honours and his body was en route to his family home in Tsaritsyn, Christina finally learned the details of her husband's death. One of Alexander's few friends came by and broke the tragic news to her. This friend, at great personal risk, was kind enough to steal several of Alex's valuable possessions before they were packed up and sent to his parents. He pawned these and brought the money to Christina. Also, among Alexander's possessions, there were several pictures that the friend found and passed along to her. One was a Mikhailov family portrait, a second was a close-up of Alex's mother, and there were also two pictures of the Mikhailov factories – one was a wide angle shot of several large buildings with tall smokestacks taken from a distance, and the other a close up of

Alexander Mikhailov, Sr. sitting behind a huge oak desk in his main office, presiding over his factories.

Christina Mikhailov had little time to grieve. She was eight months pregnant and had to plan for her future and the future of the baby she was carrying. The small amount of money she had received from her husband's friend was enough to buy food at least for a little while, and enough to pay for the services of a doctor. When the time came to deliver her baby, she checked herself into a tiny nursing home, and with the assistance of a midwife, she gave birth to Alexander Mikhailov, the third.

Tiny Alexander was a good baby. He ate, slept, filled his diaper, and grew. Christina found joy in looking after him. Here was a tiny human being whom she loved, and who loved and accepted her as she was. He did not judge her for whatever she may or may not have done, and like his father, never made her feel unwanted or unloved. In spite of deeply grieving her husband's death, Christina looked back upon this time in her life with a certain sense of contentment and satisfaction.

The friend who had brought the news of Alexander's death to Christina visited her on one or two occasions. Each time he brought her a little food and also left her a bit of money that she promised to repay. He played with the baby, and whenever little Alexander smiled, he declared that the little fellow was the spitting image of his father. Christina loved to hear this. Aside from the fact that she was poor and her money was dwindling, her life was beginning to improve. She considered writing the Mikhailov family in Tsaritsyn to inform them of their grandchild, but was discouraged from doing so by Alex's friend. Apparently rich families of fallen soldiers were inundated with letters from girls who claimed to have married their sons who had fathered their babies. On one occasion, she did write the Mikhailov family and included a photograph of herself and her baby. As expected, she never received an answer, but at least the Mikhailov family now had a picture of their grandchild. She wished that someone had taken a picture of Alexander and her on their wedding day. Then her claim to being his wife would have gained credibility. Christina was not prepared to part with the one picture she had of Alexander in full military uniform.

Christina continued to get by as best she could, but her money was vanishing quickly. Returning to work at the army base with a newborn baby was totally out of the question. Alexander's friend, who visited her on occasion, had now completed his army term and dropped by to say farewell before he returned to his home. She could not find employment, she had no friends, and now she was two months behind in her rent. But Christina was never helpless. She decided to write a letter to her *Oma* Friedrichsen. Almost two years had passed since she left Rosenthal, but so much had happened in the meantime. She simply did not know where to begin. Not that there was any conflict between them, but she and *Oma* had simply drifted apart. Each was consumed with the huge events that had overtaken their lives, and as a result, both had not written for several months.

Once Alexander entered Christina's life, relatives in Rosenthal were simply not as close. She knew that in the minds of the Rosenthal people, she had run away from home, fallen into a worldly lifestyle, and was on her way to hell, as some would no doubt judge. When she was with Alexander, the inner strength and confidence he provided helped her overcome negative thoughts, including the bad memories of her life in Rosenthal. Now that she was alone again, these thoughts crept back into her mind. She missed her *Oma* very much and she longed to show off her baby, but how could she share all the events of the last few years without upsetting her grandparents? But the cold reality was that Christina needed help and a place to live.

Oma Friedrichsen was also contending with difficult changes in her life. *Opa* Friedrichsen had suffered a stroke and was no longer able to work. Both their daughters had married and moved away to far off villages in the Molotschna Colony. *Oma* Friedrichsen was unaware that Christina was married, and certainly knew nothing of her baby. Christina sent a letter and was relieved to receive a quick reply from *Oma* inviting her to come home, at least for a while. Christina neglected to give any details regarding her marriage and her little baby. With her last rubles, she bought some food supplies and a train ticket, and returned to Rosenthal. Two years and decades of life experiences had passed since she first left home.

***

Returning to Rosenthal, the place of her youth, and the place from where she had escaped, wasn't as difficult as Christina expected. Physical hunger clearly took precedence over bad memories and emotional abuse. Food and a place to sleep for herself and her baby were such immediate needs that nosy, gossiping neighbours were quickly reduced to minor irritants in her mind. By now Christina had totally left the name of Raisa behind, and for the second time in her life, now as the widow Christina Mikhailov, she attempted to gain acceptance among the Mennonites of Rosenthal. To the local gossips, it was no surprise that Christina had a baby, and the story that the father was an army officer – a phantom army officer or probably a number of army officers – was clearly ridiculous.

She had been a little apprehensive about using her married name "Mikhailov" for fear that the association with a wealthy munitions manufacturer could raise unwanted attention among local Russian dissidents, but no one ever made the connection. Few people in the Mennonite village believed that a Mikhailov had ever been a part of Christina's life. Most of the Russian workers were more preoccupied with their own need to grind out a daily existence than to know who might be the father of her baby. The new political philosophy of communism was beginning to push such minor issues into the background.

The changes that had taken place in Rosenthal during her two-year absence amazed Christina. Many of her fellow schoolmates had grown up and moved on with their lives. Several had moved away. Most of the local residents, oblivious to the world around them, enjoyed more than enough of everything – to them the good life would go on forever. There were ominous rumblings, however. Those who were aware of current events heard that political tensions existed between Russia and her European neighbours. There were suspicions that these could easily erupt into armed conflict. The militant attitudes of many of the Russian peasant workers also should have raised serious concerns, but to those whose lives were comfortable, the ideas of a movement called Bolshevism were not taken seriously.

Most of the Mennonites continued to live well within their own self-constructed bubble of reality. But in the Friedrichsen family, changes could not be ignored. *Opa* Friedrichsen no longer worked. Both he and *Oma* had aged a great deal and were barely able to care for themselves. Their daughters had moved away, and Peter, Christina's father, had immigrated to the United States with his second wife, Margarete.

Upon her return to Rosenthal, Christina quickly called on the resourceful optimism she had come to rely upon. She was not about to allow problems to pull her down. Christina rolled up her sleeves and determined to make a life for herself and for her baby here in her former home. She walked up and down the streets, reintroducing herself to neighbours and acquaintances, and promised to work hard in exchange for food and any money they could spare. *Opa* Friedrichsen's stroke was debilitating and caring for him was all *Oma* Friedrichsen could handle. The elderly Friedrichsen couple had a small garden that needed attention. They got by with a cow, a few chickens, and the little money Christina was able to earn, as well as the alms the people of Rosenthal saw fit to send their way. And little Alex brought sunshine back into their home. Sadly, a few months after settling into their new life, things changed again as *Opa* Friedrichsen suffered a second stroke and died.

***

Christina Mikhailov's life continued to twist and turn within the new challenges that steered her into directions she had not planned to go. Just as she settled into a routine that allowed her to meet life's basic needs, a new person appeared on the scene – a man who provided immediate financial stability and some badly needed, yet short-lived, optimism. Ironically, she had the czar's government to thank for this new turn of events.

Following the poor showing of the Russian military in the 1905 conflict with Japan, the national government decided to institute a number of changes that would profoundly affect the lives of the German colonists who lived under the czar's rule. One change, known as *russification*, immediately impacted the Mennonite colonies. The Mennonites, who lived their isolated idyllic lives, had never felt comfortable using the Russian language and chose to embrace very little of the surrounding Russian culture. Many spoke only German, mainly a Low German dialect, and placed little emphasis on teaching Russian to their school children. Some elderly Mennonite people born in Russia, who had lived their entire lives in Russia, spoke no Russian at all, and this, according to the authorities, needed to be addressed. The czar's government correctly reasoned that the best place to institute a program of *russification* was in schools. To teach the Russian language to Mennonite children became an immediate priority.

Unfortunately, many Mennonite teachers were unqualified to teach Russian, and in some cases, the Russian teachers in the Mennonite colonies were unqualified to teach anything. To find a gifted teacher fluent in Russian became a challenge. When the school authorities of Rosenthal were presented with the opportunity to hire a gifted teacher who was also Russian, they quickly engaged this person's services and considered themselves to be very fortunate. Nikolai Kotelnikov, the new teacher, was a quiet, middle-aged gentleman who had attended university. He was a very good academic and a highly qualified teacher with many years of valuable experience. He felt he had wasted too much time attempting to teach lessons to children in tiny schools in insignificant little villages who had little desire to learn, so he was happy to relocate to Rosenthal. While it wasn't Odessa, at least it was a thriving little town located only a short distance from Aleksandrovsk, a city with a viable cultural life and a good library.

Nikolai loved books and studies, but certainly not horses, cows, or chickens. His academic talents were everything that his practical skills were not, nor ever would be. The people of Rosenthal found a tiny house for him located a short walking distance from the school where he would teach. Fortunately for Nikolai, his lack of practical sense was soon noticed by concerned neighbours who took it upon themselves to introduce him to a young widow named Christina Mikhailov, who needed employment and could keep house for him. Few believed that she really was a widow, and behind her back, some cruel people referred to her baby as a bastard – a child born out of wedlock. But Nikolai, ignored the local gossip and eagerly hired Christina to set his house in order, asking her to clean on a regular basis and cook one meal a day for him. This arrangement turned out to work well for everyone.

The Rosenthal residents were astute enough to realize that Nikolai Kotelnikov was of great value to their community. To keep him happy, they supplied him with milk and eggs, produce from their gardens, and some meat for the winter months. Christina was grateful for the employment and worked hard for him. As a mother to her baby, as well as a caregiver to her widowed grandmother, and now a cook and cleaning lady to Nikolai Kotelnikov, she discovered new meaning for herself. Alexander was a happy little fellow who easily won the hearts of both *Oma* Friedrichsen and Nikolai Kotelnikov. Every day, Nikolai looked forward to returning home after school to a clean house, a hot meal, and some company.

Christina was satisfied with her new lot in life and would have been content to see it continue. She did not realize there were changes on the horizon. One day, after she had cleared away the dishes and was preparing to return to the home that she shared with *Oma* Friedrichsen and her little boy, Nikolai asked her to come and sit down. He wanted to speak with her. As soon as Christina settled into the chair he had pulled out for her, and without so much as a few words of small talk, Nikolai took her hand and directly addressed the matter that was on his mind.

Christina was totally taken aback. She was not sure she understood the situation correctly. Surprised and bewildered, she stared directly into his eyes, possibly for the first time in her life, and asked him to repeat what he had just said. Nikolai did, and indeed she had heard correctly. Using as few words as possible, he candidly proposed marriage to her. Christina felt as if a bolt of lightning had struck her. Her heart almost stopped, yet instinctively she did not remove her hand that was gently cradled in his.

Thoughts raced through Christina's mind. Did she really need this? Did she not have a settled, if rather unassuming life? Her situation was not the luxurious standard of living promised to her by her late husband, Alexander Mikhailov, but it was enough for herself and her baby. They had plenty to eat and they slept in a clean bed without the company of lice that infested her mattress in the army barracks. She had her baby and her *Oma*. She couldn't fathom pursuing a marital relationship with a new spouse whom she barely knew. Besides, shouldn't marriage be based on love, and didn't love between two people begin as a spark and grow over time into a flame before holy matrimony could ever be considered? This had been her experience with Alexander. Yet, here was a man whom she hardly knew – her employer who was much older than she – who now wished to marry her. There had been absolutely no personal contact between them, no touch, at least not until now, that could be interpreted as being intentional. Certainly, there had been no hug, not even an interesting glance. They had barely even spoken to one another.

Christina was still grieving the loss of her first husband, Alexander Mikhailov, and holding out the faint hope that his family might contact her. If they would embrace her and her baby as their own, maybe they would help them financially. Many people, including her, considered Nikolai to be a person whose academic interests had totally squeezed out all romance from his life. Did he not view love as something to be studied, to be read about, but certainly not practiced? Later she discovered that Kotelnikov, in addition to being a good teacher, was also a poet and a writer of short stories that were filled with scenes of passionate romance.

When Christina finally arrived home, she was still in complete shock and had no recollection of responding to Nikolai in any way. She never looked on him as anything other than a kind gentleman. He was middle-aged, introverted, and rarely made conversation. He certainly did not portray the dashing image of an Alexander Mikhailov who, when dressed in full military uniform, made many a girl's heart flutter. Baby Alexander was able to elicit more emotion from Nikolai than she ever could. Once or twice, she even caught him crawling after the child on the floor, making funny noises, enticing the baby to laugh.

Once she got over the initial surprise, Christina began to warm to the idea and see the advantages of this unusual marriage opportunity. As Nikolai's wife, she and her baby would be looked after and she would have a little extra money to help *Oma* Friedrichsen. For a day or so, she tried to avoid Nikolai, but wherever she went, he followed her, eagerly awaiting a positive answer. Christina finally reached a decision, decided to accept his proposal, and two weeks later, in a simple Orthodox ceremony at a church in Aleksandrovsk she and Nikolai Kotelnikov were married. The tongues of the Rosenthal gossips immediately sprang into action. Within days, all eyes were focused on Christina's belly to see if anything was growing to determine whether or not something had been planted before the wedding ceremony. She had never received so much attention. The Rosenthal men, who prided themselves with their own virility, made derisive comments that doubted Kotelnikov's ability to father a child.

After a few months of marriage, when it became apparent that Christina was indeed pregnant, the gossip intensified. Many boldly assumed that someone other than Nikolai had fathered this child, since he was a man seen to be too cerebral for such an act. Several months later, her second baby, a healthy boy, was born and Christina named him Nikolai after his father. This was perhaps the happiest time in Christina's life. She felt valued as a mother, as a wife, and for a while, as a caregiver to her aging grandmother. The only sad event during this time was *Oma's* death – the woman who had raised her as her own and whom Christina had grown to love more and more as she grew older. People from the community sympathized with her as she buried her beloved *Oma* and began showing Christina a little more kindness.

Life in the Kotelnikov home continued to go well for the young family. Baby Nikolai began to crawl, and little Alex learned to speak the vernacular Low German from his mother and excellent Russian from his stepfather who accepted him as his own. Everyone was content and everyone had enough. The war, as devastating as it was for the many Russian families who lost sons in the conflict, had little effect on the Kotelnikov home. Even the revolution of 1917, eagerly watched by Nikolai, a student of history, initially had little influence upon his position as a teacher. After all, he was an educated Russian. The Bolsheviks needed his kind and believed they could conform his views to their new way of thinking. Little did they realize how deeply seated his convictions were and to what length Nikolai would go to stand up for his principles.

Shortly after Lenin assumed power, Nikolai was invited by the educational authorities to become part of a local committee to advise a newly-formed commission charged with the responsibility of examining and rewriting the school curriculum. His work as an academic had been noted and highly valued. Several of his poems and short stories had been published and some now appeared in school readers. Nikolai was asked to submit written evaluations of certain aspects of the school curriculum that were currently being taught. His evaluations of science and math courses were straightforward, causing no trouble, but the new material on history and religion that he was expected to rewrite and teach, conflicted with what he knew and what he believed.

Had Nikolai's views been a little more flexible and had he been more willing to bend just a little, there would have been less scrutiny of his teaching by the educational authorities and he might have retained his position. But this was not to be. The persistent inquiries by the authorities about what he thought and what he believed finally forced Nikolai to take a stand. At first, he received subtle suggestions by those in authority to adjust his thinking a little, but these soon developed into thinly veiled threats, finally turning into outright demands that he change his views.

The pressure to conform to communist philosophy gave Nikolai great stress. He could not sleep, he could not eat, and he developed several physical ailments as he wrestled with his conscience and the effects his stand might have upon the family he so dearly loved. The pressure to adopt the Bolshevik teachings would mean that his family would be better cared for – there would be enough to eat and the boys could receive a decent education. But Nikolai just could not compromise his views. He simply was not that big a hypocrite. Finally, the local police intervened. The demands that he change his views escalated into severe reprimands until the police were sent to his school, to arrest him, and take him in for questioning.

Following several days in prison Nikolai was released, but his position as a teacher had been terminated. The authorities realized that although his views must be silenced, there was nothing to be gained by keeping him locked up. He was now an old man, stripped of his position and social standing. His hair was grey, the lines in his face were deep, and the slight limp from a childhood accident had clearly become worse. He could still read and write, and interpret the directives that came down from central authorities. For those who had arrested and imprisoned him, this service became of value. They needed Nikolai's skills. Interestingly, some boys who now were in authority over him had been his former students.

"Thank goodness," Nikolai reasoned, "I didn't make a greater effort to teach these lazy scoundrels the basic skills of reading and writing." He was threatened and treated badly, but in order to keep him alive and useful, they paid just enough to keep him and his family above the starvation level. Christina tried to help out the family by accepting odd neighbourhood tasks she could do in exchange for food and clothing, especially for her boys.

The situation became worse as the health of Nikolai Kotelnikov began to seriously deteriorate. For consolation, he sought out the company of an old priest whom he deeply respected and who had also been stripped of his position by the new authorities. Together, the two dissidents reaffirmed their religious faith, both declaring themselves to be followers of Christ, and in secret they celebrated the Lord's Supper. This brought some solace to Nikolai, but still he could not find peace over the hardship his principled stand had caused his wife and children. He had made his decision, and now he and his family had to endure the consequences.

Very few people attended the funeral of Nikolai Kotelnikov. A short eulogy gave basic details of his life but no one read scripture and no one prayed. The police presence at this sad event saw to that. Within weeks, Christina's life slid from reasonable comfort to hardship and desperate need. She and her boys were now alone without any income. Their lives, and those of their neighbours, continued to slip from want into chaos and devastation as the armies of the czar and the forces of the Bolsheviks waged war against each other, each attempting to gain control of the area. As the front moved back and forth through the Mennonite villages, troops requisitioned horses and food at will, and resources necessary to sustain life were ravished or wasted.

Christina became deeply concerned for her boys as she saw them growing up and becoming teenagers. But what terrified her the most and kept her up at night was the realization that they were being influenced and recruited by the anarchists, these lawless bandits led by Nestor Makhno who stole from the people, and who terrorized, murdered, and raped at will. In the absence of law and order, these bandits were taking over. The boys soon realized that riding with these anarchists meant they could eat. To live by principle as their father had done, was to starve. The lessons were obvious.

Chapter 6
Alex and Nikolai – 1926

"GET OUT!" SCREAMED THE COMMISSAR AS HE BURIED HIS NOSE STILL deeper into the pile of chaos that littered the top of his desk. His sudden enraged retort froze the surprised intruders dead in their tracks.

"I'm sorry, sir," stammered the secretary. "This woman claims that she…"

"Get her out of here!" came a louder, even more belligerent reply, this time delivered with enough force to cause those within earshot to shudder in fear. Instantly, the commissar's face turned deep purple as the normally hidden veins in his neck bulged red with blood threatening to burst. He was not to be taken lightly. His word was law and any indication that someone might not pay him the deference he felt he deserved could result in that person being forcibly removed and severely beaten. Everyone knew it.

Christina Kotelnikov, using the name of Raisa Brodsky, had somehow talked her way through the front door of the headquarters of the regional Communist Party. Somehow she had slipped past an armed guard, past several functionaries sitting at their desks, and past the commissar's personal secretary whom she half-persuaded and half-dragged into the inner sanctum of his office – the very place from where Commissar Brodsky imposed his will upon those under his authority.

The scene was both dangerously explosive, as well as totally ludicrous. Someone dressed as poorly as she, without influence, a woman no less, should be thoroughly intimidated by the power and pomposity that emanated from this office, but not Raisa. Furthermore, the brutality with which this commissar imposed his will upon those within his jurisdiction was known far and wide and she surely must have been aware of this. Also, his complete control over those in her position as affirmed by the many framed diplomas, certificates, awards, and pictures that hung on the walls was not to be missed. Yet, here she was.

Raisa wasn't even sure that the official in charge, whose private office she had dared to invade, was indeed the person she hoped to see. But once inside, a quick glance at the furious figure fuming over his papers diminished her anxiety and confirmed to her that this commissar was indeed Yitzhak Brodsky, the uncle she had not seen since her childhood days in Blumenau. The resemblance he shared with his father was too strong. Furthermore, the garish décor and the poorly matched, over-stuffed furniture suggested to her that the occupant of this office was punching a little above his weight class. Her chances of surviving this bold intrusion were improving.

Raisa's audaciousness was true to her character. She had inherited enough chutzpah from her maternal grandmother to survive many a tight situation, and more importantly, she had learned not always to take no for an answer. Her mission on this day was not for herself. Not that her own needs were insignificant, but she was here to fight for her boys whose situation had become desperate and this desperation drove her to invade this office, regardless of what adverse consequences she might encounter.

The mild-mannered secretary still frozen to the floor, instantly recognized the gravity of the situation. He had allowed a stranger, a woman no less, to enter the commissar's inner sanctum. Before he could address his blunder, Raisa broke the icy silence and with her most confident, yet unusually calm voice, said, "Hello, Uncle."

The commissar still had not acknowledged the short, under-nourished, inwardly trembling woman standing before him. Instead of noticing her, he directed his scowl towards his secretary, glowering directly over Raisa's head. "If you don't get this little presumptuous piece of shit out of here, I'll kill you," he screamed to the cowering assistant. As the secretary attempted to grab Raisa's skinny arm, she instinctively jerked it away, looked directly at the commissar, and with her last ounce of courage, softly replied, "It's me, Raisa."

The sound of her voice brought the commissar's impetuous tantrum to an abrupt halt. Brodsky dropped his glasses, grabbed his desk with both hands and for the first time stared directly at the intruder. His well-rehearsed, haughty demeanour, now stripped of its authority, gave way to a look of wild disbelief.

Is this a ghost? he frantically thought. *Do ghosts speak?* Brodsky, now clearly knocked off his pedestal, motioned to the secretary to leave the room and ordered the door closed. With the voice of a whipped schoolboy, he turned to the woman and asked, "*Who* are you?" Commissar Brodsky was visibly shaken. The mixture of shock and fear, emotions he had learned to suppress in his position of authority, now wiped all fury from his face. Before she could reply he asked again, "*Who* are you?" .

The two stared at each other. Before Raisa could offer an answer, Brodsky's mind began to race about from one implausible scenario to another. Could this woman be his older sister? Could this really be Raisa, the girl who had died in Blumenau, the big sister for whom he had mourned all these years? Had she not been buried? Could she have been resurrected? Christians tend to believe in this sort of thing, or so he thought. He knew that Raisa had become Christian, but was this not a religion imposed upon her against her will by the Mennonites at Blumenau? His knowledge of Judaism and recent conversion to Bolshevik atheism did not have an answer for people resurrected from the dead. Yet here standing before him was his sister, Raisa Brodsky, or at least an exact likeness of her.

Memories flooded back from his childhood as he still grieved for her, the big sister whom he loved, the sister who had bled to death giving birth to a daughter. He had been present at her graveside, numb with grief as he, his siblings, and parents clung to each other for support, surrounded by a sea of strangers. He recalled his anger at seeing a mob of Mennonites encircle the grave and shovel clumps of dirt upon the coffin that contained his sister's life-depleted body. These people who had trampled upon his family's customs and beliefs had haunted him since that time. But here, standing before him was Raisa and the conflicting emotions were tearing him to shreds. Many times in his mind, he had taken her husband, the rascal who had impregnated his sister, to some dark secluded place and tortured the son-of-a bitch to death. Yet here stood this woman, perhaps that bastard's daughter and probably his sister's child. What was he to do? All the Commissar could do was fight the urge to gather her into his arms and release his pent up emotions in a flood of tears.

Before the Commissar could compose himself, Raisa interrupted his emotional turmoil and again spoke softly, "Hello, Uncle." She was smart enough not to call him by his first name. With lightning quickness, he regained his composure, suppressed his emotions, and answered her question from the position of a restored rational thinker. He had often used this ability to wiggle out from under tight situations, and now, yet again, it helped him regain control of the room.

"I am not Yitzak Brodsky. My name is Gregoire," he firmly stated, quickly realizing that he had disclosed his full birth name and given away more information than she had requested. Nor had he denied the fact that he was her uncle.

Raisa stood her ground proving that she was every bit as much in control of the situation as he. As her shaking subsided she thought, *How clever! He uses a French Christian name and a Jewish surname. This should sufficiently obscure his background to allow him to rise rapidly through the Bolshevik ranks, leaving behind any racial or religious baggage that might impede his upward progress.* Her mental processes were as quick as his, and her next question, stated with unusual calmness, disarmed him even further. "How is Grandmother Sarah, your mother?"

The expression on the commissar's face told her she had struck a sensitive nerve. Her question exposed a vulnerability that he, as a rational thinking Bolshevik, had not yet learned to suppress. At this point, he made no attempt to hide anything and coldly replied, "My mother and father are both dead. They starved to death because the damn kulaks, people like your damn Mennonites, had no regard for the needs of the poor people."

This was a well-rehearsed line, partially true and part of the party philosophy that he frequently preached in his speeches.

Raisa quickly interrupted, "I am not a Mennonite."

"And I am not a Jew," he asserted. "I have buried my past. I am now a Bolshevik Communist. Furthermore, I am in a position to decide what happens to people like your Mennonites."

Again Raisa asserted, "I am not a Mennonite."

"Your father was a Mennonite. Where is your father, that dirty son of a bitch who got my sister pregnant and tore my family apart? He killed her, you know."

"Yes, I am your sister's daughter, and no, I don't know where Peter Friedrichsen is." Raisa distanced herself from her father by stating, "The last I heard, he and his new wife had moved to the United States."

Commissar Yitzak or Gregoire, or whatever he called himself, dropped back into his overly stuffed chair and called for his secretary. "Bring me some of those American cigarettes," he ordered. "Let's toast the fact that Peter 'what the hell he calls himself' is no longer on Russian soil."

For the first time in her life, Raisa understood the full extent of the hurt inflicted upon the Brodsky family by the circumstances of her parents' marriage. But she was shocked at how deeply the pain was still felt, after so many years, nor did she assume responsibility for her parents' actions. "I am not to blame. I did not ask to be born," she said.

The Commissar softened his tone as he drew calmness and courage from the foreign cigarette that only he and others in his position were allowed to enjoy. As he looked directly at this woman, his anger and sarcasm gave way to gentleness and sorrow as he remembered his older sister, Raisa. Her daughter did look just like her. How could he throw her out? As his emotions continued to subside, he bluntly asked, "What do you want?"

"To talk to you," she replied.

"Everyone who comes here wants something, so I will ask you again, what do you want?"

"For myself, nothing," said Raisa.

"Then for whom?"

"For my boys."

"Where are they?"

"They are riding with Nestor Makhno."

"That asshole!" shouted Brodsky. "Stay away from that idiot," he yelled. "Do you know what will happen to Makhno and his bandits? Once they have softened up the Kulaks, Trotsky will deal with them." He spoke as though he and Leon Trotsky, head of the Red Army, were intimately acquainted. With renewed pomposity, he asked, "How old are your boys?"

"Sixteen and thirteen."

"Are they smart?"

"They are related to you."

Raisa's quick retort brought a disarming laugh from the Commissar – something he not allowed himself to enjoy for some time. But renewed coldness and severity quickly returned to his next question, "Are they Mennonites?"

"No, I told you that they were smart."

Again Commissar Brodsky broke character and rewarded her quick comeback with an even greater laugh. The civility of the conversation now allowed him to believe that he was back in control. Now he could relax and cross his legs, sink back into his stuffed chair, and be magnanimous toward his niece. He knew what would be best for her boys and quickly proceeded to help them.

The commissar called for his secretary and instructed him to contact someone named Andrij. Within minutes, the telephone rang and Andrij was on the line. The tone of the conversation between Brodsky and Andrij was cool, but cordial. Commissar Brodsky began with small talk, and then subtly, yet deftly, re-established his superior position over this person, slowly working toward the question that Andrij dare not ignore. Brodsky extended greetings to Nikita Khrushchev, Andrij's boss, and freely dropped names of persons in authority with whom he claimed to be intimately acquainted.

"We need to find suitable work for two young and exceptionally intelligent men. We have singled them out as future military leaders, but

Trotsky feels, and I completely concur, that they must first experience life as workers – you know, get a little dirt under their fingernails." In spite of the friendly tone of the conversation, Andrij knew better than to ignore Brodsky's wishes. He was probably another ambitious underling whose job it was to fix things, and the better he could fix things, the quicker he would ascend the ladder within the communist hierarchy. Andrij hung up and within minutes called back with the suggestion that these highly intelligent young men could be assigned to work as apprentices to a train crew. They would be required to work physically, learn something about the railway system, and also travel to several Russian cities where they would rub shoulders with other rising military leaders. Brodsky thanked him most heartily for his insightful suggestion. "My secretary will get the details from you," he replied and hung up.

At that moment, Raisa broke all protocol. She walked up to the commissar and hugged and kissed him – her uncle, her mother's brother. He, for his part, made no attempt to resist this expression of heartfelt affection. Immediately, they both discovered a familial bond, something neither of them had pursued with anyone else for some time. Through all this, Brodsky never once asked the boys' names, nor ever arrived at the conclusion that Alex and Nikolai were sons of Kotelnikov, the man whose career he had probably helped to ruin.

***

A week or so later, two precocious young leaders, Alex and Nikolai Kotelnikov, were escorted to the hiring authorities at the regional office of the People's Commissariat of Railways at the Aleksandrovsk rail yards. Aleksandrovsk was a large central hub from where grain grown in the surrounding rich agricultural area was transported to larger Russian cities and to the ports of Odessa and Berdyansk for export to foreign markets. Rail executives and members of train crews were fully aware of the reality behind such new hires, but for the sake of their job security, everyone fell in line with the official position that highly gifted future leaders needed to experience life as workers. The new recruits were greeted warmly, interviewed briefly, and promptly introduced to members of Crew No. 84. These were not the first super intelligent youngsters to be assigned to Crew No. 84. Most others had shown such promise that after a few weeks on the job, they were promoted to higher positions elsewhere, much to the relief of crew members who feared for their own safety when lazy, incompetent boys attempted to move long trains and operate powerful steam locomotives.

Alex and Nikolai, fully aware of the reality of their job appointments, were smart enough to keep their mouths shut and do as they were told. The survival skills they had developed in their young lives were now essential in this new job. The boys were extremely polite and performed the simplest tasks assigned to them, be they ever so menial, with diligence and competency. They also shrewdly absorbed all the information they could regarding rail traffic and especially the operation and maintenance of steam locomotives. Alex showed sufficient mechanical aptitude to win the confidence of Uri, the chief engineer. In the minds of the crew, perhaps these polite and hard-working boys might indeed be future leaders chosen for rapid advancement in the new Russian order of things. And it might be to everyone's best interest to treat them with respect and teach them all they would need to know. Alex and Nikolai were also astute enough to keep personal information about themselves to a minimum and avoid giving direct answers to questions regarding their backgrounds. This, in turn, only helped encourage the mystique surrounding their presence about who they were and how far up the line their connections might be traced.

More importantly, Uri, the chief engineer responsible for the smooth operation of the train, liked the boys. He was an excellent mechanic, a terrific problem solver, and generally a good person who got along well with others. Uri, however, had a problem that couldn't be hidden. In the morning, he was an exceptionally competent engineer and mechanic, but by noon, his skills began to deteriorate. Then by late afternoon, he was unable to walk straight, and by evening, he was often seen falling down drunk. But the members of Crew No. 84 liked him and covered for him, so the trains under his direction generally ran well and arrived at their destinations on time.

Alex and Nikolai enjoyed working with Crew No. 84. The train routes were mainly to Berdyansk and Mariupol, but some days they travelled to further destinations, including once or twice to Odessa. They received little pay, but enough for food, and warm clothing – luxuries they had rarely enjoyed during their short lives.

Raisa missed her boys, but she was happy that they were now gainfully employed. She was immensely relieved they were no longer under the influence of Nestor Makhno, the anarchist who promised his men food and clothing that was usually stolen from terrorized people, and in return, offered little more than typhus, lice, and filth. She continued to live under the name of Christina Kotelnikov, the name given to her by her late husband, Nikolai Kotelnikov, but worried that someone might associate her name and that of her boys with him – the man who had been disgraced for his unwillingness to teach the official Bolshevik Party line.

By the mid 1920s, Russia's economy was improving as the political system under Lenin and Stalin began to provide stability. World War I had cost the USSR many lives and vast recourses. For a period of time, it even had to relinquish chunks of territory in exchange for peace and bread, at least for those employed by the state, as had been promised by Lenin. The country's industrial output was beginning to grow and this necessitated a reorganization of the railway system. Trains became longer and more locomotives were coming on line. The numbers of workers increased, and train crews were expanded and reorganized. These changes also effected Crew No. 84. One day they were informed that they were being reassigned to operate from the main rail yards in Moscow. By this time, Alex and Nikolai had worked their way up in their jobs, and Uri, the chief engineer, had grown to like them and even depend upon them. He fought hard to keep Crew No. 84 from being split up, succeeding in doing so.

The boys' first reaction to the news was one of excitement. They had proven themselves to be competent, reliable workers and had won the confidence of the train crew, who in turn had become more convinced than ever that these were indeed hand-picked young men who needed to be closer to Moscow, the centre of action. The move also meant the boys were now officially leaving home and striking out on their own. This development was more difficult for their mother to accept than for the boys. Moscow was located about 800 km from Rosenthal. Her sons assured Christina that they would be rolling through Aleksandrovsk from time to time and would have opportunity to visit her and even spend holidays with her. Most importantly, they could save a little money and send any extra cash to their mother so she could live more comfortably and eat nutritious meals on a more regular basis.

***

Before the official transfer to Moscow, each member of Crew No. 84 received a two-day pass to bid farewell to friends and loved ones and prepare for the move. Alex and Nikolai returned to Rosenthal to spend their final days with their mother before striking out on their own. Christina knew she would miss her boys, but took solace in the fact that they were now earning a wage and eating properly. She hoped they would have opportunities to visit her. At the same time, she realized she was entering a new stage in life, and the family life with her boys, as she had known it, would no longer be the same. She might rarely get to see them and this gave rise to a maternal need to pass along to them the lessons she had learned in life, and what they would need to know to get along without her guidance. During their visit, the boys noticed that their mother did not look well. Her face was gaunt and drawn, and her clothes hung loosely from her thin, undernourished frame. Her claim that she was healthy and had enough of life's necessities did not convince her sons, and yet the smile on her face partially allayed their concerns.

On the first evening together, Christina shared events from her childhood that she thought the boys should know – events that had taken place in Blumenau and Rosenthal. She talked about the Brodsky family, especially her grandmother, and about the Friedrichsen grandparents who had raised her and provided for her. She also talked about Peter Friedrichsen, her father. She spared few details of the events from her youth, including the account of her escape to Odessa and the brief but wonderful times she had spent together with her first husband Alexander Mikhailov. Christina thought that somewhere there must still be wealthy members of the Mikhailov family, and although she did not know how to contact them, she held out the faint hope that her boys might one day connect with them, and be accepted and cared for.

She described in great detail the foyer of the Odessa Opera House with its ornate staircase that she had dared not ascend, the numerous gilded figures, and the beautiful chandeliers that defied description. She told the boys the story of *Eugene Onegin* that Tchaikovsky had set to music, and mourned the fact that she and her husband had not been able to realize their dreams of careers in opera. Christina wept as she recalled the tragedy of her husband's death and leaving Odessa as a seventeen-year-old widow with a baby in her arms. She spoke to them about returning to Rosenthal and being greeted somewhat coldly by her Friedrichsen grandparents who had meanwhile grown old and were no longer able to provide for her.

Christina also described her brief courtship and marriage to Nikolai Kotelnikov, a man almost thirty years her senior, whom she had learned to love and with whom she had baby Nikolai. Kotelnikov was an excellent teacher, a caring husband, and a good father to both boys. Alex and Nikolai were most amused by details of the brief and unusual courtship between Christina and Nikolai and expressed surprise that such a good marriage had resulted from such an unlikely relationship.

Christina wept as she recalled the pain she and her husband, Nikolai, had experienced as he wrestled with his conscience over the discrepancy between what the authorities required him to teach and what he believed to be the truth. *Could he not have given just a little?* she had reasoned. *Just enough to see his family looked after?* On nights when she put her boys to bed, she could sense the hunger in their little stomachs. These memories still haunted her. Why had she lost two husbands? Why did they both have to suffer and die? Why did her little boys have to grow up without a father? Was all this pain and suffering simply a result of a clash over political ideas?

In spite of the difficulties she had experienced, Christina had learned to accept life as it was. She had grown to love and admire her husband, Nikolai Kotelnikov, and respect the position he had taken. Initially, she felt resentful toward the authorities, even toward Nikolai who had been forced to choose between principle and falsehood, and between a life of relative comfort and a life of poverty. Yet she deeply empathized with him over the agony this dilemma had forced upon him. The stress of Nikolai's stand had killed him emotionally long before physical death relieved him of his pain. He was far too principled a man to survive in the new order.

Young Alex clearly remembered the family hardship that came down upon them after Nikolai Kotelnikov was removed from his teaching post, stripped of his salary, and forced to deal with the consequences of living according to his conscience. For the first time in her life, Christina informed the boys that in her view the communists were a bunch of liars. Although this bold assertion flew in the face of the information preached to railway employees during the lectures they were forced to attend, it was a point of view the boys were also slowly coming to realize for themselves.

Christina had experienced many difficulties in her short event-filled life. She had learned many lessons and wanted to pass along to her boys what she had come to understand. "Appreciate the good things you see around you," she advised, "your friends and what you have been given. And ask God to help you let go of the bad. Above all, learn to forgive those who have wronged you."

The boys had heard these words before, but this time the reference to God caught them by surprise. On the one hand, they knew that religious practice was being discouraged, even outlawed, but on the other hand, they heard their mother, the one who had always cared for them, advocate the opposite. She related events from her childhood – some good, others not so good. She bluntly stated that upon leaving home for Odessa, she had wanted nothing to do with religion, least of all what she had seen practiced by the people of Rosenthal where she had grown up. The kind priest in

Odessa, who officiated at her baptism and performed her marriage ceremony, had encouraged her to take a second look at the Christian faith. But at that time, her interest in faith went only so far as to accept baptism to please Alexander and lessen his family's possible objections to their marriage. Nikolai Kotelnikov, like Alexander Mikhailov, was also a deeply religious man who had encouraged Christina and the boys to regularly attend religious services with him.

Christina proceeded to tell her sons that she had recently begun to attend Bible study sessions and she was learning to see the Christian faith in a new way. According to her, the most important message she wanted to communicate to her boys was that she had become a follower of Jesus Christ – something she encouraged them to also consider. This struck the boys as odd. The words of Adolf Reimer, the leader of an underground Christian group whom she had recently met, had influenced her very deeply. Reimer echoed many of the same arguments the kind priest in Odessa had presented to her at the time of her baptism.

But now, at this stage in life, these ideas had taken on new meaning for her – the acceptance of a faith in Jesus Christ as Lord and Saviour had become personal. It was more than a church's statement of faith and more than a belief a husband wished her to accept. It was between her and the God she worshipped. Christina felt that this is what Nikolai had tried to tell her shortly before his death, and what he wished for her and their boys to accept. In his last weeks of life he had met privately with a priest who had also been mistreated by communist authorities and also removed from his position. At that time, Nikolai had affirmed his Christian faith. He had requested Christina to do the same and to teach this to the boys.

Hearing that their mother had become a follower of Jesus Christ was a strange idea to them. Who was Jesus Christ? During their childhood they had heard the name, but where was He and what was He all about? Could a person approach this God directly? Through prayer? These questions would need to be considered. But there was no denying the fact that something had changed in their mother. At a time when her body was losing its physical strength, she was gaining inner strength. She was at peace.

Christina had always approached life's challenges with fortitude and determination, and these qualities were now becoming stronger. Those who knew her were always amazed at the emotional resiliency her tiny physical being could produce. After hearing all that Christina shared with them, the boys left home with a great deal to reflect upon.

Christina hoped to leave Rosenthal and return to Odessa, so she decided to pass along her personal belongings to her boys. Alex received a photo of his father in full military dress, along with several pictures of the Mikhailov family and the Mikhailov factories in Tsaritsyn. She also gave him the letter that young Alexander had written to his parents before his death informing them of his recent marriage. This letter had never been sent. Nikolai received a wedding photo of his parents and a sheaf of unpublished poems written by his father describing events in his life – the happiness that he experienced at meeting and marrying Christina, and the incredible joy he felt at holding his new baby son Nikolai for the first time.

Christina bid farewell to her boys. She held each one in her motherly arms, kissed them and said goodbye. She wasn't sure when they would meet again, so she committed them to God, the One who loved her and accepted her as she was. Raisa Christina Brodsky Friedrichsen Mikhailov Kotelnikov now found herself alone, in an empty nest. She was an old woman, widowed twice. She was thirty-five years old.

***

When possible, Alex and Nikolai carried most of their earthly possessions with them. These included the pictures their mother had left, plus a gold pocket watch, a woman's diamond necklace, and a gold wedding band. These treasures had been acquired under highly unusual circumstances – a direct result of riding with the anarchist Nestor Makhno.

One evening, after the bandits had filled their bellies with food taken from some village in the Molotschna and with vodka pilfered from somewhere, they decided to open a communal bag of stolen articles to examine their ill-gotten treasures. Buoyed by the alcohol in their systems, they felt safe and invincible as they relaxed in a remote campsite, securely hidden by a thicket of tall bushes. At some point during the evening, the peace and tranquility of the gathering was shattered as gunshots rang out from somewhere. Fearing an attack, possibly from the *Selbstschutz*, the surprised bandits grabbed what they could, ran for their horses, and frantically scattered in all directions leaving Alex and Nikolai behind, abandoned and terrified.

During the ensuing chaos, most of the bandits escaped on horse, while the less fortunate ran for their lives. Most of the treasures had been quickly scooped up, but in the alcohol induced confusion, several valuable pieces had been scattered about and left behind. No further shots were heard and no counter-revolutionaries ever appeared. After some time, the boys came out of hiding, extinguished the embers, and waited anxiously for the confusion to settle. As they left the campsite to retrieve their horses, they saw a small loot bag left on the ground. Inside, they found a gold pocket watch, a necklace, and a ring. Since there were no markings identifying the rightful owners, the boys took the stolen goods and left the site.

Life on the trains with Crew No. 84 continued to be tolerable. Days were long and the work physically taxing, but as state employees their basic needs were looked after. A heavily subsidized communal kitchen provided train crews with meals of varying quality at a reasonable price, and for lodging the boys shared a room in a very modest dormitory subsidized by the state. Trains rolled out of the Moscow rail yards in every direction. The schedule, though not strictly adhered to, was designed to keep train crews within a one or two-day ride from Moscow, if trains ran on schedule.

When crews were stranded somewhere for more than one night, the boys tried to find a room in some state-supported dormitory, but all too frequently there were none available. Consequently, they would be forced to catch a few hours of sleep in a baggage car, especially if they found themselves on some remote sidetrack. If the train carried freight deemed priority, or if some dignitary were on board, the train would reach its destination on time. But, if it were merely a freight train with one or two passenger cars, then the delay could be for days at a time.

As the Russian industrial output grew, greater demand was placed upon the transportation system. Train crews worked longer hours, had fewer days off, and were assigned to travel greater distances to strange and faraway places. Working conditions were certainly not ideal, yet Alex and Nikolai reminded themselves that they at least were gainfully employed and could pay for life's basic needs.

Following yet another strenuous multi-day trip to some remote destination, the boys looked forward to returning to Moscow to set their feet upon solid ground that did not sway from side to side, and place their tired heads onto pillows that were clean and free from unrecognizable vermin. Although the train had travelled day and night, it was still thirty hours behind schedule. The long and arduous journey had taken them to some obscure destination near Siberia where they had slept most nights on sacks of something loaded onto freight cars with rodents as company.

As the brothers left the train, they staggered like drunken sailors along the lengthy platform that would eventually return them to the large terminal. Dizzy with exhaustion and starved for decent food, they reached the main passenger waiting area and continued to stumble along through the huge building toward their dormitory room. In the distance, they spotted a face that stood out from the others and appeared to be someone they knew. At first, Alex blamed his bloodshot eyes for playing tricks on him, but as he drew nearer he was delighted to recognize the friendly face of Walter Friesen, an acquaintance from Rosenthal, whose family had recently befriended their mother. Walter also recognized the boys, walked directly up to Alex and Nikolai, extended his hand, and said, "Please accept my deepest sympathies."

The boys were so overjoyed to see someone from home that they completely missed his expression of condolence. Instead, they launched into conversation and questions about Rosenthal, especially about their mother whom they had not seen for several weeks. Walter calmly restated his expression of sympathy. This time the look on his face convinced the brothers that they needed to keep quiet and listen more carefully to what he had to say. With a trembling voice, now choked with emotion, he relayed the tragic news to them that their mother, Christina, had died. Upon hearing this, the boys stood there in stunned shock and total silence. Neither could breathe.

"Has no one told you?" Friesen gently asked. The looks on their faces confirmed to him that no one had. "Your mother died two weeks ago," he softly repeated. Alex and Nikolai remained frozen in disbelief. Friesen continued, "The funeral was last week. Has no one told you?"

Alex and Nikolai left Walter standing alone in the terminal building and hurried back to their room to see if any mail had arrived. There it was, a white envelope with a black border with a letter inside confirming the shocking news that Christina Kotelnikov, their mother, had suddenly taken ill with pneumonia and died several days later. The letter had been sent two weeks ago, on the exact day that she had died. Russian mail was always late and sporadic at best. They had not heard from her for several weeks and had falsely assumed that all was well.

A second letter had also arrived. Friends from the disbanded group of Christians led by Adolph Reimer, of which she had also been a part, had arranged a funeral service. They had written to Alex and Nikolai, and also informed her uncle Gregoire Brodsky of her death. Brodsky took responsibility for her burial and agreed to move her remains to some city, perhaps Odessa, and bury her in some old family plot.

Alex and Nikolai were in shock. They read and reread the letters. Deep grief enveloped them, compounded by a sudden and bewildering sense of being alone and of being left behind. They felt overwhelmed by questions of where to go, what to do, and how to respond to the situation – if any response was at all possible. Alex was filled with a consuming urge to run away and escape, but from what and to where? Nikolai reacted much differently to the tragic news. He sat in silence and barely breathed. At an age where he still needed the care of loving parents, he found himself away from home doing hard physical labour and now dealing with shock, grief, and a sense of aloneness. Alex was three years older, a little taller and stronger, and emotionally a little more mature, but then again, for his brother's sake he had to be. There were no other options.

Over the next few hours, Alex's shock began to thaw and give way to anger and resolve – he needed to do something. He paced from one end of the room to the other, but no matter which way he turned, he could not escape the tightness in his chest, nor could he run away from the burning sensation deep in his gut. Worst of all, he realized that these surging emotions were taking him nowhere. Alex knew he had to say something or do something for the sake of his brother, but he could think of nothing other than to escape... anywhere, in any direction.

"Let's get out of here," he finally blurted. Nikolai remained quiet. A few more paces and Alex turned to ask, "Do you want to spend the rest of your life working like a dog, wearing filthy clothes, and sleeping in cold, rat-infested baggage cars?"

Nikolai stiffly shook his head and strained a reply, "I like to eat."

"Gravy-soaked fat and gristle, coloured water they call borscht, while the Bolsheviks eat sausage and real meat. This is what you want for the rest of your life?"

While Alex needed to move, Nikolai remained frozen to his chair. He just wanted to close his eyes and hope that this bad dream would somehow go away. Any action seemed overwhelming to him, but unlike his mother, he was not a risk-taker. He longed for stability. He remembered the feeling of hunger in his stomach that drove him to ride with the Makhno bandits, yet he also recalled the terror he experienced while associating with them. Memories of being bullied by the anarchists and shot at by the Mennonite *Selbstshutz* were still all too real for him. He longed for the comfortable life that his mother's people had enjoyed, living in their sanitized Mennonite villages and having enough to eat, but he had also learned to make do with what he had.

Alex, on the other hand, was more restless by nature and this restlessness finally took over, driving him to action. The spark of hope of a better life still burned somewhere inside his gut. At nineteen years old, he had worked hard, and longed for what the Mennonites had. But he also felt that his mother had been denied the comforts of Mennonite village life, and believed that he and Nikolai would be similarly deprived. There must be a better life than what they were currently facing. Anger continued to build in Alex. Somehow he sensed his life was at a crossroads and that an important decision lay before him. If he did not take hold of this opportunity now, then he might die in a baggage car along with filthy rats on some abandoned sidetrack.

"Let's get out of here, Nikolai," he repeated with urgency.

"To Rosenthal?" asked Nikolai.

"No no, let's go to Canada."

The brothers recalled their brief conversation with Walter Friesen at the train terminal. They learned that he was travelling with a group of Mennonites that hoped to leave Moscow by train for Riga the next day. The boys realized that their crew could possibly be assigned to this very same train. Trains had taken several emigrant groups to Riga, and as far as they knew, all had travelled to Canada and no one had ever returned to Russia. They had heard Canada described as the land of a thousand opportunities.

"Do you want to become a Mennonite?" asked Nikolai.

"Hell no," shouted Alex, "Let's just go to Canada. Once we're there, we'll be on our own. Surely it will be better than what we have here."

Alex and Nikolai just sat and thought, overcome with emotion. They worked through various stages of shock, grief, and worry about what to do next. They also reminisced about their childhood, recalling better times with their mother and speculating on what may have killed her. They were convinced, and rightly so, that malnutrition had compromised her overburdened immune system. They tried to list the names of friends and relatives to whom they could turn for help or advice, but unfortunately there were none. After some time, an emotionally driven Alex got up, gave his brother a long hug with a customary Russian kiss on each cheek, and told him that he loved him. With reckless resolve, he walked out the door telling Nikolai that he would be back before night. As he walked away from the dormitory, his quickened step took on a clear decisiveness. Alex boarded a streetcar marked "Kremlin," rode several kilometres, and got off near a complex of government buildings. From here he walked briskly toward the building that housed the Foreign Office.

Once inside this huge, multi-storied structure, Alex asked directions and soon made his way toward the department where visas, passports, and travel documents were processed. It was almost closing time and workers were starting to leave the building. In 1929, very few people were emigrating and even fewer were returning to Russia, so this department was not very busy. With purpose in his step, Alex smiled his way past several security guards and moved quickly enough to avoid the questions normally posed by inquisitive receptionists. His reasonably clean clothes identified him as a Russian railway employee. Alex walked confidently into the main office, past several clerical workers sitting at their desks, and entered the private office of what he considered to be the highest-ranking person in authority.

The official sitting behind his desk, almost asleep, was caught totally off guard. In a state of disbelief, he remained seated and stared directly at Alex, unsure of how to respond to this bold intruder. The audacity of someone walking past security and entering his office unannounced was completely unheard of. As he rose, to re-establish his composure and prepare himself to deliver his most denigrating sneer, he took note of an expensive gold watch loosely wrapped around Alex's fingers. Fortunately for Alex, this director was a perceptive man who grasped an unusual situation very quickly and knew how to turn it to his advantage. A sharp wit was needed to survive in this strange new political system – a wit that had helped the director move upward in rank and ascend to his present position. He immediately recognized the value of the gold watch, softened his look of scorn, and asked, "How did you get in?"

Alex looked directly at him and with every ounce of chutzpah he had inherited from his mother, he firmly stated, "I have come for my travel documents."

The official recognized Alex's railway clothes and realized that he may be dealing with a person who had some standing. The young man before him certainly had guts. The two stared at each for several seconds as Alex fidgeted deliberately with the gold watch. Inwardly though, he was sweating profusely and scared out of his mind.

The official deliberately walked to the door and shouted loudly, "Aleksa come here at once." Alex froze in fear. Had he heard "Aleksa," or had he heard "Alex?" Was the person being summoned an accommodating female clerical worker named Aleksa, or was this an oversized gun-toting security guard named Alex, who would grab him by the collar and drag him away to the authorities. He could feel the hair on his head stand on end. He feared that he might be arrested, accused of bribery, and charged with attempting to leave the country illegally – a much greater offence. He could lose his job and be exiled to some obscure internment camp. But worst of all, Nikolai would also suffer the consequences of his ill-conceived plan, also lose his job, and end up on some Siberian work detail where once again he would go hungry.

Alex decided to risk everything. There was no turning back. Before Alex or Aleksa, whoever he or she may be, could walk in, he removed the gold watch from his hand and gently laid it on the desk. Above the sound of his own pounding heart he could hear footsteps as someone walked into the office behind him and shut the door firmly. Chills ran down his spine.

"This gentleman needs travel documents that must be expedited immediately," demanded the director in his most commandeering tone. To Alex's relief, Aleksa was a petite secretary who looked perplexed at this highly irregular request so late in the day. But she also knew that for her survival she needed to obey her superior's every whim. She returned to her desk, found the necessary blank forms, and began to fill in the information that would change Alex and Nikolai's identity, allowing them to legally exit Russia, and hopefully thereafter, gain entrance into Canada.

Concealing his cold sweat Alex followed her to her desk and carefully guided her eye across the page with a small gold ring that hung loosely on his little finger. She pretended not to notice and worked quickly and efficiently. An hour later, after two Mennonite boys now named Alexander Friedrichsen and Nicholas Friedrichsen had been successfully added to the list of those permitted to legally leave Russia, the ring was gone. Photos were required for the documents and again the gold watch and gold ring did their job. Two smudged and blurry pictures were retrieved from some file, one with a vague likeness of Alex and the other, probably a young girl, was made to look like a dark haired, brown eyed, sixteen year old boy. The official seal was applied across each face with sufficient force to further obscure the image of each applicant.

Shortly after 6:00 p.m., Alex walked into the dormitory room he shared with Nikolai who quickly jumped up and frantically screamed at him, "Where have you been?"

"Changing your identity," Alex calmly replied. "You have now become Nicholas Friedrichsen." The blood drained from the face of the newly-christened Nicholas, as his countenance turned from crimson red to bleached white. His mouth dropped open and there it stayed.

"Let's go eat," suggested Alex.

"Eat! Now?"

"You had better eat, this may be your last meal on Russian soil."

"What are you talking about?" The newly-named Nicholas, though relieved to see his brother, yet still full of panic and anger, was now bewildered by Alex's calm demeanor. Hours before, the fury of Alex's emotions had caused him to pace from one end of the room to the other. Now an unusually tranquil expression replaced all his nervous energy. This upset Nikolai even more and he clammed up in an even tighter silence.

"Tomorrow we are leaving for Canada," stated Alex with assurance.

Nikolai could barely breathe.

Their last meal in Moscow consisted of boiled potatoes and tasteless gravy with pieces of gristle and fat oozing to the surface to be sopped up with a few pieces of stale bread. Over dinner, Nikolai finally found his voice and adamantly uttered his main belief. "Have you lost your mind?" he asked. Now it was his turn to be angry. Frozen emotions began to thaw and churn up as his once paralyzed voice exploded with, "I am staying here!"

Alex told Nikolai about the entire episode at the foreign office and again explained his plan for leaving Russia. Nikolai lapsed back in speechlessness, yet remained firmly unconvinced. "Not me," he decisively stammered.

The brothers' disagreement became quite heated. Nikolai had experienced more upheaval in one day than he had in his entire life. He desperately needed to regain some sense of stability, to reconnect with roots rather than be further torn away from all that was familiar. Learning of his mother's death was traumatic enough, but leaving everything and everyone he knew to go to a land he had never seen, speak a language he did not know, and adjust to customs with which he was totally unfamiliar was just too much for him. At only sixteen years of age, he felt he needed to cling to the roots he still had. Alex, on the other hand, had risked too much to turn back. Besides, he was not sure that he could trust the director in the foreign office whom he had conned, or his secretary, Aleksa, who remained so unusually quiet. They could still blow the whistle on him and have him arrested. He had reached the point of no return.

For the next several hours, Alex tried every argument he knew and every trick at his disposal to shake Nikolai free from his entrenched resolve to stay in Russia. Even the awful evening meal was better to Nikolai than the feeling of hunger that he still remembered all too well from his earlier years. Somewhere between 3:00 and 4:00 a.m., the two brothers found a way through the impasse that separated them and hammered out a compromise. Their mother had encouraged them to pray and seek guidance from God, especially in the face of difficult decisions. This is what Alex suggested they do.

"Does God really listen to those who lie and bribe others to gain what they want as you did this afternoon?" countered Nikolai. The moral and theological implications of this astute observation normally would have concerned Alex, but not at 3:00 a.m. Ever since hearing the news of his mother' death, his heart had ruled his head, and the line between right and wrong had become blurred.

"Besides …" said Nikolai, "how do we know that the train won't be rerouted to Siberia? This has happened before."

"That's it," said Alex. In the dimness of the early morning, a light had gone on in his head and a way through the impasse became visible. "If the train is sent to Siberia, we will accept this as a sign from God that we are meant to stay in Russia. But, if the train goes to Riga, this will be our sign to immigrate to Canada."

Nikolai was too wasted to argue any further. He was totally exhausted and emotionally spent. Although he was deeply consumed by his mother's death, somewhere within himself, he found enough resolve to reluctantly accept the compromise as suggested by his brother, if only to escape from under the weight of the huge decision being forced upon him. Could he really become Nicholas Friedrichsen?

Chapter 7
Alex and Nicholas – 1929

BY THE EARLY 1900S SIGNIFICANT CHANGES HAD TAKEN PLACE IN THE newly-established province of Manitoba. Settlers from various parts of the world had arrived to take advantage of the attractive land offers made available to them under the terms of the Dominion Lands Act of 1872. Some came to flee the persecution they had experienced in their homeland, while others driven by a desire to escape their current realty came in search of that elusive pot of gold at the end of some rainbow.

Some had experience growing crops and raising livestock, while others simply came. Some were honest and hardworking, and others were not. Many possessed the necessary physical and emotional determination to create a new life out of raw opportunity, but others found the physical work too back-breaking, and the emotional strain of eking out an existence so dependent upon weather and fluctuating commodity prices too overwhelming.

Tiny dwellings began to break up the monotony of the wide open prairies. Where sod was the only building material at hand, living quarters were dug into the ground and covered with a layer of turf. In areas where wood was more plentiful log cabins, a little more stable yet still very basic, began to appear. Over time, and with the availability of better construction materials these primitive dwellings developed into complete farmyards with house, barn and livestock. Eventually, as more settlers arrived, the growing number of buildings began to cluster together into communities that became the foundation for the development of towns such as Harwood, Manitoba.

Hubert J. Harwood, the popular British writer, traveler, and adventurer who lent his name to the town of Harwood, helped to fuel interest in this part of Western Canada. His books and magazine articles extolled the beauty of the land with its vast agricultural potential in such glowing terms that pioneers from all over the world felt compelled to come here and check it out. The first to arrive were settlers from Eastern Canada, soon to be followed by immigrants from various parts of the British Isles. The persistent ones, possessing the stubborn courage to stare down adversity, stayed and survived, at times in tents and sod huts. The next groups of pioneers came from Iceland, France, and Germany. These were later joined by Eastern Europeans: Ukrainians, Poles, and Russian Mennonites. All came prepared to stake their future on the precarious prospect of growing crops and sustaining livestock in this vast open region with its extreme temperatures. Into this mix of newcomers came settlers from the United States, lured north by the attractive land deals. The Americans, many of whom brought livestock and machinery with them, experienced a much easier beginning than those who arrived from Eastern Europe with almost nothing.

By 1929, the small settlement of Harwood had grown into a viable little community with small businesses, a general store, several offices, two churches, and a branch of the Imperial Bank of Canada. The Canadian Pacific Railway fuelled further development in the region by constructing a spur line that ran near the town. This in turn encouraged grain companies to erect grain elevators along these new rail lines and take advantage of potential profitable business opportunities.

Across the vast region, settlers of similar language, religion, and culture homesteaded together to form homogenous settlements where they could preserve their heritage and practice the values they held in common. Russian Mennonites were happy to live together in such tight communities. This is how they had existed in Russia, how they had built their economy, and how they had developed and maintained their unique culture. Some Mennonite groups, such as the Bergthaler and Old Colony congregations, expected, even mandated their people to build their homes in close proximity to each each together within the confines of closely-knit little villages.

But just as the rural areas of Western Canada began developing sustainable communities, and farmers and business people began making a living, in 1929 the American stock market suffered a calamitous crash. The period that followed, known as the Great Depression, brought progress and enterprise to an abrupt halt as economic development stalled completely. People across North America, including those in smaller Canadian towns and villages such as Harwood, became overwhelmed. The depletion of assets and material goods was hard enough to accept, but the influence of this economic collapse on the psyche of the people was even more serious. Hopelessness and desperation, not normally associated with a pioneer spirit, now showed itself. The price of wheat, the main crop of the area, lost over half its value and the market for livestock dried up. Merchants were caught with inventory that customers could not afford, and farmers were stuck with mortgage payments and bank loans they could not repay. Farms were repossessed. Tractors and farm machinery were returned to dealers or simply abandoned on fields where they had last been used. Bankrupt owners left their land, homes, and dreams, and simply walked away. Even those who stayed and tried to tough it out saw the spirit of adventure that had brought them here wither away into worry and deep concern. People faced the sinister belief that all was for naught. Perhaps the move to this isolated and dreadfully cold place had been a mistake. Perhaps they should return to their former homes, but was this even possible? In most cases, it was not. Some felt that by staying on their land, they would somehow survive, at least for a period of time. Plans for additional land purchase or any form of economic expansion were abruptly abandoned.

Into this bleak environment, appeared a new voice, a prophet of hope, a religious leader named Konstantin Nazarov – a man some believed was sent by God to proclaim a strange new gospel. Here was a local person from Harwood whose ability to stir the hearts and minds of the people vastly exceeded his capacity to successfully manage a modest-sized farm. When times were good, his influence was minimal, but when times turned bad, his message became credible, especially to those who had lost hope. Within a short time, his influence extended beyond the local Doukhobor community, the church to which he and most Russians in the area belonged, to include converts from among German and English farmers. Nazarov's message of hope and relief provided an answer to those overwhelmed by loss and adversity. According to him, the land that did not yield a livelihood was condemned. By abandoning this sin-infested land and following him, people could again find the will of God in some new place, and there gain a new even greater prosperity. His most audacious prophesy claimed that he personally had heard the voice of God, and that God was leading him to gather his followers and move farther west to search for and discover a New Canaan. The converts who embraced his passionate message began to sell their belongings and take what livestock they could, abandoning their farms, machinery, and financial commitments, and follow this new prophet. They hoped to practice the teachings of their charismatic leader in a new land in tightly-knit communities where there would be no interference from skeptical neighbours who did not understand the leading of God.

The financial institutions, banks and government agencies that held the mortgages on these abandoned and repossessed farms knew even less of God's leading. They simply wanted to reclaim some of their investment and avoid further financial loss. They had their own economic difficulties to deal with and they did not need more land to fall back into their possession. Nor did the Hudson's Bay Company or the Canadian Pacific Railway want any territory returned to them. Banks were caught in a dilemma. The only way out of this bind was to resell the land and machinery at whatever price they could get and thereby recoup at least part of their investment. Consequently, they offered attractive financial terms to new settlers. The Mennonite Central Committee (MCC) heard of these offers and encouraged Mennonite immigrants to explore these purchase opportunities.

This was the scene at Harwood that greeted one of the last groups of Russian Mennonite immigrants to enter Canada. These people, who had been forced from their villages in the Molotschna and Chortiza colonies, had travelled to Moscow and succeeded in escaping Russia. Once in

Canada, this group came into contact with representatives from the MCC under whose guidance, and with the encouragement of local Mennonite farmers, they approached the banks with plans to purchase some of this newly reacquired land.

Financial institutions were not in the farming business and were anxious to dispose of their bloated inventory. This situation allowed MCC officials to present offers to banks to sell this newly-vacated land to these immigrants, many who were experienced farmers, at terms they could afford and thereby recoup at least a portion of their losses. From the bank's perspective, this arrangement meant accepting purchase agreements with very little money down and with very favourable mortgage terms – conditions they really didn't like. Furthermore, the lenders were told that much of this land, although possibly well suited for farming, had never been properly proved up, that is, cleared and ploughed. Therefore, in its present condition, it was to be considered of lesser value. The banks also did not like to hear this. Yet somehow they accepted these arguments as valid and reluctantly negotiated a plan whereby a monetary value would be placed upon the number of acres cleared and ploughed each year. A portion of this would then be credited toward the mortgage principal. By creating conditions for farmers to succeed, the banks would rid themselves of surplus land and hopefully win back these farmers as customers for future banking needs. Fortunately for everyone, the local Mennonite farmers had established a reputation as being honest, hard-working citizens, and this helped convince banks and governments to take the risk and resell the land to these people. The federal government, keenly interested in seeing the land developed with viable communities established, decided to offer financial incentives to the money lenders to sweeten the pot and encourage banks to sell to these people.

The Harwood area was similar to the landscape initially described by Hubert J. Harwood as gently rolling terrain with large trees, pretty creeks and relatively few stones to obstruct farming implements. After accomplishing the back-breaking task of removing trees and stumps from their land, the more ambitious farmers had indeed found the soil to be fertile. Others, in search of quick solutions, had simply sawed off the trees at ground level and attempted to till the soil around the stumps. This was actually a partial violation of the terms drawn up between the government and the pioneers for proving up land. Owners were expected to clear stumps and large stones in order to properly prepare the land for planting crops.

For their part in meeting the terms of these financial agreements, some of the Russian immigrants, including Heinrich Gerbrandt, had brought, or smuggled, a little money out of Russia and now used these modest funds as down payments on their new farms. Perhaps smuggling was too strong a term. The money Heinrich brought with him was actually his, as he repeatedly pointed out, and a government that, in his view, lacked legitimacy had drawn up the Russian monetary rules regarding money leaving the country. The seams, belts, and straps of his and his family's clothing may have seemed a little thick to Russian border authorities, but no official ever decided, or even had time, to conduct a thorough body search on any of the emigrants. For this they had Alex and Nicholas to thank. Had the boys not made such a ruckus aboard the train car on which the Gerbrandt family was travelling, and had they not hassled the Russian guards at the Latvian border with fabricated stories about the train needing to be back in Moscow by the next morning, the search may have taken longer with a more unpleasant result for the emigrants. Whenever Heinrich's wife, Helena, complained about the treatment that she had received on the train ride to Riga, Alex would bite his tongue rather than remind her that the outcome for her could have been quite different.

With most of his money used as a down payment, Heinrich Gerbrandt secured a purchase agreement with the local Imperial Bank to buy 160 acres of partially cleared land. The bank manager gulped as he drew up mortgage papers with terms that his head office had somehow approved. Thomas Krueger, the local lawyer, crossed his fingers and uttered a small prayer that the financial arrangement negotiated between the bank and Heinrich Gerbrandt would allow a viable farming operation to succeed and that other farms sold under similar terms would also survive.

Approximately half of the Gerbrandt quarter section had been cleared of trees. The former owners had originally intended this farm to become a livestock operation, so they had allowed most of the land to be turned into pasture and had not bothered to clear away all the stumps. In order to grow grain, the land now needed to be ploughed. This meant cutting through a layer of thick sod interwoven with stumps and tree roots – no easy undertaking. On the positive side, the farm had a large sturdily built and freshly painted barn that could be seen for several miles around. The barn was built to comfortably shelter ten to fifteen horses, an equal number of cows, with a haymow large enough to feed even more animals throughout a long Manitoba winter. This barn, no doubt, was intended to serve the farming needs of a large extended family.

The house was the exact opposite – old and small, with only three rooms held together by wallpaper and whitewash according to Alex Friedrichsen. The roof needed constant repair to keep out the rain, the cracks in the window frames and doorways were forever being plugged, and very little could be done to evict the rodents who constantly devoured the foodstuffs and terrified the Gerbrandt family living there. But at least there was a roof over their heads. The land could feed them, and most importantly, no bandits rode across their property at night rattling windows, shooting dogs and terrifying the people.

Ever since their initial meeting, Alex and Nicholas Friedrichsen had tagged along behind Heinrich Gerbrandt. On paper they had succeeded in becoming Mennonites, at least according to their immigration documents. Initially, they met Heinrich's group on the train ride from Moscow to Riga and had travelled with them from Latvia to Liverpool, across the Atlantic to Halifax, then by train to Manitoba and to his barn in Harwood, where they now lived.

The first few nights in the Gerbrandt barn were all too reminiscent of the ugly times they had ridden with Nestor Makhno and his bandits, hiding and sleeping in barns on piles of straw infested with mites, ticks, and goodness knows what. The gnawing hunger in the pits of their stomachs also reminded them of that time. But now, added to their list of unpleasant experiences, was the feeling of aloneness and abandonment. The realization that their parents were dead, and their relatives, wherever they might be, had no interest in reconnecting with them was difficult to accept.

This feeling of being alone and left behind was especially troublesome to sixteen-year-old Nicholas. He had been reluctant to leave Russia and continued to question the wisdom of his brother's decision to escape their homeland. But once he learned of his mother's death and realized the depth of Alex's grief and anger as shown by his insistence that they leave this godforsaken land of hardship and constant trouble, Nicholas had finally agreed to come along. Now, more than ever, Alex had to be strong for his brother as well as for himself for he knew all too well that there was no turning back.

Feelings of aloneness and abandonment were driven even deeper by the treatment they received from their fellow travellers. And why should anyone be surprised by this reaction? Were these not the same boys who marched up and down the train aisle on its final border inspection before leaving Russia, yelling at passengers and threatening to beat anyone with rifle butts who failed to obey their commands? How does one forget such terrorizing experiences?

The trip across the ocean and the train ride from Quebec to Manitoba, with its wide array of new sights, had greatly interested the Friedrichsen brothers. Fortunately for them, Heinrich Gerbrandt and some of the Mennonites had given them food and a little money to fend off starvation with the stern reminder that any debt would need to be repaid. Once in Canada, the boys' offer to ride the Canadian Pacific Railway engine and feed the boiler in exchange for a little money was rebuffed. The language barrier between them and CPR train crews was simply too great.

Once they had arrived in Harwood, the Gerbrandt family continued to share food provisions with the brothers from what they had received from the MCC. Others, however, were less generous. Several even suggested that the boys be turned over to authorities for questioning, not merely for what they had done, but also for who they were — a couple of *Russe Bengels* — lazy, stupid, thieves who were masquerading as law abiding citizens.

On more than one occasion, Heinrich subtly reminded the boys that Mennonite women had suffered terrible crimes at the hands of Russian bandits. Alex usually managed to mask his sarcasm and suppress his anger at these remarks by agreeing with Heinrich, fully understanding the pain that the women must have endured. His own mother had also suffered abuse and unwanted sexual attention at the hand of at least one Mennonite Christian whose relatives were a part of this self-righteous group of immigrants.

When his mother had returned to Rosenthal from Odessa, alone and destitute, she became vulnerable to abuse, especially when she reintroduced herself as a Russian widow rather than a Mennonite girl. Isbrand Riessen, the son of the perpetrator of these offences, had followed Heinrich to Harwood. Alex knew it was only a matter of time before he and Nicholas would confront him. The situation was complicated by the fact that Isbrand Riessen was somehow distantly related to Helena Gerbrandt, Heinrich's wife.

Gerbrandt remained kind to the boys. Over time, he and his wife, as well as their daughter, Marusia, warmed toward them, eventually offering them trust and respect, treating them as worthy individuals rather than charity cases. For little Suzanna, Marusia's daughter, the friendship with the boys grew much more quickly. Alex and Nicholas played with her, teased her, gave her lots of attention and soon earned her friendship.

The fact that the boys could understand, and even speak a little Mennonite Low German dialect certainly helped to warm their relationship with the Gerbrandt family. On the voyage across the Atlantic, Alex and Nicholas earned a little money by working for the ship's crew doing odd jobs. When a wicked influenza virus spread throughout the ship laying low a number of passengers and sailors, they helped buy some tonic for Helena Gerbrandt who had become emaciated from the effects of the flu. They also located and purchased more nutritious food for her daughter Marusia, who was attempting to nurse her crying baby with as much milk as she could produce. But the other Mennonites viewed the boys with suspicion. All too frequently, the brothers interrupted groups of men off to the side speaking in low tones while looking over in their direction. Had someone recognized them as members of Nestor Makhno's gang?

Alex and Nicholas had ridden along with the anarchists on several raids through the Molotchna and had eaten meals supplied by Mennonite women who, under duress, had been forced to give up food from their own meagre provisions. They had eaten this food, but did hunger make them thieves? Were they expected to starve? The boys had been horrified by the indiscriminate acts of hostility many anarchists perpetrated upon victimized individuals, especially violations toward women and children. Ironically, they themselves were children at this time, only marginally tolerated by Makhno's men, and never fully accepted by them. They had been bullied by many of the riders, especially young Nicholas, harassed by certain men with looks and touches that he only later understood. On one occasion, several of Makhno's men cornered girls in the back room of a house. The screams that the brothers heard and only later understood would haunt them for the rest of their lives.

"Why didn't we grab a gun?" lamented Nicholas. "Why didn't we blow their damned heads off?" He felt that many of Heinrich Gerbrandt's references to forgiveness in his sermons were directed toward him. They probably were.

***

Survivors who weathered the Great Depression in the 1930s frequently detail the many hardships they were forced to endure. In some cases, Manitoba farmers saw their income shrink by as much as eighty per cent as the value of wheat was cut in half and the production of all crops further reduced by drought and insect infestation. Yet many immigrants were still better off in Canada than they had been in their homeland. Many newcomers were familiar with food shortages caused by drought and crop failure and had experienced famine made worse by resource mismanagement and political chaos. Many had also endured the ravages of unscrupulous armies and roving bands of anarchists who not only stole their food, but also terrorized their people. Chaos, anarchy, and the chronic lack of life's basic needs were experiences the Gerbrandt family and also the Friedrichsen boys had endured in Russia. They knew what it meant to scrounge for food, look for work, and deal with scoundrels and criminals. This is what Alex and Nicholas had known for much of their young lives. Aside from the few years their father had held a teaching position in Rosenthal, and the three years that they had worked for the Russian railway, this had been their life.

Here in Canada, they still had no money, but at least the brothers usually had enough to eat. The fear and dread of being bullied by either the communist police or by Makhno anarchists was now replaced by hope for a brighter future. Alex and Nicholas were in good health, had adequate clothing, and usually enough food to battle the gnawing feeling of hunger. In 1929 and the years following, this was more than many people even in Canada enjoyed.

Memories of life during the first few months in Harwood were a blur. The Gerbrandt family moved onto their property in late summer – a very poor time for prospective farmers to take possession of their land. People who occupied their farms in early spring had the opportunity to plant and harvest gardens. But now these new immigrants did not have time to prepare for winter and had reason to be concerned that food sources for the impending cold season would not be enough.

For several weeks before the heavy frost arrived, the boys helped the Gerbrandt family dig through garden plots in search of potatoes, beets, carrots, or anything edible that had escaped the tines of a harvesting fork. They also searched for berries along hedges and fencerows that could be dried or canned. When there was nothing left to do, they swept cobwebs from the cavernous Gerbrandt barn that now housed two cows, two horses, and one or two cats – all this in exchange for food.

Neighbours were kind. They gave the Gerbrandt family a few chickens, one or two turkeys, and even a few geese. The empty chicken coop on the farmyard was now partitioned with wire mesh into separate compartments for chickens, competing roosters, turkeys, and geese. Heinrich managed to buy a milk cow that had recently birthed a calf and could supply milk for the family for several months. The second cow that came with the farm was too old and eventually at the end of her milk cycle was butchered for meat. The cows were expected to share the huge barn with two horses that also came with the place. The haymow had sufficient feed for these few animals, and a pile of grain, found in a corner of the barn, could be cleaned and ground into flour and chicken feed. Fresh seed grain would need to be purchased next spring.

Soon after the Gerbrandt family had settled into their house, the Friedrichsen boys moved from the barn into a reclaimed old log cabin built by early property owners that had been converted into a chicken coop. They thoroughly cleaned the one-room structure and patched the holes in the roof and outside walls. A new floor was constructed from salvaged building material and several coats of whitewash were applied to walls and ceiling. The tiny cabin again became suitable for human habitation. The shallow slope of the roof could hold snow for insulation. Straw packed and tied into bales was piled against the outside walls to help keep out the cold, and a functioning potbelly stove with a chimney pipe extending from one end of the cabin ceiling to the other could heat food and provide warmth. And there was even a window.

Work during those first few months was difficult to find. Employment that actually offered pay was nonexistent. Days were filled with a variety of make-work projects or simply whiled away in boredom. Along with other newcomers, the Friedrichsen boys relied upon their own ingenuity to survive. They learned to market themselves and the services they could provide, at times for simply for a plate of food when payment of money was unavailable.

Alex and Nicholas's social standing within the community was tenuous at best. Not only the Mennonites, but other neighbours questioned the legality of offering the boys residence in Canada. Were they refugees or were they illegal immigrants? These terms needed to be clarified. Even the MCC, the organization that provided support for the newcomers, was wary of sponsoring illegal aliens and thereby running afoul of Canadian law. This was the gossip circulated in the town by one or two uncharitable people.

In the absence of meaningful work, boredom became a problem. One way to pass the time was to walk six kilometres to Harwood just to look around. Sometimes Alex and Nicholas would catch a ride with Heinrich Gerbrandt, who was forever sizing up and training his team of two totally mismatched horses hitched to an old, rickety farm wagon. There was little to explore in Harwood. If they could saunter along the wooden sidewalks and dirt paths slowly enough, they could usually see the sights of the town in a matter of minutes. Their favourite game was to speculate about the activities that might be taking place behind the doors that were closed to them.

The hamlet of Harwood, the largest village within walking distance, was a unique little place for them to visit that did not resemble in any way the towns or cities that they had passed through during their time as Russian Railway employees. Harwood had a sizeable general store stocked with everything from farm and garden supplies to dry goods, as well as an assortment of groceries and household articles. The boys speculated about the contents of the little cans and jars that lined the shelves.

"Must be medicine," said Nicholas as he spotted an interesting looking jar placed off to the side.

"Probably for constipation," laughed Alex.

"That's easily cured by eating the gravy-soaked food served to the train crews in the kitchen near the Moscow station," Nicholas mused. Alex agreed.

When they entered the general store, the boys felt intimidated by the foreign words directed at them and the unfriendly expressions on the faces of the proprietors. Were they being viewed with suspicion? Did people think they were drifters or thieves? Obviously, this was not an enterprise for the curious, nor could anyone mistake it for a place where charity was handed out. This was a business, a general store for people who had money. Heinrich Gerbrandt appeared to fare a little better in this establishment, but then again he could actually buy things ... he had money.

Beside the general store was a vacant lot and next to it, a school. When classes were not in session, Alex and Nicholas loved to walk up to the school building, peer in through the windows, and wonder aloud what it would be like to again sit in clean desks and write with chalk against a clean blackboard. Alex recalled the happy times he spent attending school, wearing clean clothes and writing with real pencils in real scribblers. His stepfather had been his teacher. But school also held unpleasant memories for him. Alex vividly recalled the morning that the police rudely interrupted the class and arrested his stepfather, hauling him away for questioning. The expression of horror on his stepfather's face as he was pushed toward the door is one Alex would never forget.

Before the boys left for Canada, their mother informed them that the cause of this upheaval was the fact that their father's views were not sufficiently hardline enough for the Bolshevik authorities, who were determined to fill the children's minds with only the purest communist teaching. The authorities were fully prepared to fire anyone who would not comply with their philosophies. The boys were left to wonder how the situation would have ended had their father been more flexible, more amenable to the demands placed upon him, and more prepared to compromise just a little. He might have kept his teaching position a little longer, his family might have been cared for, and the boys could have received a decent education. Unfortunately, Nikolai Kotelnikov was not that great a hypocrite. Principle and integrity were qualities he simply could not set aside. This is a lesson he passed along to his boys.

The brothers recalled the stress-filled days and nights following their father's dismissal, of hearing their parents cry over the situation. Alex and Nicholas experienced hunger, yet now understood how much worse it had been for their parents who rarely ate anything. Worst of all, they vividly recall seeing their father lapse into despondency, physically wither away, and finally die. These were memories they wished to forget, experiences they hoped never to see repeated. Was this repression of a person's basic beliefs not sufficient reason enough to leave Russia?

Beside the school stood a stately wooden church with an Orthodox cross positioned on top of a tall steeple. The church needed a coat of paint and other minor repairs, but no doubt served as a dignified house of worship. The boys weren't sure who attended here and speculated that both Orthodox and Doukhobor congregations probably shared the building. They had little experience with church. Their parents had initially introduced them to the Orthodox faith by having them baptized, but as infants they simply were too young to fully appreciate the Orthodox mass, or any other practice of faith for that matter. After their father's death, their mother had decided to explore her Mennonite roots and began attending Mennonite churches in Rosenthal. These services seemed so cold and austere, like the people who attended, and the sermons so mind-numbingly boring. But the singing in Mennonite churches was memorable. Anthems and songs set to themes of joy, love and hope were sung most beautifully in four-part harmony. Yet, at times, the music was performed with no joy being reflected in either the people's facial expressions or in their actions – at least not toward Christina and her boys. Their mother always sang heartily and introduced the soprano, alto, and tenor lines of congregational songs to her little boys.

What influenced the brothers' religious views most was the instruction given to them by their mother, especially during their childhood and again in her last year. While living in Rosenthal she began attending Bible studies led by Adolph Reimer, an itinerant Mennonite preacher, and was deeply moved by his message. He preached love, grace, and forgiveness. Sermons were not about the severity of a God whose wrath would punish her for her sins, but about a God who accepted her as she was and loved her in spite of her faults and shortcomings. When not searching for food, Christina spent time travelling with his little group until the communist authorities banned religious teaching of any sort. She read to her boys from her Bible until it was confiscated, and she knelt with them and taught them to pray.

Across the street from the General Store was a run-down blacksmith shop, or was it a machine shop or an implement dealership of some sort? The disorder in and around the place made it difficult to tell exactly what purpose the proprietor of this establishment had in mind. Was he attempting to hide some illegal activity? This thought crossed the minds of many local residents who knew the owner all too well. Pieces of wood and metal were thrown about or left leaning against the sides of the building, making it dangerous for anyone to walk too close, and impossible even for weeds and grasses to find the light of day. Oil and gasoline spills left dirty dark patches of brown bald earth that prevented anything from growing in or crawling through these filthy circles.

On one of their frequent Harwood walking tours as the boys again shuffled along Main Street past the Orthodox church, past the school and past the vacant lot, the boredom of their peaceful, mid-afternoon stroll was rudely interrupted by sudden shrieks of anger. Loud abrasive language uttered by a high-pitched voice rattled the tranquility of the afternoon and filled the air with highly offensive words that belonged to a Russian dialect of some sort. The boys stopped and listened. Was this their mother tongue? Were these the words of their ancestors? Cautiously they inched forward toward the messy machine shop, the place from where the sounds appeared to originate hoping to reconnect with someone who spoke the Russian language. As they drew closer they clearly recognized colourfully crude expressions that their father would never have used, being directed toward a man who was peacefully perched on a Coca-Cola box located inside the large open doorway of the shop.

An exceptionally irate woman was spewing forth years of pent up emotion toward this poor character who reacted much like a cat that chooses to ignore a bird that's dive-bombing its head. He sat perfectly motionless without twitching a single muscle. This full-throated harangue built into a huge crescendo that abruptly ended with a loud banging noise, likely produced by a door being violently slammed shut. Within minutes, Harwood recovered from this dramatic display of emotion and returned to the peaceful pursuits of the quiet autumn afternoon. People returned to their mundane activities, horses tethered to hitching posts continued their mid-afternoon slumber, and the school children, whose play had been interrupted, returned to their comparatively quiet recess activities.

From across the street Alex and Nicholas had witnessed the entire episode. After a moment or so, an astounded Nicholas looked at the man, the recipient of all this unwanted attention, and broke the silence, "He's dead."

"Not yet," said Alex.

The boys waited a few moments, and then slowly crossed the street. Cautiously, they moved toward the open doorway, fearing that objects worse than words could be hurled their way. As they neared the shop, they walked directly toward the man still calmly seated on the Coca-Cola box and carefully addressed this poor victim of abuse in the best Russian they had learned from their father. This verbally battered man slowly got up from his dirty box, limped toward them, and returned the greeting in some Polish/Ukrainian dialect that he was attempting to pass off as highbrow Russian – not nearly the correct Russian that the boys had learned, but nevertheless, quite understandable.

After a short exchange of meaningless pleasantries, Alex looked around and asked, "Do you need help?"

Instantly, the man's eyes came to life as he spewed forth his own version of pent up emotion. He greeted Alex's innocent request with a high-pitched derisive laugh, followed by a torrent of cynical words and phrases that communicated the widely-held belief that a viable business was no longer possible in this damn country, and that even if it were, he needed no help.

Stunned by this sudden, rather belligerent, reply, Alex waited a moment, looked around until his eye noticed parts of a partially disassembled motor lying about the shop floor and blurted out the first words that came to his mind, "What are you doing?"

Again the proprietor let loose with a barrage of hopelessness, interspersed with swear words – some of which would have caused the lowest of the Makhno bandits to blush. He ended his oration by pointing to his injured hip and said he needed to get off his feet. As the boys turned to leave, he asked if they could at least help him lift a heavy engine part from off the floor as he attempted to reattach it to a partially disassembled engine block.

Alex and Nicholas stayed all day, helping the man move heavy items and locating tools hidden beneath piles of debris. They even attempted to tidy up the shop a little. Afterward, they were rewarded with an evening meal of fried potatoes, white bread with butter, and fresh milk. The woman, whose initial belligerence had intimidated the boys, now introduced herself and softened her attitude toward them, but maintained her icy grip on the poor man. This initial contact with George and Katja Zabilski grew into a friendly and mutually beneficial relationship with Alex and Nicholas. Katja Zabilski would feed the boys whenever they stopped by to help George. She was a good cook, even better on days when her husband George did not get on her nerves, which wasn't very often.

"George is a good man," she once explained to a trusted friend, "but if I don't sit on him, he wastes time with Kamiski and other reprobates and gets nothing done." According to local gossip, Peter Kamiski had a little enterprise on the side where he distributed homebrew produced at his own private distillery discreetly located in a bush near the back of his property.

Alex didn't believe this gossip. He saw little evidence of George's excessive drinking, so Katja's allegation did not overly disturb him. Over time, he realized that George was an excellent mechanic, and secretly thought that George might need the occasional belt of homebrew just to endure Katja's incessant nagging. One of the few unifying elements that kept the Zabilski marriage together appeared to be the fact that they both liked Alex and Nicholas.

Next to the general store stood a vacant lot, the other ugly sight that helped define Harwood's skyline. A partially concealed and abandoned foundation overgrown with weeds and tall grass shielded stones and various pieces of debris from view. The state of this rundown eyesore raised Alex's curiosity. He noticed that no one ever walked across the lot, not even dogs or horses. One day, after he and George Zabilski had become better acquainted, he asked George what building had once stood on this site and why the property was so badly run down.

"It's cursed by God," came the instant reply. George stopped what he was doing, lowered his voice, looked around to see if anyone was listening and then whispered some highly interesting gossip into the boys' ears. According to what he remembered, an unscrupulous entrepreneur had once operated a small pub and gambling hall on this site, and had even erected a small stage where girls of questionable reputation would dance on Saturday nights for paying patrons. The place was called "Chez Paree."

"You mean Harwood actually had dancing girls?" blurted out a surprised Alex. He could just see Helena, Heinrich's wife, turn stone-faced with shock, then go and burst into the place with some of her Mennonite friends, and throw the dancing girls out onto the street. The image reminded him of a picture he had once seen in his mother's Bible where Christ threw the moneychangers out of the temple.

Sometime later, George took it upon himself to describe to Alex in greater detail the iniquities that take place in this "wicked world of ours." Between frequent glances over his shoulder to see if his wife Katja was listening, he passed along information that he felt young men entering adulthood would need to know. He began by relating a vivid account of what, according to his reliable sources, had taken place at "Chez Paree." His narrative walked the fine line between condemning the erotic dancing on the one hand, and vicariously enjoying the sights and sounds that the provocative stage show had elicited in the minds of the testosterone-laden men of Harwood.

"Lulu, the main dancer," according to George's information, "was dressed in this flimsy see-through ..." Here his voice tapered off to a faint whisper that Alex could barely hear. Alex found himself caught in the awkward position of keeping his face close enough to George's garlic breath to hear all the juicy details, while still firmly maintaining his partially extended elbow against Nicholas's rib cage to keep the boy at a safe distance. Alex felt that he owed it to their mother to protect young Nicholas from such a blatant description of sin. Nicholas's frequent interruptions were largely ignored. He was confused. Had he heard "wiggled," or was it "jiggled," and what part of a female dancer's body would produce such an action.

"Then the men, even old man Hutchinson, stood up and ..." Here George's voice again tapered off to a whisper as the next instalment of bawdy details was disseminated into the eager listener's ear. George's face lit up with delight. Alex gasped in amazement and Nicholas would have given anything to hear what was being said. Katja, who walked into the shop to ask George a question, rudely brought the information session to an abrupt end.

Later Nicholas asked Alex, "Do you think they actually danced to music?" trying hard to piece together an image of what George had described.

"For this kind of dancing you really don't need music," whispered Alex. "Besides, if necessary, George Zabilski and his buddies could always hum a few tunes."

Wishing to shield his younger brother from further harmful information, Alex insisted upon changing the subject. George's details brought back memories of what he had once seen in Russia where he had inadvertently, according to him, stumbled into such an establishment of ill repute. The live dancing girls continued to interest Nicholas, but here Alex drew the line. The details of what he had witnessed in Russia and the account that George had relayed to him needn't be shared with sixteen-year-old Nicholas ... not at this time.

At least the school provided a buffer between the church people and the dancing girls, thought Nicholas. He was fixated on the image of scantily clad girls dancing on a stage to no music and being leered at by the police and by George Zabilski and his buddies.

Sometime later, George again took up the conversation relating how one Sunday morning this place of ill repute had caught fire and burned to the ground. Had it not been for the quick actions of some of the lesser-inebriated patrons, the school and the General Store located on either side might have also been destroyed.

"Do you think the Mennonite women burned it down?" pondered Nicholas.

"Not likely," replied Alex. "They always stay home on Saturday night to take a bath."

George Zabilski had a most interesting explanation of what happened. "God struck down this den of iniquity," he asserted, shaking his finger heavenward in response to Nicholas's question. Actually, these were not George's words. He was merely repeating the official explanation given to everyone by his wife Katja. "God saw fit to burn it down even before the police could get around to close it." This interesting observation contradicted the widely held view that accused the police officers of being among the most faithful patrons of this den of iniquity.

"Now that I think about it," reflected George, "the police did occasionally stop in for a drink or two. Besides, the girls really weren't that good and the drinks were watered down." This information was whispered in lower tones and, according to George, gathered from the only time he had actually been inside the place. "The ground around the foundation is now cursed," said George, again with the words of his wife, "Not even weeds grow where the building once stood."

Nothing could grow in that soil so saturated with the urine from the peeing patrons, thought Alex.

***

On slow days throughout the long winter, the boys continued their walks to Harwood to search for little jobs – mostly clean-up activities at George's machine shop. George took a liking to Alex, especially his youth and physical strength, as well as his total disregard for the oppressive hopelessness that now gripped the area. Alex's quickness at understanding tasks and solving mechanical problems was also impressive to George. Word got around that this young man was a very reliable worker who would do most anything in exchange for an evening meal. Soon the proprietors of the general store found jobs for him, usually lifting and carrying heavy bulky items. Alex learned to bargain with his new employers and with the people from Harwood who hired him, and they in turn grew to like and trust him. Even Thomas Krueger, the lawyer, found the occasional activity for Alex.

Nicholas found some employment on a neighbouring farm owned by Uri and Ruth Hershberger. Uri had heard of the predicament faced by the unemployed immigrants and thought he could help by offering the Friedrichsen boys who lived nearby a little work. Uri was a good man and a very good farmer. He had developed a successful grain and livestock operation that had become the victim of its own success when the manual labour required to keep the farm afloat was more than he could provide. His farm would have prospered more, had the 1929 Depression not eroded commodity prices, and if he and his wife had had sons rather than daughters – six to be exact – none of whom had even the slightest interest in cows, horses, or tractors. To make matters worse, the oldest five daughters had grown up and moved away without casting so much as a glance in the direction of the local land-owning eligible bachelors.

One day while Alex was in town helping George Zabilski, Uri rode onto the Gerbrandt yard and met Nicholas. He had come to size up the boy and his brother to see if either of them could be of use on his threshing crew. Nicholas quickly agreed to an initial proposal of a few hours of work in exchange for food and rode along with Hershberger. He performed the tasks set before him with quickness and competency. Uri took careful note of this, and found a few more make-work projects to help this unemployed lad. Nicholas, in turn, worked hard and continued to impress Uri. He had a way with horses that his brother Alex totally lacked. He also took a special interest in the well-stocked woodworking shop that Uri had built for himself. Uri was happy with Nicholas and decided to pay him a little more regularly from his own meagre income. This soon resulted in fairly steady work for Nicholas. Uri had plenty of hay to feed his animals, so he decided to keep his cows and horses through the long winter rather than sell them at bargain basement prices. With his animals needing daily chores, Uri was grateful for the extra help.

The Hershbergers enjoyed Nicholas's company. In addition to paying him a modest amount, they fed him well and accepted the challenge of teaching the boy some English. Initially, communication between them was carried on through the use of words and expressions common to the

Pennsylvania Dutch, the language the Hershbergers spoke, and the limited understanding of the Mennonite Low German that Nicholas had acquired. When verbal communication reached an impasse, the two sides resorted to wild arm gesticulations to convey their thoughts. Uri enjoyed working with Nicholas and seeing him take a keen interest in his woodworking projects. Nicholas became the son Hershberger wished he'd had.

During the threshing season, there was work for both the boys, stooking sheaves of wheat and oats, and accompanying Hershberger's threshing crew throughout the district. Alex was fascinated by the operation. Whenever there was a mechanical problem, a breakdown or adjustment that needed to be made to some tractor or machine, he was right there to offer assistance and gain any knowledge he could. Nicholas was more of a horseman. Before long, he was in charge of his own team and wagon, picking up sheaves of grain from the fields and bringing them to the threshing machine. The boys had never eaten so well. Soon their thin bodies began to fill out with muscle and their facial expressions began to reflect a sense of satisfaction at the meaningful work they had found.

Once the threshing season, shortened by limited rainfall, had ended, Alex and Nicholas again found little to keep them occupied. The Hershbergers had a room for Nicholas, but with their youngest daughter, Sarah, still at home, it was seen as inappropriate for two unrelated teenagers of opposite sex to sleep under the same roof. Sarah, with help from the local schoolteacher was attempting to complete her high school courses through a correspondence program. Every night, the two boys would return to their renovated chicken coop turned cabin and watch their threshing muscles shrink and their calluses soften.

Once the cold days of late autumn had arrived, Uri Hershberger and several neighbors came together to butcher geese and several hogs. The process of turning pig carcasses into cured hams and smoked farmer's sausage – a staple for many winter farmhouse meals – fascinated the boys. They enjoyed turning the crank of the hand-powered meat grinder and savoured the smell emanating from the cauldron of boiling pork fat that was being rendered into lard and cracklings. Those cracklings tasted so good when slathered onto a slice of Ruth Hershberger's famous homemade white bread.

Nicholas passed the time riding and training Hershberger's horses, something he enjoyed and did very well. But the skills of horsemanship that had worked so well with Herberger's fine animals were totally lost on Heinrich Gerbrandt's mismatched team. The Gerbrandt farm had inherited from the former owners an old gelding named King, and a much younger and smaller mare named Dolly. King, possibly the leader of the herd in past years, had now simply run out of steam. Consequently, he was low on energy and even lower on any desire to work. Only sudden loud noises would motivate him to move, and then only if he felt his life being threatened. Dolly, the younger, stronger, and more energetic teammate, was a good-looking horse with broad shoulders and long straight legs. From the left side, she looked like a handsome three or four year old mare. But from the right side, she had scars from some terrible accident that had taken an eye, left an ear deformed, and severely scarred the skin on the right side of her head. Like old King, she was easily spooked by loud noises. The boys reasoned that Dolly, if coupled with a good stallion, could possibly produce a healthy foal.

Alex continued to spend time with George Zabilski, gathering knowledge about farm machinery, especially the quirks of those "son-of-a-bitch" internal combustion engines. It took Alex several months to realize that the term "son-of-a-bitch" could be applied to more than just the mechanical objects that incessantly irritated George. But when it came to solving mechanical problems, George could fix most anything.

Long winter evenings became a problem. The boys embraced any activity that could take them away from their tiny cabin, even for an hour or so. On Monday evenings, Mary Stuart, the local schoolteacher, offered English language instruction to the recently arrived immigrants. She offered this service to fill her own long winter evenings, and perhaps to keep her job at the local school where enrolment was very low. Alex and Nicholas were the first to register for these English classes. Soon Heinrich Gerbrandt and his daughter, Marusia, joined them. Many other newcomers to Canada also enrolled, always with their best intentions for learning English, but unfortunately many attended class so infrequently, they soon fell behind, lost heart, and dropped out. Miss Stuart was a smart young woman, an avid reader who brought with her an excellent grasp of English language usage and grammar. The fact that she was so well read probably made her value as a teacher more suited to adults than to children. Heinrich Gerbrandt was her counterpart in the German language and literature. He understood rules of grammar and sentence structure very well, and his strong linguistic background quickly enabled him to gain a good grasp of the English language.

The Friedrichsen boys, however, found they did not fit in. Their father had spoken excellent Russian, and from the little time they had spent with him before his death, he had passed along to them whatever he could. Beyond speaking Russian and some Mennonite Low German, Alex and Nicholas were barely literate. Alex could read and write a little Russian, but neither boy could read German, and both boys knew very little English. They simply had little opportunity to attend school and receive a formal education.

But the brothers were smart, and more importantly, determined to learn. They had grown angry at the put-downs and the humiliations they had been forced to endure, and were tired of receiving sideways glances from pompous adults. They decided not to take this abuse any longer and together determined to make something of themselves. This became the driving force in their lives. Alex and Nicholas studied hard and before long found they could keep up with the pace of the class. They even managed to acquire better English pronunciation than Heinrich Gerbrandt, who became stuck in a world of "zis" or "zhat," and "zese" or "zose," rather than "this" or "that," and "these "or "those." The brothers' rapid progress so impressed Heinrich that he offered to teach them German. They readily accepted his offer, and as a result, a second night of the week was occupied.

On Wednesday evenings, Alex and Nicholas followed Heinrich to the small wooden church just outside Harwood where he led a Bible study and prayer group. The first time they walked in, they were greeted, and almost

confronted by Isbrand Riessen, the resident authority on almost everything. Isbrand saw himself as the keeper of the gate, the guardian of what
was pure and right. He reacted to the boys' presence with his usual self-
righteous condescension. He had not yet forgiven the boys for mistreating
him at the border crossing to Latvia. Actually, they had not treated him any
differently than the others. They had simply failed to show him the proper
deference to which he felt he was entitled. In his mind, they were just *Russe
Bengels*. According to Riessen's poorly disguised prejudice, any attempt to
rehabilitate these lost Russian souls was futile. Just get rid of them. His
way to achieve this was to mock their actions and ridicule their words.
When a passage of scripture was to be read, Isbrand would look at the boys
and ask them to stand and read, but then he would suddenly realize his
error and quickly correct his mistake by reminding everyone in the room
that the boys could neither read nor write. The boys simply endured this
humiliation. But after a year or so when Isbrand attempted his put-down
for the very last time, Alex rose and asked if he wanted the passage read in
German, English, or Russian. This was only a partial bluff since Alex had
an ear for languages and learned to read very quickly.

Saturday night was bath night throughout rural Manitoba. In the
absence of a large tub with sufficient hot water the reduced body surface
of the boys' skinny frames took little time to bathe. Consequently, the bath
in the Friedrichsen cabin rarely stretched into an activity of more than a
few minutes or so. Afterwards, the boys would huddle around the kerosene
lamp and speculate on what Marusia, who bathed in the Gerbrandt house
just a few hundred yards away, would look like in her bathtub and without
her clothes. Once they learned to read, and borrow books from the school
library, Saturday evening boredom was no longer as great a problem.

***

Friday night was by far the best night of the week. After harvest activities had finished and once hog butchering was over, there was little to do
on the long evenings of late fall. This was a tough time for everyone. Some

people were struggling to find employment, others were struggling to keep their farms afloat, and everyone was struggling to find a reason for believing in a better future. With money being tight and the Christmas season just a few weeks away, everyone realized there would be few, if any, store-bought presents, and even fewer extra ingredients to make Christmas baking special. To help alleviate the general pessimism in the community, Helena Gerbrandt proposed a Christmas choir at the church she and her family attended. Her idea was greeted with enthusiasm. Singers from this multicultural congregation of Lutherans, Mennonites, and a few others responded eagerly to her suggestion. Time certainly was not an issue. Very few people had work and a Friday night activity was most welcome.

Close to twenty singers arrived for the first rehearsal. A seating plan was quickly established, followed by a few welcoming remarks by Helena. Next, she introduced a few basic vocal warm-up exercises that many found to be quite amusing. Then Helena suggested a well-known Christmas carol, established a tempo, gave a pitch, and the first Harwood choir rehearsal was under way. Soprano, alto, and bass sections were well represented. By the second stanza, Helena was relieved to hear that most people in the group could maintain their respective part quite securely, and those who had difficulty could probably learn from the others.

Helena Gerbrandt had taken some voice training in Russia, so she had basic knowledge regarding proper breathing and proper vowel production. To her surprise, the choral tone was quite strong and she realized that with a few more rehearsals, this group could develop into a decent little choir. What was lacking however, as is frequently the case in small choirs, was a tenor section and for this she had no solution. The Mennonites who attended this first rehearsal noticed that the Friedrichsen brothers had also come. This stirred a little commotion among several people who wondered aloud why these boys would even bother to appear. "After all," whispered someone, "why did they come? Did they think there would be free food?"

The self-appointed leaders, important in their own minds, directed the boys to sit at the end of the last row so they could observe what was taking place. During the singing of the first two songs, the nervous and self-conscious Friedrichsen brothers looked rather bewildered and barely moved their lips. Isbrand Riessen took note of this, and in his usual pompous manner, leaned over and suggested that they could make a better contribution to the group if they at least opened their mouths to sing. Others who heard this, especially Isbrand's son, Gerhard, and a few sopranos who fancied themselves to be very good singers, laughed heartily. Helena just ignored the comment.

Once all voices had warmed up, Helena suggested as the third song, a rather ambitious German chorale she thought both Lutherans and Mennonites would know. She was right. But what happened next caught everyone totally off guard. Within two or three bars of this song, the harmonic texture of the sound suddenly became rich and full as a tenor part clearly rang out from somewhere. Surprised, Helena stopped the choir, looked in the direction of the Friedrichsen boys and asked them what part they were singing. An equally surprised Alex informed her that this was a song that their mother had taught them. They knew the melody and also two other parts and asked Helena which part she wanted them to sing.

Now, somewhat amused and slightly flabbergasted, Helena suggested that the group begin the song again and this time asked the choir to sing softly so she could hear what notes the boys were attempting to add. This time everyone distinctly heard two parts come from the end of the back row where Alex and Nicholas had been told to sit. Helena and most of the choir immediately realized that Alex was singing the tenor line, and Nicholas, with his higher voice, was attempting the alto part, switching to falsetto for only the very highest notes. Not only were the brothers singing their vocal lines securely, they were singing all notes in perfect pitch, in perfect time, and with most beautiful tone.

Again, there was laughter, but this time it was not laughter of ridicule, but laughter of amazement and delight as the choir realized the great contribution these unusual and beautiful voices could make to the group. To Nicholas's relief, he was asked to join Alex on the tenor line. He had felt that alto was a little high for him. Once again Helena cued the choir and this time a most beautiful four-part version of "Nun ist sie erschienen, die himmlische Sonne" filled the little country church. With unrestrained delight, Helena conducted the song three or four more times, first with the choir sitting, then standing, singing all stanzas each time. Helena hardly slept that night. With this little group she had visions of performing choruses from Handel's *Messiah* that she had sung in Russia. Immediately, she set aside times to further explore the Friedrichsen voices and teach these boys as many tenor parts as she knew, and, always of course, in exchange for an evening meal.

At their next meeting, Alex shared with Helena how their mother, Christina, had loved to sing. With tears in his eyes, he related to her that singing was the one joy in his mother's life that no one could ever take away from her. While living in Rosenthal, his mother would gather her boys around her and sing to them, as well as attend services with them where she knew the congregational singing would be good. She always sang soprano for the first verse and then would sing either the alto or tenor parts for the following stanzas. As Mennonite hymns always had many stanzas, it allowed her to teach the boys the three upper parts to a number of songs. Alex recalled seeing baby Nicholas attempt to stick objects into his mother's mouth while she was singing, and while she tried to keep Alex from annoying those around him with his incessant wiggling.

At one of these extra tenor rehearsals, Helena also invited Johann and Wilhelm Bergman, two brothers who together with their widowed mother had recently moved to the area. Helena hoped to convince Johann to join the tenor section. Her husband, Heinrich, had sat next to Wilhem, Johann's brother, at the first choir rehearsal and thought that the young lad had a very good bass voice. The rehearsal went well. Helena worked with the boys, checked their notes, corrected rhythmic errors, offered them breathing instruction, and before long they sang as a four-part male quartet. All four boys had good musical instincts and caught on quickly to what Helena was teaching them. Before the rehearsal was over, Helena suggested that they try to sing a four-part male voice version of a traditional Christmas carol. Once again her music teaching skills succeeded, as the boys quickly became secure in their respective parts and with beautiful tone sang the carol, "Stille Nacht."

Christmas arrived and the first Christmas Eve service in the little white church on the edge of town promised to be a simple, yet very well-attended celebration. The Lutherans and Mennonites, along with a few others that made up the congregation, joined together to plan a service that included a little something from everyone's tradition. Decorations were few, although there was a Christmas tree with some homemade candles that graced the front corner of the church near the makeshift altar. The lights did not need to be dimmed to create a festive atmosphere. At the best of times, there were barely enough candles and kerosene lamps to light anything.

The newly-formed choir under Helena Gerbrandt's direction sang several Christmas songs and led the congregation in singing three or four more carols. The new male quartet of the Friedrichsen and Bergman boys sang, "O du fröhliche, O du Selige," an old German chestnut. The boys were too naïve and innocent to be nervous. They simply got up and sang. In any other setting, the applause to their song would have been thunderous, but on Christmas Eve, the people simply received the gift of their song in appreciative silence. Following the song by the quartet, the woman who read the Christmas story could barely find her speaking voice. She was too choked up with emotion.

The Friedrichsen boys enjoyed attending church events. Actually, they enjoyed attending any social event that would allow them to escape the confines of their tiny cabin, especially on long winter evenings. Alex and Johnny, the older Bergman boy, became good friends, and Nicholas and Wilhelm, who was about six inches shorter than Nicholas, also got along very well. These relationships would grow to become lifelong friendships.

***

Uri Hershberger did his part to help the boys through the winter. He gave them farm chores, including milking cows and feeding the animals, and his wife, Ruth, provided many evening meals for them. Nicholas enjoyed the challenge of training the young horses and preparing the old plough geldings for "Olympic equestrian events," according to Alex, should such competitions ever be held in Harwood. Many times, Nicholas ended face down on the ground, but always managed to get back up onto the horse and convince the old nag who was boss. Alex reminded everyone that Nicholas should be grateful that he usually landed face first into fresh manure; otherwise, he would surely have broken his nose or chipped a front tooth. In response, Nicholas would then point out that Alex needed someone to hold his hand whenever he came near a horse. Hershberger enjoyed the friendly banter between the brothers as they teased each other about practically everything.

Whenever the boredom became too great, the boys would walk to town to visit George Zabilski, who always provided entertainment, comic relief, and the occasional minor task. George was a kind man who would dig up a few jobs for the boys just to allow them to stay for supper. George had a modest contract with the government to keep main roads in reasonable repair during the summer and free from snow in winter. This contract was not very lucrative, but it did pay real money, something the local farmers lacked, and financially it helped him get through the lean months. George had a team of horses, stupid old geldings according to Alex, and an old tractor with a blade for clearing snow. George's age however, and arthritic hip did not like the cold. Once he realized that Alex could drive the tractor and keep it running during extreme weather, George hired him to look after this part of his business. Whether this employment was offered to Alex as a gesture of kindness or perhaps reliance on Alex's strength never became clear.

George Zabilski remained his cantankerous, pessimistic, and at times, kindhearted self. He was convinced, "The whole world has gone to hell and it can only get worse." Alex, on the other hand, saw life as full of interesting opportunities. Each day, he would feed George a little more of his infectious optimism and each day George would assure Alex that he had totally lost his mind. But over time, something began to stir in George. He slowly came to realize that the world needed to eat and Harwood was surrounded by very good farmland. Eventually, the farmers would need properly functioning machinery that he could supply to allow them to plant and harvest their crops.

Alex's restless ambition took note of a number of pieces of machinery that lay scattered about the yard in various states of disrepair. George had initially sold these to farmers who had returned them once they could no longer afford the payments. George also had managed to collect two old Rumley tractors and an even older Hart Parr from farms that had been abandoned when families simply left their operations and moved away. Alex was eager to try his hand at repairing some of this equipment. The first few sparks of optimism appeared in George the day he reluctantly agreed to look at several small implements that were collecting rust behind his shop. Once retrieved from under piles of debris, then cleaned and lubricated, these pieces of machinery again became functional. Where minor repairs were required, George was happy to show Alex what needed to be done. Next, in response to Alex's continued aggravating persistence, George turned his attention to ploughs and seed drills, implements with more complicated mechanisms that also needed to be cleaned, greased and, if necessary, rebuilt. Where needed, parts were usually salvaged from the huge piles of junk that surrounded George's property.

Eventually under duress, George reluctantly agreed to drag a huge Rumley Oil Pull into the shop. The engine was "seized up" according to him, and needed to be completely "tore down."

"Furthermore," he vehemently asserted, "this thing won't run in a million years." With great curiosity, Alex watched in amazement, as George, the old cynic, became the master mechanic, who amidst many colourful expletives, carefully and methodically began to disassemble the engine. Each gear, sleeve, bolt and washer was examined and cleaned, and where necessary, replaced with spare parts reclaimed from George's junk pile. George was at his best, finding and correcting one problem after another while continually directing a torrent of colourful terms toward the incompetent owner who had allowed the tractor to reach such a complete state of disrepair.

Once every part had been carefully checked, tested and greased, George with the accurate precision of a Swiss watchmaker began reassembling the engine. As he worked through each step, he explained to Alex why it needed to be done exactly this way. Alex could feel his grasp of proper Russian language usage erode and be replaced by a wide variety of swear words and vile expressions not found in the dictionary, directed toward each step of the operation. During this time, Alex learned a great deal about internal combustion engines and transmissions – invaluable knowledge for years to come.

On a cold winter afternoon, the large doors of the shop were opened and the newly-restored Rumley was allowed to catch a sniff of fresh air. Under George's watchful eye, Alex was instructed to turn the flywheel while George began making many minor adjustments to the choke, the throttle and the spark. Initially, and for many minutes thereafter, nothing happened. Again and again, Alex was directed to pull the flywheel. His exhausted arms were ready to fall off, but his spirit was continually spurred onward by George's oration of colourful expressions directed toward the tractor. Were it not for Alex's growing discouragement, the scene would indeed have become quite comical.

Now it was George's turn to show optimism. With uncharacteristically renewed perseverance, he asked Alex to pull the flywheel for what seemed to be the hundredth time. From out of nowhere an eruptive blast pierced the cold air. This was followed by an enormous belch of smoke that nearly set Alex onto the seat of his pants. From up in the rafters, pigeons immediately vacated their favourite perch and flew out through the main doorway scattering feathers in every direction. Alex quickly recovered from the blast and watched in amazement as the flywheel slowly began to turn on its own, threaten to stop, and then rotate again with a little more speed. A second eruptive blast, even louder than the first, escaped through the exhaust pipe. George, sweating like a work horse, feverishly worked the levers in an attempt to preserve the spark of life the tractor was attempting to create.

After a few more belches, first sporadic and then with greater regularity, the newly-created coughs and puffs gradually gained momentum until the old dormant Rumley roared back to life. Startled shopkeepers rushed out onto the street, dogs cowered for cover, and Katja Zabilski ran into the shop, applauding wildly as tears flowed down her face. This was more than a tractor springing to life – this was the rebirth of optimism and hope for all who were watching. Life had returned to the old Rumley, to despondent George Zabilski, and perhaps soon to the entire town of Harwood.

The day that old Rumley started may have been a turning point of the Great Depression for the people of Harwood, for it seemed that thereafter things improved. George sold the tractor to an optimistic owner of a lumber mill and pocketed a tiny profit. He began looking for other abandoned tractors and machines, and with Alex's help, developed a tidy machinery restoration business. Whenever George paid him, Alex would share his newfound gain with the Gerbrandt family. The family began to eat more nutritious meals, and Heinrich's wife, Helena, began to gain weight.

Chapter 8
Life in Canada – 1930s

HEINRICH GERBRANDT WAS A MAN OF PRINCIPLE WHO RARELY DEVI-ated from his deeply held convictions. No one doubted Heinrich's love for his wife, his two daughters or his grandchildren. His attitudes and actions toward people in his community were never questioned, even under adverse circumstances. Furthermore, the exemplary leadership he provided for the diverse, and at times divisive, group of Mennonites whom he led out of Russia allowed them to begin life anew in Canada. These qualities made Heinrich an obvious leader, a position he naturally fell into, though one for which he never volunteered. People trusted his ability to negotiate tough situations without compromising the principles for which he stood. Therefore, no one should have been surprised that he advocated so strongly for the Friedrichsen "outlaws," or orphans as he chose to call them, when others held them at a distance with fear and prejudice.

In spite of Heinrich's many fine qualities, he lacked the knowledge and practical hands-on skills to earn a living as a farmer. This ineptitude in all things practical became painfully clear the day he attempted to till some land and plant a few acres of wheat with his team of mismatched horses. "Surely the knowledge to grow crops could be learned from a book," he reasoned, but the skills required to put such information into practice had not been part of his academic education.

All winter, Heinrich schemed and worried about the wheat, oats, and hay crops he would need to grow for his farm to become profitable. He and his family couldn't continue to rely on the generosity of neighbours to provide them with the necessities of life. At some point, they had to learn to become more self-sufficient. A vegetable garden would not be a problem. Helena, his wife, had a green thumb and could do wonders with vegetables, flowers and most anything that grew out of the ground. In the farm's large barn, Heinrich found some basic pieces of horse harness, along with several implements including a plough, a disc, a set of harrows, a seed drill, and a wagon that could be converted into a sleigh once the snow arrived. All winter, Heinrich worked his horses, trying to teach Dolly to wait for King, and trying to encourage old King to show a little more life … a little more spunk … a little more of anything.

Once spring arrived and the frost was out of the ground, Heinrich managed to prepare a garden plot for seeding. He was encouraged by the fact that his horses could pull the implements through the loose soil with reasonable ease. Surely, they could do the same with ten or even fifteen acres of farmland. But King, the old gelding and the larger of the two horses, was well past his prime and should by now be grazing in some peaceful pasture for retired horses. The young mare, Dolly, his teammate, was not quite full-grown and was barely halter broke.

A second problem that threatened Heinrich's quest to establish a successful farming operation was the thickness and depth of the sod he would need to break. The surface of the field he was attempting to plough had become thoroughly intertwined with decades of old roots and partially rotted tree stumps. This made the soil much denser than expected. The first few feet of Heinrich's ploughing attempt went reasonably well as the plough cut through the almost impenetrable soil, turning it over and exposing rich black dirt. The two horses and an optimistic Heinrich were relieved to see a straight furrow form behind them. But after a hundred yards or so, Heinrich noticed that the young mare was pulling both the plough as well as the old gelding, who by now was panting heavily and sweating profusely, on the verge of giving up.

Before old King could collapse completely, a miracle sparked vigour into his body and life back into his bones. Like a young stud sensing the presence of a mare in heat, King pulled back his ears, reared up on his hind legs, and began pawing the air with his front hooves. Fear – that great motivator – had struck terror into his heart. Panic and foam shot from his eyes and nostrils, causing Dolly to spook as well. The two would have taken off in any direction, were it not for the fact that they were harnessed to a plough that had by now sunk deeply into the sod.

Up the driveway roared the cause of the chaos, as an ugly steel colossus coughed and sputtered its way toward the barn, clearing away all birds and rodents from its path. Perched high up on the seat behind the steering wheel of this moving monster sat Alex Friedrichsen. Heinrich immediately understood the reason why the former owners of the farm had abandoned these two horses and why the beasts reacted so frantically to every foreign sound whenever they left the security of their barn. They were simply terrified by any loud noise and this impairment was probably incurable. Had Heinrich had access to a horse tranquilizer, or maybe a gun, he would have been tempted to use it.

Alex immediately recognized the problem. He stopped the tractor, turned off the engine and ran toward Heinrich. Together they calmed the horses, unhitched them from the plough, and led them away to the safety and security of their stalls. While a dejected Heinrich contemplated his next move, Alex returned to the tractor and cranked the motor of the colossus into life. He then turned it into the field and sank a three-furrow plough into the sod. Heinrich was speechless as he watched the Rumley roar into action and drag the plough through the thick turf, cutting, lifting, and gently turning the sod into beautifully even rows. Neither the deafening noise nor the vile smell that belched from the exhaust pipe could dampen his renewed optimism in any way.

All morning, Heinrich watched in disbelief as the Rumley muscled its way back and forth from one end of the field to the other, as the plough uprooted thick sod, rotten fence posts, and remnants of partially decayed roots and stumps that lay hidden beneath the surface. George Zabilski had loaned Alex his sturdiest plough and shown him how to attach pieces of metal to the underside of the worn points to keep the plough at a constant depth. Alex viewed the results with immense personal satisfaction.

Heinrich, who by now had been joined by his wife and daughter, stood at the end of the field and cried. Perhaps he realized that the horse era was coming to an end, or perhaps he was choking on the smell from the Rumley exhaust. Or just perhaps he was appreciating the glimmer of hope that was now unfolding before him. The land could be worked and planted, the plough could expose the rich black earth, and old King could now enjoy retirement in a peaceful pasture, free from the roar of motors that so terrified him. Yet again Heinrich's prayers had been answered. The God whom he worshipped had intervened on his behalf and sent Alex Friedrichsen, the tractor, and implements to help the family begin to earn a living.

Many farmers in southwestern Manitoba thought these heavy tractors had limited value. The weight that rested on the huge steel rear wheels packed the soil more tightly than ploughs and discs could work up. Furthermore, the cost of fuel during the lean years of the 1930s strained the farm budget, not to mention the fact that the sound of the Rumley when roaring at top speed scared the livestock silly. But when it came to lugging heavy loads, removing tree stumps, and ploughing several furrows of virgin soil at a time, the Rumley was worth its weight in gold.

Tractors, according to the philosophic wisdom of George Zabilski, were "as tricky as a woman and even harder to keep running." As any of his neighbours would attest, however, he had absolutely no control over his wife, Katja, and could not influence her in any way. But George had learned to control the Rumley. He knew how to adjust the spark, the throttle or the choke, and with one or two pulls on the flywheel, along with colourful expletives and a little of Kamisky's home brew under his belt, he could usually get the thing running and keep it going. For most of a year, Alex had watched George tinker with tractors and by now had become quite knowledgeable with the intricacies of the Rumley. George paid Alex very little money for his assistance, but he generously loaned him tractors and machinery from his rich inventory of partially functioning equipment.

By the third summer, Alex and Heinrich Gerbrandt had ploughed and seeded about eighty acres. Some of the land had been tilled before and worked up quite easily. But twenty acres of dense pastureland had not been ploughed for several years, with the rest of the land covered with scrub bush and mature tree stumps that needed to be removed and ploughed for the first time. Upon Heinrich's insistence, twenty-five acres had been kept for hay and pasture for horses and cows. "Handsome feeding for two horses, one of which is too old and too sickly to chew, and the other too blind to see the grass," muttered Alex to Marusia.

Marusia was caught in the middle. Like her father, she had a nostalgic love for animals, especially horses. She remembered the times in Russia when their beautiful horses were led from the barn by bandits and abused, even ridden to death, by people whose cruelty knew no bounds. She also appreciated the cows that produced milk and cream that could be made into butter and cottage cheese for *verenicki* and other foods that they had not enjoyed since before the Russian Revolution. Heinrich firmly believed that farms still needed horses and cows. Alex was convinced that Heinrich believed the Rumley and the anemic gas-powered McCormick-Deering tractor owned by Hershberger would cough out and the job of farming would again be left to the horses, as God intended it!

Thomas Krueger, the Harwood lawyer who looked after the financial dealings of most people in the area, was impressed at the progress he saw on the Gerbrandt farm. The soil was blacker and richer than expected, fewer stones had been found, and even under dry conditions, the land had produced encouraging quantities of wheat, oats, and hay. This is exactly what the government and the bank holding the mortgage on the land had hoped to see.

***

Between the Gerbrandt and Hershberger properties lay an abandoned quarter section of land completely overgrown with weeds and neglect. The Friedrichsen boys, continually restless and never satisfied with the work at hand, were always inspired by new opportunities. They took careful notice of the vacant property and speculated that the land could be coaxed into production if the farm were to become theirs. This abandoned land would need to be worked by someone with limitless optimism and an incredible capacity for backbreaking work – qualities they possessed. Some of the land was low and sloped quite steeply toward a winding creek that passed through the quarter section and curved through a corner of the Gerbrandt farm.

There were trees that covered about twenty-five acres, and another twenty-five acres of weeds and scrub vegetation that had grown up once the large trees had been cut down, leaving thick stumps sticking out of the ground. The Friedrichsen brothers realized that land producing such a heavy cover of trees could also grow good wheat, oats, and other crops, and they were right. Some of the land near the Hershberger side of the property was of poorer quality, more suited to pasture and possibly hay. Alex muttered to Nicholas that the poor land would be perfect for Heinrich's horses. They could build a small enclosure, move the horses to this area, and forget about them. Nicholas did not share his brother's low regard for horses and teased him about being frightened of the big beasts.

Near the creek, on the Hershberger side of the property, sat a partially constructed house, abandoned when the foundation on one corner had collapsed during the flood of 1927 when water eroded the groundwork. Someone's partially-completed new home in this gorgeous setting had not survived the heavier than usual spring rains that, for the first time in years, had turned the entire creek valley into a torrent of rushing water. Farmers had lost buildings and livestock, and had not been able to get onto the soaked land until late June that year. The discouraged owners of this property had walked away from the farm, leaving the house and the land to revert to the mortgage holder.

The government was not interested in keeping the re-acquired land. It might be prepared to secure long-term mortgages to be administered by local banks, but its interest was to see the land cleared and farmed. The government wanted families to move into the area, build towns and communities, and to vote Liberal whenever an election was called. Krueger, the lawyer, was aware of this. In a casual conversation with the Friedrichsen brothers, he pointed out to them that the terms of the Dominion Land

Act of 1872 might still apply to this property, especially if it could be proven that the majority of the land was still virgin soil. Under the terms of this Act, agricultural pioneers might still be able to settle and "prove up" a quarter section of land for a small filing fee, plus several years of improvements, as long as they resided on the land. Krueger also made the argument that land susceptible to flooding was of lesser value, and therefore worthy of some special financial consideration.

Again, Krueger asked the bank to consider special terms for abandoned land to allow new purchasers to establish profitable farming operations. And again, the local manager of the Imperial Bank accused Krueger of staying out in the sun too long. But the manager did agree to drive out with the lawyer and see the property so he could make his own assessment. On the way to see the land, Krueger drove the banker onto the Gerbrandt farmyard. Spring rain had allowed the grain to germinate and a beautifully uniform colour of green was beginning to emerge from the carefully tilled soil. Stumps and large stones had been removed and were nowhere to be seen.

"If they get decent rains," stated Krueger, "this farm will produce bumper crops and everyone, including your bank, will be happy." The banker could not disagree with this argument. He was clearly impressed by the transformation of this neglected farmland into beautiful fields of grain and hay in such a short time. He also recognized the ugly truck with the blue box and nondescript cab that sometimes parked in front of the bank. He had noticed how often this truck, with the name Friedrichsen clearly painted on the side door, rolled through town carrying loads of wheat, oats, hay, cows, and horses destined for somewhere. To him, this enterprise smelled of profit.

A purchase agreement was drawn up, references were submitted, including one from Krueger, and again the central authorities of the Imperial Bank were asked to approve a somewhat risky mortgage. Krueger's reference was particularly strong. It probably provided the tipping point between the bank either accepting the terms or rejecting them completely. Krueger had prepared many purchase agreements for immigrant farmers, and based upon his dealings with other Mennonites, had written a positive letter of reference on the Friedrichsen brothers' behalf. Krueger was always careful not to associate his name with poor business investments. If any of the new farmers were to default on their financial obligations, it could reflect negatively upon his reputation and some of the lucrative legal work that came his way with the bank and government could be lost.

During the summers of 1930 and 1931, the rainfall had been light and this worried Krueger a great deal. He spent time walking across the fields with the newly-arrived farmers and encouraged them as best he could. Nicholas claimed that at times he had seen the lawyer talking directly to the plants, commanding them to grow. The Friedrichsen brothers' activities interested Krueger. He enjoyed hearing them sing in the local church choir, where he also sang, and was amazed that Alex could continue to work with George Zabilski, a man whose mechanical ability vastly outshone his competency to keep his financial dealings in order. Krueger had prepared the tax statements for the Gerbrandt and Hershberger families and had seen the influence that these two brothers had upon the operation of these two farms. From what he knew of these boys, he was fully prepared to support their financial expansion.

The Imperial Bank approved the Friedrichsen application and the government authorities decided to take another chance. The purchase price was certainly more than the ten dollar filing fee that Krueger had initially proposed, but the financial terms were manageable. The land was not a handout, and the terms of purchase signed by the Friedrichsen brothers required many hours of backbreaking work to satisfy the requirement to have a predetermined number of acres cleared and planted each year. Neither Alex nor Nicholas was as yet a naturalized Canadian citizen, so they felt fortunate that the government authorities had approved their application.

The first order of business was to clear the required number of acres in order to comply with the terms of the purchase agreement. But before the requisite papers could pass all the bureaucratic hurdles, the middle of summer had arrived. By then, Alex had welded together an implement with a steel prong that could sink deep into the soil to uproot large, stubborn stumps. The virgin soil had to be ploughed to a depth of ten inches, a task that might have taken forever, even with a team of four or more horses. Again the Rumley came to the rescue. A three-furrow plough was found and the Rumley was put to the test. For days it belched and sputtered its way from one end of the farm to the other as it turned over rich black earth. Tree roots and stones were dragged to the surface, picked up, and disposed of. Plough points quickly wore down, but were reinforced with metal pieces attached to the underside to allow the tip of the plough to maintain a constant depth.

The old Rumley smoked and spewed its toxins into the air as it pulled the implements and transformed the abandoned land into a viable farming operation. More than once Alex came home with an imprint of the steering wheel firmly imbedded upon his chest as a stubborn root had won the pulling contest between tractor and tree, bringing the Rumley to an abrupt halt. Heinrich considered the entire venture to be far too risky, and Uri Hershberger betrayed no emotional response once he learned that the boys had purchased the farm. Perhaps Hershberger was planning to eventually purchase the land himself. Many an evening after the Rumley had roared for twelve to fourteen hours, Heinrich or Marusia could be seen at the end of a field motioning for Alex to come home before he collapsed in total exhaustion. By late fall, the yearly quota of cleared and tilled land had been reached. As Alex and Nicholas's farm began to produce, Heinrich Gerbrandt and Uri Hershberger saw their respective levels of blood pressure return to normal.

A new condition stated in the Dominion Land Act directed the new owners to live on the property for at least a period of three years – a condition the government authorities strictly insisted upon. The partially completed house next to the creek was structurally unsafe and too costly and impractical to repair. A year later, this house was moved onto the Gerbrandt yard, and over the course of several years, it was totally rebuilt to become the principal residence for both the Gerbrandt and the Friedrichsen families.

There was also an old shack and a well-constructed barn on the newly-purchased property, along with several small chicken coops and a fair sized granary. Uri Hershberger took note of the good barn on the premises and asked the boys if they were prepared to sell it to him. The barn could easily be dragged over to his place and attached to his existing barn. The shack, a hovel or shed at best, was a sight to behold. The Gerbrandt house and the cabin where the Friedrichsen boys lived were palatial mansions when compared to this shabby structure that was totally unfit for human habitation. The door had not closed properly for several years, inviting the elements to blow in through the open doorway and out through a broken window. Wild animals had probably checked out the place and agreed with Heinrich that the shack was unfit for habitation. Even rats and mice had given up and moved on once all the food sources disappeared. Heinrich Gerbrandt considered the structure to be beyond repair. Marusia walked around the shack and promptly agreed with her father that any attempt at restoration was hopeless. Little did she realize that one day she would spend her honeymoon in this place.

The boys were undaunted. They soon determined that the wooden shingles on the roof could be reattached. The doorjamb could to be repaired with new hinges to allow the door to hang properly. A chicken coop on the farmyard was dismantled and any salvageable lumber was used to reinforce loose boards to both the inside and outside walls. Finally the boys felt confident that the structure could be jacked up, the rotten foundation could be replaced, and a proper wooden floor could be nailed down. The dismay at seeing a dirt floor brought back far too many unpleasant memories of their earlier years in Russia.

Once the ceiling and inside walls had been properly washed and given several coats of paint, the musty smells and vile impurities that filled the house were sealed away forever. The potbelly stove still functioned well. Once the stovepipes and the chimney had been cleaned, a roaring fire cremated the last few rodent carcasses and mouse droppings uncovered during the thorough cleaning. A small entranceway with a second door was built to discourage the wind from blowing directly into the main room. It also served as a space for hanging coats and storing boots. On a Sunday afternoon in late fall after all the work had been completed and once a few pieces of furniture had been scrounged, salvaged, and painted, Alex and Nicholas invited the skeptical Gerbrandt and Hershberger families for an open house with appetizers that consisted of bread, butter, sausage, as well as coffee and a little wine. A good time was had by all.

***

While most of Western Canada was stuck in the demoralizing morass known as the Great Depression, the people of Harwood were slowly beginning to crawl out from under the economic burden of the last few years. Fortunately, Manitoba farmers had been spared the severe drought that created the Dirty Thirties in many parts of Western Canada. Although rainfall was sporadic and not enough to produce large crops, there was sufficient moisture to allow modest quantities of wheat, oats and hay to be harvested. But even where agricultural commodities were produced, low prices kept the farmers poor.

Alex spent the winter months working for George Zabilski who needed help to keep his modest business from collapsing. George's arthritic hip prevented him from lifting heavy objects. He had difficulty walking, wincing at the slightest movement that required him to turn sideways. Katja realized that without Alex's help, George's business could not be sustained. She took it upon her to feed the boys at least once or twice a week in hopes of keeping them coming back. Alex knew that he was learning a great deal from George, and although he was poorly compensated, he was able to borrow tractors and implements for use on the farm. George now traded and bartered tractors and implements in various mechanical conditions, repaired them, and resold them at a modest profit.

On one of his many transactions, George reluctantly took a truck in trade for a tractor that he and Alex had repaired. George had no use for this piece of junk, as he called it, and wondered how best to dispose of it. Perhaps he should simply add it to the growing pile of scrap metal behind his shop and sell it off as parts. Alex, on the other hand, saw opportunity. With George's help and constant complaining he carefully disassembled the engine head and determined that the motor could be restored. Next, he examined the transmission, and removed and disposed of the rotten lumber that had once been a box. The engine was worn, but with George's help and a few motor parts salvaged from George's junk pile along with a few new parts ordered from Winnipeg, the engine was restored.

The gears in the transmission had been stripped beyond repair and the clutch assembly needed an overhaul, but the fenders and bumpers could still be banged out and welded back into shape. Cords could be seen sticking out of the tires, yet somehow the remaining rubber still held air. Alex invested a few more dollars in another wreck with useable tires and a workable transmission. This vehicle, once owned by the municipality, had met its tragic end by colliding with a tree just a few miles north of Harwood. Once a fully functioning body, chassis, and motor had been assembled, he and Nicholas with Hershberger's help constructed a sturdy box with racks solid enough to hold grain, horses, household furniture, and any number of objects that needed to be hauled. Finally, they painted the box a sky blue colour with paint purchased on sale, but never got around to painting the cab that in its better days had possibly been a green colour of some sort. "Ugly as sin!" spouted George.

By the third year, Alex had developed a tidy business using the truck to haul grain, cattle and larger farm and household products to places within a wide radius of Harwood. One day while returning from Brandon, he noticed an interesting business establishment with a large sign that advertised "Feldman and Gladstone General Store." In smaller letters below the name he read, "Specializing in new and used items." Curiosity got the better of him and Alex decided to stop in and check out the place. As he walked in, he overheard the owner conversing with a customer in a language he partially recognized. He recalled his mother using similar words and phrases that she had learned from her contacts with the Brodsky family and that she tended to mix together with the Mennonite Low German or *Plautdietsch* she had spoken in Rosenthal.

Once again, Alex drew upon his mother's limitless courage and addressed the owner in what he believed to be a very polite Yiddish greeting. His words were almost right – just right enough to catch old Gladstone's attention. Alex's strange linguistic mix clearly intrigued Gladstone. From there on a conversation slowly evolved between the two. They muddled through several languages and dialects and, with the help of a wide variety of hand gestures, finally managed to establish communication with each other. Before he left, Alex had successfully introduced himself to Gladstone and managed to inform him during the conversation that his maternal grandmother was named Raisa Brodsky.

Gladstone took an instant liking to this young man and whenever Alex came to Brandon, he would stop in at this general store to warm his hands over the potbelly stove. He would always purchase something if he had any money, or simply help Gladstone the proprietor move some heavy items. One day he purchased a used Sunday suit for himself from Gladstone, as well as a pair of trousers for Heinrich Gerbrandt that required only minor alterations. "Probably removed from some corpse prior to burial," quipped Nicholas the day Alex modelled the suit for him. Alex also managed to buy some mismatched dishes, cutlery, and cooking utensils – some new and some used – for the Gerbrandt kitchen. Over time, he became more familiar with these people and their business practices. He and old Gladstone would enjoy bargaining for practically everything. Gladstone liked Alex and frequently let him win. Gladstone also knew that if a heavy item needed to be hauled within Brandon or to some outlying town, Alex and his truck were reliable and the job would be done quickly and competently.

**

Within days of setting foot onto Canadian soil, Alex Friedrichsen had convinced himself that this is where he wished to be and this is where he hoped to build his future. He was relieved that the train transporting him from Halifax to Western Canada was putting distance between himself and Russia, the country responsible for the early death of his parents and the pain and hunger that he had experienced. There were not enough happy memories from his childhood and youth in Russia to bind him to his country of birth. Canada, on the other hand, was a wide open place, a clean slate of opportunity where he as a young adult could start anew to build a future. Now five years later, he had patiently waited the required period of time to apply for citizenship. But now he faced the daunting prospect of either being accepted as a naturalized Canadian and seeing his dream come true, or having his application turned down and being deported back to Russia. This issue needed to be faced directly.

Alex and his brother Nicholas had settled reasonably well into their new life. They were beginning to feel confident with a new language and comfortable with customs that initially felt strange. The Gerbrandt farm and the adjacent property he and Nicholas had purchased were providing them with a modest living. The truck they jointly owned added to their income in their business of hauling grain, livestock, and heavy articles for farmers and business people in the area. They had a social circle of good friends, and aside from the cruel Manitoba winter, Harwood was beginning to feel like home.

Yet there was the fear that the circumstances under which they had entered Canada would come to light. If the details from their past were discovered, their application for citizenship could be in jeopardy. Also, deep down inside, Alex was dealing with feelings of guilt that he had escaped Russia while his friends, equally as worthy as he, had been left behind to deal with the chaos many Russian people were now experiencing. Alex correctly believed that Russian citizens under Joseph Stalin, especially those living in Ukraine, would be further deprived of life's necessities and forced into a new way of thinking. If they failed to comply with the rules of the new regime, they could be humiliated, severely punished, or possibly stripped of their means of livelihood. This is what had happened to his stepfather, Nikolai Kotelnikov.

Why were we worthy of Canadian citizenship and its many opportunities while others suffered want and hardship, he asked himself. Many days his thoughts went back to his former coworkers on the Russian trains. These were good people and many had become his friends. He wondered how they had reacted once they realized that he and Nicholas had not returned to the train in Riga. Would they have suspected that the Friedrichsen brothers, their friends, had boarded a ship and immigrated to another country, or would they have assumed that some horrible criminal act might have befallen them? The Stalinist regime was tightening its grip on its people, making it almost impossible to legally immigrate to another country. Also, there were stories – uncorroborated and probably spread by Russian railway authorities – that Russian workers had been known to disappear from the streets of the port city of Riga.

Alex was also concerned about what might have befallen the train crew that he and Nicholas had abandoned. Were they sufficiently competent to guide the train safely back to Moscow? What would the gullible conductor have thought once he realized that no dignitary had come to the Moscow station to meet his train? The understanding with the crew was that Alex and Nicholas would leave the train in Riga to attend to a personal matter, and if they were not back within two hours, the crew was to depart on schedule without them. They would catch the next train to Moscow and would settle the matter with their superiors upon their return.

Within minutes of deserting the train in Riga, the boys had checked into a cheap hotel near the harbour where they bathed and changed clothes. Next they repeatedly re-examined their new travel documents to assure themselves that these appeared valid. Then they set out to locate Heinrich Gerbrandt. Their request to travel to Canada with this group of Mennonites had placed Heinrich in an awkward position. On the one hand, he wanted to help the boys, while on the other he needed to placate a group of confused and deeply divided Mennonites who had gathered on the pier and were preparing to board their ship, hopefully without the two renegade railway workers.

Heinrich had reluctantly agreed to add the two Friedrichsen names to the list of emigrants, and had also guaranteed the Canadian Pacific Railway authorities that the travel costs for each person, including these two boys, would be repaid in full. This made even the kindest, most compassionate members of Gerbrandt's group very nervous. No one knew that the boys' travel documents were bogus, the pictures were false, and the signature by the new Russian Minister of State on their exit visas was a pure forgery. Fortunately, the Canadian immigration official, an astute fellow, found nothing out of the ordinary with the Friedrichsen travel documents. He even directed a few humorous, rather insulting remarks about the work of the photographer who had taken the pictures of the boys. Alex reacted to the official's attempt at humour with a hearty laugh, but almost passed out with relief when permission to board the ship received the final stamp of approval.

That day the personal effects of Alex Brodsky Mikhailov Kotelnikov and Nikolai Brodsky Kotelnikov were added to a pile of dirty clothes and discarded in an abandoned trash barrel found somewhere near the wharf. In their place, Alex and Nicholas Friedrichsen, two cleanly shaven young men sporting acceptable clothes and carrying the necessary travel documents, watched from the deck of the ship as the port of Riga disappeared into the distance. At that very moment, their train was departing the Riga station and steaming back toward Moscow without them. To further bury their Russian past, Nikolai began referring to himself as Nicholas, a more common name in the English world and the new name appearing on his travel documents. Spelling, however, was of little concern to him – he was barely literate.

Now that they lived in Canada, the pretence under which they had been allowed to enter the country continued to worry the boys. Would they someday be exposed? Would someone blow the whistle on them to inform the immigration authorities that they were Russian boys instead of Mennonite immigrants, and that they had procured travel documents under false pretences? Did anyone know they had actually bribed an official with stolen jewelry in order to obtain these? Furthermore, an investigation into their baptismal records would reveal that these boys had been baptized in the Russian Orthodox Church and their connection with Mennonites was tenuous. Their knowledge of the teachings of Menno Simons was questionable at best. If discovered, would these facts prevent them from becoming Canadian citizens and possibly lead to their deportation?

Alex and Nicholas had found a home in the Harwood Mennonite Church where they attended services on a regular basis and sang in the choir, where they as tenors were heartily welcomed. This congregation was made up of people from several Mennonites conferences, several Lutheran families who appreciated the music and the German language, and a few others who simply liked the people. Two Russian Orthodox Christians easily blended into this church. According to Heinrich Gerbrandt, keeping peace within this congregation was more difficult, and finding consensus on the finer points of theology was not even considered. Although the boys had won the acceptance and respect of many of the members of the Harwood community, they were never really sure as to where they stood with the Isbrand Riessen clan.

To assist them in their application to become naturalized citizens, Alex and Nicholas engaged the services of Thomas Krueger, the Harwood lawyer, and told him their entire story of sordid details and ambitious aspirations. Krueger did not see a problem, but like a good lawyer he presented to them all the strengths and weaknesses of their application. According to him, a successful outcome in such matters was never a foregone conclusion. Yet Krueger agreed to appear on their behalf before the judge and willingly agreed to provide a letter of reference supporting their application. Krueger advised the brothers to also seek a reference from the Hutchinson family, owners of the Harwood General Store.

He did warn them, however, that under no circumstances were they to mention anything about their applications to George Zabilski. George was a rather opinionated "loose cannon" – a free radical who constantly spouted his ideas on any number of subjects to anyone who would listen. Most troubling were his political views. He strongly supported communism, which according to his understanding was a system of governance whereby the rich, namely Krueger and Johnson (the bank manager) would be forced to share their wealth with people like "him and Kamiski."

One final concern was the matter of the truck. Alex had gained entry into Canada as a farmer and he did indeed work both the Gerbrandt land, as well as the quarter section he and Nicholas jointly owned, but during these lean years, much of Alex's income continued to come from making deliveries with his truck – a truck without insurance and a driver without a valid driver's licence.

The day of the court appearance arrived, and Alex and Nicholas Friedrichsen along with Thomas Krueger travelled to Brandon to appear before Judge Stuart, who just happened to be a relative of Mary Stuart, the Harwood schoolteacher who had taught Alex and Nicholas English. The sight of the courthouse relieved everyone's stress. The place was not nearly as threatening as Alex had imagined it to be, and the courtroom to which they were assigned was smaller and much less imposing than his worst fears had led him to believe.

"Looks like a church," quipped Nicholas.

"Keep quiet," said Krueger.

The proceedings got off to a good start as the judge greeted Alex, Nicholas, and Thomas Krueger in a friendly, yet formal, manner. Nicholas and Krueger were invited to sit, but Alex, whose case was being considered first, was asked to come forward and stand before the bench. Alex looked around, wishing desperately to find some friendly face to ease his stress level and make him feel more comfortable. The judge betrayed little emotion as he began examining Alex's file. By now, Alex had given up trying to synchronize his rapid heartbeat with the loud ticking of a clock hanging on the wall. The judge adjusted his glasses several times as he thoroughly scrutinized the documents. After what seemed like many minutes, the judge complimented Krueger on the judicious preparation of this application. He also appeared satisfied with the written references submitted by Krueger and the Hutchinson family. Without looking up, he fired his first question at Alex, "State your name."

"Alex Friedrichsen."

"Your place of residence."

Alex hesitated.

"Where do you live?" demanded the judge.

"Harwood, Manitoba," came the reply.

The judge paused. From the tone of his voice, it was difficult to determine his mindset. Furthermore, a black robe partially hidden by a tall imposing bench behind which the judge sat, carefully concealed any nuances in his body language. The length of each pause worried Alex. Had the judge discovered the truth that Alex's real name was either Mikhailov or Kotelnikov, and not Friedrichsen? This information was not stated on the documents given to the judge. Krueger had informed Alex that he might be required to answer several obvious questions in order for the court to enter his answers into the record. Also, the judge might wish to determine the level of conversational English that an immigrant applying for citizenship had achieved.

"Do you pronounce your name Fredrickson?" asked the judge.

"No sir. My name is Friedrichsen. It's of Danish origin," countered Alex.

"Way to go," muttered Krueger under his breath.

From here on, Alex's ancestral background was of little concern to the court. His diverse racial origin would likely not have barred him from Canada, but his German and Jewish ancestry, as well as the fact that he attended a Mennonite church – a church that preached pacifism – were all details that could complicate the situation.

"Give as little information as possible," Krueger had advised. "Remember that knowledge is power."

The judge determined from the documents that Alex was a member of a group of Mennonites that had left Russia and entered Canada legally. Besides, it was clear to him that any sane person residing in Russia should apply for asylum elsewhere. Russia had become a country firmly fallen into the grips of a crazy idea known as communism and led by an even crazier and unpredictable tyrant named Joseph Stalin.

More pauses in the judge's interrogation unnerved Alex further. He had never completely accepted the fact that he was worthy of Canadian citizenship. He was plagued by recurring dreams of being dragged from his bed by Russian railway authorities, sent back to Russia, and confronted by the coworkers whom he had betrayed and abandoned in Riga. Even Yitzhak Brodsky, his mother's uncle, who by now was no doubt a high ranking Bolshevik, frequently invaded his nightmares, appearing as someone who judged him and sentenced him to prison – the same prison where Nikolai Kotelnikov, his stepfather, had suffered and been starved.

«Your occupation?" asked the judge.

Alex hesitated.

"Do you have a job? What do you do?"

"Farmer," stammered Alex.

So far, so good, thought Krueger, *all the right answers.*

"Why are you here?"

"I want to become a Canadian citizen." This statement flew out of Alex's mouth like a bullet from a gun. It had been carefully rehearsed in his mind many times.

The judge softened his tone as he launched into a variety of technical questions to determine Alex's knowledge of land cultivation, especially the growing of grain and hay. He, himself, had been raised on a farm and knew what questions to ask.

"How many horses do you have?"

"Two," replied Alex.

"It's not possible to farm as many acres as you claim with only two horses."

"We also have a Rumley tractor and a three-furrow plough," answered Alex.

This piqued the judge's curiosity. He had also attempted to farm with a tractor. He had even done battle with a Rumley and had probably directed his own share of colourful words toward this impossible beast. Perhaps everyone in southern Manitoba had learned the language of George Zabilski – the mantra of vile words and expressions needed to start the Rumley tractor and keep it running. Alex's few tips on starting a tractor engine convinced the judge that this young man had sufficient mechanical aptitude to successfully till a large number of acres with a tractor. Krueger's written reference confirmed this.

"How do you remove stumps?" asked the judge.

"We cut the roots and pull most of them. Sometimes we use dynamite."

The judge also seemed impressed by Alex's command of the English language. Slowly the onslaught of questions took on a more pleasant tone, as he appeared to enjoy this question and answer exchange that explored several topics, some unrelated to the matter at hand. All answers pointed to the fact that Alex would become a productive citizen and a successful farmer. The matter with the truck gave him no concern. It was clear to him that a farming operation needed a truck to haul grain and livestock, and if Alex could earn a few extra dollars transporting goods for others, then the court certainly had no objection.

The interview had gone well. The judge wanted to get home, but he needed to complete the process of asking the required questions. This had been a long day for him and he looked forward to relaxing in his favourite easy chair with a newspaper, a pipe filled with his preferred tobacco, and a glass of scotch. Krueger also wanted to get home. Representing immigrants who applied for citizenship was normally a routine procedure for him. Often it was a rather boring waste of his time. Alex's case however was different. Krueger liked the Friedrichsen boys, but Alex's incessant worry over being deported back to Russia had worn on him and taught him to consider this as a real possibility. On his less optimistic moments he could see Alex handcuffed, led away and imprisoned in the Brandon jail until arrangements could be made to deport him back to Russia.

Alex slowly began relaxing, the judge was smiling. Nicholas heaved several sighs attempting to loosen the tightness in his chest, knowing he would be next to face the judge. Krueger began checking his watch. The last question, however, changed all that. Judge Stuart was a stickler for the rule of law and Krueger should have known this. To him minor regulations, ever so insignificant, were there to be obeyed. It was obvious to him that as a new province, Manitoba could only prosper if its citizens, especially immigrants, obeyed the rules and regulations drawn up by governing bodies. When he asked if Alex's truck was registered and licensed, Alex truthfully replied that it was not.

Immediately, his demeanour stiffened, and he demanded, "May I see your driver's licence?" Alex turned white with shock. "Where is your driver's licence?" insisted the judge.

The judge was visibly annoyed. How could a bright young man be so disrespectful toward the law as to own and operate an unregistered truck, and do so without a valid driver's licence? Fortunately for Alex, Krueger immediately intervened. He assured the judge that these matters were being attended to, and as proof, he provided copies of the application forms that had already been filled out. Krueger went on to argue that this oversight was in no way an indication that Alex was anything other than an honest young man who fully respected every aspect of Manitoba law.

The judge calmed down. He did not question Alex's church affiliation. To him there was no discrepancy between attending a Mennonite church and having been baptized Russian Orthodox. Alex's religious practice was of no concern to the court. Also, Alex's status as a refugee or illegal alien, as contended by his critics, was not questioned. All that mattered to Judge Stuart was the fact that this young, healthy, seemingly successful farmer spoke reasonably good English and was applying for citizenship. The circumstances that led Alex to come to Canada were of lesser concern.

The final question caught everyone by surprise. The judge, partially in jest and perhaps to tease Alex a little, asked him if he knew the words to the Canadian national anthem. This song had been taught to adult students in the evening English classes that the boys attended. Alex, whose emotions were now totally on edge and still feeling apprehensive over the driver's licence and insurance issues, thought that he had been asked to sing the national anthem.

Still somewhat concerned that he could be sent back to Russia, he immediately launched into "O Canada" with the richest and most resonant tone that only a mixture of fear and determination could draw out of him. Because there was no instrumental accompaniment and because of his raw nerves, Alex lost his tonal centre and began singing the anthem in the key of B-flat, five notes higher from where it is normally sung. The judge and all those in attendance stared in stunned disbelief. They had never heard anything like this before. Krueger looked around him for a hole in the ground he could sink into. But Alex was undaunted. He continued toward the end of the song with strong tone and rugged determination.

By the time Alex reached, "True patriot love, in all thy sons command," the judge was on his feet. The court clerk, RCMP officer, Krueger, and everyone in attendance got up out of their chairs and also stood to attention. Whether this was a gesture of patriotism, or simply curiosity on the part of the judge to see if Alex could hit the high note will never be known. The judge was a decent singer himself who sang in the Brandon Oratorio Choir and, with his wife who conducted this group, was constantly on the lookout for good tenor voices. Alex ignored all distractions and continued to sing in this unusually high key. As he reached the melodic climax, he confidently belted a high B-flat and even managed to stretch the notes on the word "Can-a-da" a little longer than written.

After he finished, the atmosphere of patriotic reverence he had created not only in the courtroom, but also in the hallways and adjacent rooms where everyone clearly heard him, lingered for several seconds. Everyone in attendance was obviously deeply moved by his singing. Such a passionate expression of allegiance to a new country had never been stated as eloquently, as beautifully, or as boldly by any immigrant. All in attendance were sure that Judge Stuart would most affirmatively approve this young man's application for Canadian citizenship.

Before the judge completed the proceedings he looked at Krueger and said, "For goodness sake, see to it that he gets his vehicle registration and a valid driver's licence!"

***

Romantic love between a man and a woman remains one of life's most baffling mysteries. How does one understand the inexplicable fact that two people, initially attracted to each other, fall in love, and then live together in marital bliss for the rest of their lives, while others struggle to find that special soulmate and choose to remain single. Does Cupid indeed shoot arrows into the hearts of those who are meant to be together? Do they instantly recognize their mutual attraction for each other and then act upon this impulse? Or is marriage a contractual arrangement entered into for the sake of convenience? Do people with this belief find it in their best interest to come together, hope that love will take root and grow, and allow them to live happily ever after?

These are valid questions to be raised by anyone who observed the relationship between Alex Friedrichsen and Marusia Kampen. Undeniably, there was a spark of mutual attraction between them, but why it took so long for this spark to ignite into a flame is difficult to understand. In their case, Cupid chose to take the form of a little girl, one who had only recently learned to speak and could not possibly be aware of all the vagaries and intricacies that need to fall into place for a marriage to even be considered. But this little one who one day would blurt out her strongly held opinions would change the course of history, at least for the Friedrichsen, Kampen, and Gerbrandt families.

Marusia first met Alex Friedrichsen, the newly-converted Mennonite, on the train ride from Moscow and Riga. Her first impression of him was anything but good. As the train rolled to a stop at the border crossing, the passengers felt somewhat relieved that they were almost safely out of Russia. However, they were also fully aware of one final impending threat, one more interrogation with unknown consequences before they were free – free from the Bolsheviks, from the Makhno terrorists, and from the ugly memories of persecution and starvation they had experienced these last few years. They thought the Latvian border guards would treat them with respect and civility, but the stories of what they could expect from Russian guards – these newly-minted officials whose authority came from their allegiance to the Communist Party – made them fearful as they approached the border.

Shortly after the train rolled to a complete stop at the Latvian border, Marusia and the other passenger's fears were confirmed. As they patiently sat in their seats, their anxious silence was suddenly interrupted by a loud banging noise as the door to their passenger car was rudely kicked open and their coach invaded by two imposing figures, followed by a slightly smaller Russian border guard. Wielding guns and yelling instructions at the frightened passengers, the officials burst into the compartment and demanded to see travel documents. The bulky railway issued coats and hats made Alex and Nicholas Friedrichsen look larger and much more menacing than they were, and their faces - blackened with soot - concealed the fact that under this camouflage stood two scared teenage boys who also shook with fear.

Alex's shrill shouts and feigned rage struck terror in the hearts of the passengers. His anger, mixed with the grief of his mother's death, fuelled his "don't-give-a-damn attitude." Both he and Nicholas were angry at the world, and angry at Russia with its endemic chaos that inflicted grief and pain upon innocent people. They were angry with these bloody border guards, all newly-appointed and totally ignorant Bolsheviks, who exercised what little authority they had, yet did not know their ass from a hole in the ground. They were also angry with the Mennonites who had mistreated their mother. Nicholas was even angry at Alex for forcing him to leave Russia — a decision that did not sit well with him. This stew of emotional confusion boiled over into threatening shouts directed at innocent travellers and backed up by guns that they barely knew how to use. All along, their only intention was to protect these people from the corrupt and stupid guards and help them keep the last few personal articles they carried, hopefully later joining them in their escape from this blood-drenched land.

To expedite this border crossing from Russia to Latvia, Alex had cooked up a story that at best was only partially true. He convinced the conductor, and later, the border guards, that the train was due back in Moscow before morning. He even altered the times on the train's log to make this appear plausible. The conductor, a rather dim fellow, bought the story wholeheartedly and eagerly looked forward to meeting some non-existent dignitary who, according to Alex's story, would be awaiting his train upon its return to Moscow. As a result, he did everything within his power to keep the falsified plan on schedule.

As soon as the train rolled to a stop, both Alex and the conductor, who was forever attempting to expand his sphere of authority, accosted the

Russian border guards with threats of what might happen to them if the train was not allowed to proceed immediately. To help speed up the final border check, the Friedrichsen boys volunteered to interrogate the emigrants who rode in the first two cars where they knew the Mennonites were riding. They would check each person's documents carefully to see that no one on this train was attempting to leave the Soviet Union illegally. The Russian officials agreed to check the rest of the train and everyone could be on their way within an hour. One Russian guard, probably the kindest of the lot assigned to assist Alex and Nicholas, even reminded them to treat the people with a little more civility. Nevertheless, Alex's strong voice and menacing demeanour could only be interpreted by the passengers as threatening. This first impression of Alex would take some time to erase. His first shouts as he opened the door caused Marusia to cry out, clutch her baby, Suzanna, and scream for help.

Once the train was released and had crossed into Latvia, the emigrants realized that they were safe and had not been robbed. Now they slowly began to relax. Long after Alex and Nicholas had legally joined the Mennonites, their loud voices still struck fear in the hearts of the people. After the train had safely crossed into Latvia, it stopped to take on coal and fill the tank with water. Many of the passengers disembarked. Some hugged, some cried, while others prayed, and all spontaneously joined in to sing the hymn, "Nun danket alle Gott." With tears in his eyes and a voice choked with emotion, Heinrich Gerbrandt, the leader of the group, offered a prayer of thanksgiving. Several emigrants even kissed the ground.

The next sight, as incredulous as it was, brought the exuberant celebration of the passengers to a complete stop. With shock and disbelief, they noticed that the two loud, ugly members of the train crew, the same ones who terrorized them, now stood at the rear of the engine and appeared to sing along with them most heartily. From his vantage point, Alex spotted Heinrich Gerbrandt whom he correctly identified as the leader of the group. Alex climbed down from the engine and slowly walked toward Gerbrandt. Before Heinrich could say a word, Alex astounded him with a most unusual request delivered in *Plautdietsch*, the German dialect most familiar to the Mennonites. He asked for, and was granted, a private meeting with Heinrich. Off to the side of the track, he introduced himself and his brother as Alex and Nicholas Friedrichsen of Rosenthal. Heinrich was speechless. In their short conversation, he learned that the boys had lost their parents and had lost all contact with any of their relatives. They wished to reclaim their roots and asked to travel to Canada as Mennonites. They explained that the charade at the border was a ruse to keep the corrupt guards from molesting the passengers and stealing their last few belongings. Later, when reflecting upon the traumatic border crossing, the passengers had thought it strange that Alex, the terrorizing "border guard" who had succeeded in frightening the people, had not harmed anyone and had actually returned all gold rings and watches he had taken from them and could easily have stolen. He had also refused to take the money Heinrich Gerbrandt had offered him as a bribe in exchange for safe passage.

After Heinrich Gerbrandt got over his total surprise, he felt compassion toward these two young boys and was the first to soften his stance toward them. Once the brothers had earned a measure of his trust, and convinced him that their escape from Russia was serious, his views toward them changed even more. Marusia, however, continued to shield her baby from Alex and Nicholas, while others from the group also remained apprehensive and found it difficult to trust them.

A second interaction between Alex and Marusia took place on the ocean voyage across the Atlantic. The fear, terror, and grief that Marusia had endured during her last few months in Russia were passed along to her baby in the form of colic. At the age of twenty, Marusia was a single mother, a widow who had very recently lost her husband Leonard Kampen to typhus, the dreaded illness that decimated both the Mennonite as well as the general Russian population. She had been married for less than a year and gave birth to her baby daughter several weeks after her husband's death.

The rough sea compounded Marusia's physical condition, as seasickness further depleted her strength. Many felt that her baby was simply not receiving enough milk. Little Suzanna screamed day and night with every ounce of energy that she could muster. Food rations for the passengers, although adequate, were hardly sumptuous and certainly not sufficiently nutritious for a nursing mother. There was also a virus that was travelling throughout the ship that infected many passengers, even seasoned sailors. Alex and Nicholas didn't catch the virus. It was quite possible that in their short lives they had weathered such adverse living conditions that they had developed immunity to a wide range of germs, lice, and other forms of vermin. But people wondered if they were the carriers of the dreaded germ that infected passengers and crew.

A few days after the widespread flu epidemic broke out, even members of the crew were sick. The boys were hired to shovel coal and help maintain the engine room, doing whatever sailors stricken by the flu were normally assigned to do. The boys gladly accepted the work and exchanged the little money they received for food that Marusia could keep down. This enabled both mother and the baby she was nursing to gain sufficient strength to survive the ocean crossing. This gesture of kindness was the first sign that a bond between the Gerbrandt and Friedrichsen families was possible. After the voyage, the relationship between Heinrich Gerbrandt and Alex and Nicholas continued to warm.

After the group had settled in Harwood, the people assumed that Alex and Nicholas would move on and seek a life for themselves elsewhere. During the first two years in their new country, the brothers successfully weathered the winter in the log cabin turned chicken coop that had once again been converted into living quarters. Food was scarce. Were it not for the kindness shown to the boys by the Gerbrandt and Hershberger families, they would have gone to bed hungry on many a night. Circumstances, however, kept the two brothers from realizing their initial plan to learn English and then move on. On the trip from Halifax to Manitoba, their train passed through Winnipeg on a beautifully warm late spring evening. The trees were in leaf, flowers in bloom, and the city was a beautiful contrast to the stark landscape of northern Ontario. This was a place where Alex and Nicholas hoped to return someday, but they kept experiencing delays. They needed to help Heinrich with his farm work, yet they did not wish to become a burden to the Gerbrandt family, which was struggling to keep food on the table.

The Gerbrandts, their daughter, Marusia, and the Friedrichsen boys continued to live in peaceful co-existence, but any thought of a romantic attachment with anyone, let alone Marusia, simply did not enter Alex's mind. His main objective was to simply survive. Just meeting the basic needs for the next few days or so took up all his time and energy. Love was a luxury he simply could not afford. Under George Zabilski's tutelage, his knowledge of tractor and auto mechanics, along with English and Russian swear words were growing exponentially. Time passed quickly when spent with George, who was a fun person to be with. Katja Zabilski also helped to keep the boys fed. Eggs, milk, flour, and some meat were available, but meals were basic and no one had money for any extras. George had a gun that he loaned to Alex, who was able to shoot a good-sized deer that first year. Each spring, Alex's plan to move on was delayed by the need to clear more land and prepare it for planting. He enjoyed ploughing the Gerbrandt fields, seeding a large garden together with Helena and Marusia, and watching everything grow. George Zabilski paid Alex very little, but was generous in loaning him an old Rumley tractor and some farm equipment so he could work the fields.

Cupid, small in stature but big in heart, can be a most persistent fellow. Even independent Alex, somewhat thick-skulled according to his brother, was not immune to Cupid's arrows. But Alex was slow to respond. To quote the baseball term, Alex was always behind in the count, entering situations with two strikes against him. This prevented him from stepping up to the plate to claim the prize that was there before him.

Alex must have been aware of the little niceties Marusia was directing toward him. She would cook his favourite foods and set the table as beautifully as possible when her parents were not at home. Goodness knows she spent enough time helping him tie his necktie until it was just right, and would do her best to make herself look attractive. He must have noticed this, but failed to respond to such telltale signs. Alex succeeded in convincing himself that she was being nice to him because she needed him, and that her family needed his help to harvest the garden, provide meat for the table, and also bring back grocery and dry good items from his trips to Brandon.

Both Alex and Marusia must have noticed the friendly relationship that existed between Alex and little Suzanna. He teased her, played games with her, and brought her little treats. During one of their first Christmases in Canada, when Alex was invited to share Christmas Eve and Christmas day with the Gerbrandt family, he secretly placed a small Christmas present on the table where each family member sat. Suzanna had little cause to believe in Santa Claus or to expect anything for Christmas, yet at her place she found a colouring book with a box of crayons. Marusia and her mother, Helena, were given lovely scarves, and both Grandpa Heinrich and Alex received English and Russian Bibles, all from Santa Claus. Since that time, Alex encouraged Suzanna to believe in Santa Claus, especially when Christmas drew near. After Christmas, she was allowed to lapse into her usual skepticism regarding his existence.

At some point in time, possibly the third winter in Harwood, Alex failed to notice the frequent visits that Isbrand Riessen and his family, including son Gerhard, were paying to the Gerbrandt family. The presence of Isbrand and Gerhard was reason enough for Alex and Nicholas to avoid the Gerbrandt house whenever these people came for a visit. According to Isbrand and his son, Alex and Nicholas simply did not possess the right bloodlines to gain acceptance into their inner circle.

One night at the supper table with Alex in attendance, little Suzanna blurted out the news that mommy was going to marry Gerhard Riessen. Earlier, her grandmother, Helena Gerbrandt, had talked to Suzanna, to prepare her for such a possible change in family relationships. Little Suzanna understood her mother's marriage to Gerhard to be a fait accompli, and had very strong views on the matter. Such a marriage, at least in her young mind, made absolutely no sense. The little girl loved Alex and thought of him more as a doting big brother than as a father. With this in her mind, Suzanna boldly made the statement at the table that if her mother should marry anyone, it should be Alex. Helena Gerbrandt froze in horror, Heinrich choked on his soup, Alex became unusually quiet, and Marusia left the room in tears. Little Suzanna now had the floor. Before anyone could silence her, she went on to list several reasons why Mommy should marry Alex and not Gerhard Riessen, whom she did not like.

Isbrand Riessen, on behalf of his son, had indeed proposed marriage to Marusia via her father, who subsequently informed her of this marriage proposal. The Riessen family had brought money with them from Russia and had successfully established a viable farming operation. A marriage between Gerhard and Marusia made sense. Heinrich and Helena had talked about selling the farm to the Riessen family and moving to Winkler. With a solid marriage proposal, they were probably relieved that their daughter and granddaughter would be looked after. Grandma Gerbrandt had broken the news to Suzanna as a strictly guarded secret, but to Suzanna this secret was not one she felt entirely comfortable keeping.

Alex finished his supper. Before Marusia returned to the table, he quietly walked back to the little cabin on the yard. He was in shock and feeling very much alone. He felt abandoned, much like this old cabin must have felt when he and Nicholas purchased their own farm and moved into their larger, yet equally decrepit, shack. It is difficult to say what drew him back to this old place. Was this the site of happier memories, the place where hope had finally won out over the withering pessimism that he witnessed around him? Or was this the place where he first realized that he had feelings for Marusia? But why hadn't he acted upon these feelings? This was a question that now haunted him. Was he too poor, or perhaps was he not worthy of someone like her. The negative thoughts raced through his mind.

Alex walked into the log cabin through the unlocked door, felt around in the darkness and located matches and several partially burnt candles left on the shelf above the stove. Next, he found some kindling in the old firebox with a few pieces of wood that had been left behind. Alex lit a fire in the old potbelly stove and sat back on a wooden crate used as a chair, waiting for the fire to warm and to console him. He needed to be alone. It was difficult to reflect upon what might have been. Right now, he didn't want to return to the cabin on their new property where he and Nicholas now lived. Hershberger had taken Nicholas with him on a short trip to Morden to help some relative for a few days. They were expected back tonight. Alex just didn't care to answer any of Nicholas's questions. He sat in stunned silence as he contemplated his future.

Should he have made a move on Marusia? Would she and her family have considered him worthy? Now he would never know. Now he would need to move on, to Brandon or possibly Winnipeg, and seek a new life for himself. Zabilski did not have enough work for him, so it was pointless to stay in Harwood. Gerbrandt had talked about selling the farm and would, no doubt, now attempt to forge some financial arrangement with Isbrand Riessen. The land that Alex jointly owned together with Nicholas could probably be sold to Hershberger. Nicholas would likely stay in Harwood and marry Sarah, the girl he spoke about endlessly. All Alex's earthy possessions could easily fit into a small suitcase, if only he had one. These were his thoughts as he stared into the fire for a long time, watching it flare up and then slowly burn down.

A gentle knock at the door interrupted his thoughts. No doubt, Heinrich Gerbrandt had come to fully explain the situation to Alex and give him suggestions as where to go from here. Heinrich, always a decent and honest man, would probably offer him some sort of financial settlement for his work in developing the farm once he had sold out to Isbrand Riessen. Listlessly, Alex walked to the door and prepared to hear what Heinrich had to say, but to his surprise instead of Heinrich, there stood Marusia. Her eyes were red from crying, her face was pale, and she quietly asked, "May I come in?"

Alex was speechless. He invited her in and offered her his wooden box as chair, as he prepared to sit down beside her on the corner of the old bed frame. Before Marusia could launch into any gratuitous explanation as to why she had decided to marry Gerhard Riessen, Alex offered her his congratulations. In the dim light, he noticed that she had fixed her hair, and changed into a better dress from what she had worn at supper. Her eyes were red and swollen. Marusia opened her mouth to speak, but no words came out. Again he wished her well, and again she attempted to speak, but this time he noticed tears beginning to reappear in her eyes.

Alex forced out some small talk. "You and Susie will be looked after," he said. "The Riessen farm has good land and someday will become a prosperous operation." Under his breath he thought, *Perhaps by then, Gerhard will have learned to become a man and to stand up to his father.* Something Nicholas was convinced would never happen.

Marusia did not look directly at him. Alex did not know what else to say. The lengthy silence was beginning to become awkwardly deafening. From somewhere in his broken heart, Alex blurted out the question, "Are you happy?" Marusia began to cry. "Are you all right?" he nervously continued.

At the exact moment when he touched her hand to console her, Marusia totally broke down. Instinctively, he gently put his arm around her back to comfort her. The next instant, she fell toward him and put her arms around his neck. Alex immediately took her into his arms and held her in a tight embrace. Words were no longer necessary. His actions finally acknowledged his feelings and confessed to her what Nicholas, Cupid, and George Zabilski had been telling him for over a year. He loved her, and if he weren't so darn stupid, he would see that she loved him, too.

Marusia began to regain composure, but Alex did not readily release her from his embrace, nor did she attempt to move away. Before long, words between them began to flow. The next few hours flew past as thoughts and emotions were shared, explanations given, misunderstandings cleared up, and declarations of love finally expressed. At approximately 2:00 a.m., hours after the fire had died, Alex walked Marusia to the back door of her house. Heinrich and Helena were sitting at the kitchen table, anxiously awaiting the outcome of this encounter. Only Suzanna, the one who started this avalanche of emotion, lay in her bed sound asleep, entirely oblivious to the fact that many lives and situations would now change just because she had not been able to keep a secret.

Chapter 9
Peter Friedrichsen – 1948

BY 1946, THE WORLD HAD BEGUN TO RECOVER FROM THE DEVASTATING events of the previous years, events that had taken the lives of millions of people, displaced millions more, and inflicted poverty and hardship upon communities across Europe and Asia. Very few countries remained untouched by the wanton destruction brought about by World War II.

As the decade neared its end signs of physical and economic recovery were creating a sense of optimism. Canadian soldiers had come home, rains had returned to the drought stricken parts of Manitoba, and agriculture and commerce were on the rise. Better crops and higher commodity prices were providing more disposable income to Manitoba farm families. On many fields, one could see modern tractors, riding on rubber tires rather than steel lugs, pulling newer, more efficient farm implements. State-of-the-art combines were replacing threshing machines, making large thresh-ing crews unnecessary, and sending hundreds of horses to the glue factory.

The Gerbrandt and Friedrichsen farming operation was also beginning to experience growth and modernization. The flood-damaged house, found in the river valley of the land purchased by Alex and Nicholas, had been moved onto the Gerbrandt yard and restored, and the original shack where the family once lived had been converted into a garage. The tiny cabin that Alex and Nicholas had once called home reverted to a chicken coop. King, the old gelding, had left this earth. One morning, he was found dead in his stall and Dolly, his teammate, had been assigned the painful task of drag-ging his body out to some trees in the river valley where he was buried. In the ensuing years, Dolly had been bred twice to a strong stallion from a neighbouring farm and had produced two colts, named Dick and Tom who were now reaching maturity. Now that tractors and trucks did all the farm work and cars transported the people, Heinrich finally had his team of beautiful, cooperative and equally matched horses. The family now looked forward to heavy snowfalls that forced them to park the car and travel to town on a sleigh pulled by Dick and Tom.

George and Katja Zabilski had sold their business to Alex and Nicholas and retired to Brandon to live with their daughter and her family. The roof on George's old shop had finally collapsed. The Friedrichsen brothers salvaged what they could and rebuilt the structure to make way for a new John Deere dealership they now owned. George's mountain of junk and scrap metal survived the site upgrade and became a favourite topic of conversation whenever members of the Friedrichsen families travelled to town. Nicholas referred to this pile as an artistic installation that spoke to the hearts of the people who stopped to appreciate it.

Alex had married Marusia, and Nicholas had married Sarah Hershberger. The noise of children delighted both families, especially the grandparents. In 1936, Marusia gave birth to a son named Aaron. Two years later, Jacob arrived, and in 1942, baby Stephanie joined the family. Suzanna, the little girl who survived the boat journey across the ocean, had now completed high school and was enrolled in a nurses' training program in Brandon.

Heinrich Gerbrandt had finally received guiding light from above. According to several of Alex's witty friends, the Lord had clearly revealed His will to Pastor Heinrich and convinced him that he was neither a farmer nor a businessman. Alex and his father-in-law, Heinrich, enjoyed an interesting relationship, one that allowed them to support each other's interests, yet also upon occasion see things quite differently. Alex once complained to his brother Nicholas that Heinrich would still be tending the same ten-acre field if he had not been prodded out of his comfort zone. He would still be ploughing with the same mismatched team of horses and milking the same old cow.

On the other hand, Alex's reckless business expansion was a worry to Heinrich. He feared that his son-in-law's ambition was exceeding his financial reach, he could lose everything, and end up being jailed by his creditors. Alex was truly thankful that Heinrich had been engaged to teach courses at the Winkler Bible Institute, located 150 kilometres from Harwood. He would miss Heinrich's leadership in the Harwood Mennonite Church, but getting the old man out of town for a few months each year was a hardship he was quite prepared to endure. Unfortunately, Heinrich's cautious nature was continually being stretched when upon his return home in spring, he would see a new tractor pull a new piece of machinery across a newly purchased piece of land.

Poor Marusia often found herself positioned uncomfortably between her husband and her father's competing points of view. On one hand, she would try to soften her husband's ideas to her father, and on the other, she would mediate her father's concerns to her husband. Summers went by when she doubted that she ever told the complete truth to either of them. Perhaps this is where son Jacob inherited his ability to survive in politics. However, when matters of agriculture and economics were not involved, Heinrich's wisdom and good common sense carried the day. He was a good academic and an excellent teacher as reported by his students, and the classroom was exactly where he belonged, according to Alex. Heinrich was also a wise and capable church leader, and as everyone would agree, he was an excellent preacher who received frequent speaking invitations across southern Manitoba.

In 1948, the Winkler Bible Institute, a tiny prairie school of Mennonite biblical studies where Heinrich taught, decided to convene a summer conference to readdress the Mennonite position on non-resistance and non-violence. The war had raised this matter into a contentious issue, causing the views of many young men to be at odds with the teachings of their church. Some boys joined the Canadian Armed Forces, some claimed the status of conscientious objectors, while still others enlisted in the army medical corps. To give these boys some direction, a conference was convened to study the Mennonite position on peace. A teacher and preacher from Reedley, California was invited as special guest to present several lectures. By reputation, this man was known as a thinker, a biblical scholar, and a man with a university education – something very few Mennonite preachers of the time could claim. The churches felt they could afford his fee and travel expenses, and were anxious to hear what he had to say. His name was Reverend Peter Friedrichsen.

It was midsummer and a quiet time in Harwood. Everyone was sure that the farming operation could spare Heinrich's services for a day or two to allow him to attend the conference. In reality, he was only too happy to escape the dust and smell of the farm, as well as the tedious job of pulling weeds from his wife's garden. The sessions in Winkler were all he hoped they would be. The guest speaker presented stimulating and thought-provoking ideas that were discussed, argued over, and, in some cases, tabled for further consideration because of their contentious nature. Social times at meals and coffee breaks made the conference still more enjoyable.

On the final day of the sessions, Heinrich found himself sitting across the lunch table from Peter Friedrichsen, the guest speaker. Friedrichsen had just addressed the topic, "The church as a witness for peace," and Heinrich was anxious to discuss with him certain points that he had raised. Their conversation began with the usual pleasantries and from there progressed to friendly banter regarding events that both men had experienced during their youth in Russia. Because Friedrichsen was not a very common name among Russian Mennonites, Heinrich was curious to know where Peter came from. He wanted to see if Peter might be related to his son-in-law who shared the same family name. Peter laughed heartily at this suggestion and replied, "No doubt," and in typical Mennonite tradition the two gentlemen began searching for common roots.

Heinrich continued, "Then you must have attended the *Halbstadt Zentralschule?*"

Peter Friedrichsen's face lit up as he thought he might be reconnecting with a former school buddy of his. "Why yes," he replied. "Were you there?"

"No, but I had many friends who were," replied Heinrich.

Friedrichsen immediately launched into a lengthy monologue describing details of his studies at Halbstadt, identifying this as one of the best times in his life. "These were wonderful years," he continued. "I enjoyed my studies, made many friends, and this is where I met my wife."

Heinrich interrupted this flood of happy memories by asking, "Where you there in 1902 or 1903?"

"Yes!" came the enthusiastic reply. "I graduated in 1904."

The conversation meandered about through a recollection of additional happy times as both men recalled events from their youth and childhood that happened before the war and the revolution had ruined things forever.

"Did you ever know a Christina Friedrichsen?" asked Heinrich innocently.

Peter Friedrichsen's expression went blank in an instant. His jovial smile collapsed into an empty stare as he abruptly ran short of words. "Why yes," he replied in a somewhat subdued voice. "I had a sister named Christina."

The total change in Friedrichsen's demeanour made Heinrich realize that he had better tread carefully. If this was a close relative of Alex and Nicholas, as he was beginning to suspect, and if their information about this man was correct, then he may either be in total denial of past events or he may be carrying an elephant on his conscience.

"Did she come to Canada?" asked Heinrich. With this question he hoped to defuse the man's obvious discomfort.

"I don't know," came the reply. "Since 1937, we haven't heard anything from anyone in Russia." Friedrichsen wanted to continue the visit, but had to excuse himself to speak with Johann Wiens and Gerhard Reimer, who interrupted the conversation in order to settle a few details regarding the afternoon session.

Heinrich was left to reflect upon this information. If Alex and Nicholas were right, then this man could be their grandfather – the person who had abandoned his daughter, their mother, Christina Friedrichsen. According to the boys, her father had marginalized her as his sister rather than accepting her as his daughter. Had he even assumed an ounce of responsibility for her, she might still be alive. These were heavy thoughts to process.

Following the final session, Peter Frederichsen walked directly toward Heinrich, backed him into a quiet corner, and peppered him with questions. "What do you know about Christina Friedrichsen?" A myriad of emotions raced through Frederichsen's mind as he alternately choked up and also interrupted every answer, only to learn for the first time in his life that Christina, his daughter, was dead. This fact struck him deeply, but the news that she had two sons shook him to the core.

"Are they in Russia?" he asked.

"No," said Heinrich.

"Are they alive? Where are they?" stammered Peter. He needed to know.

"They live here in Manitoba, two or three hours away."

Peter Friedrichsen could barely breathe as he absorbed the news that both boys, his grandsons, had taken his name and were married with families, and that the eldest, named Alex Friedrichsen, was Heinrich's son-in-law. Tears began to roll down his face as he, in good Russian custom, kissed Heinrich on both cheeks. Friedrichsen then left, but not before requesting Heinrich's address.

Heinrich returned to Harwood trying hard to process the information Peter Friedrichsen had unloaded upon him during their final conversation. Several weeks later, an unusual letter addressed to him arrived from Reedley, California. The letter began: *Dear Brother Gerbrandt*. It started with the usual cordial greetings, followed by a few pleasantries. Then the letter became serious.

Since our conversation in Winkler several weeks ago I have been dealing with a heavy matter that is giving me great difficulty. I am an old man and will likely be called to my heavenly home within the next few years. As it is my hope to die in a right relationship with my Lord and Saviour Jesus Christ, and also with my fellow man, I come to you with a very large request and beg for your assistance. I have tried to address the mistakes of my youth and beg forgiveness of anyone whom I have wronged, but regarding the matter I am about to share with you, I hardly know where to begin.

As you may have gathered from our final conversation in Winkler, Christina Friedrichsen was not my sister. She was my daughter by my first marriage.

Her mother, Raisa Brodsky, was a Jewess who died in childbirth. With tears of regret, I recall my failed relationship with Christina. I drifted out of her life, allowed my parents to raise her, and now must assume responsibility for the negative experiences that befell her. As she is now with the Lord, I can no longer make things right by her. I dearly wish, however, to meet her sons, my grand-sons, and hopefully receive their forgiveness. If they do not wish to see me, then I must learn to accept this. But I deeply wish to meet them, perhaps get to know them and personally ask for their forgiveness. Can you please advise me as how best to go about this?

Your fellow servant in the Lord,

Peter Friedrichsen

Heinrich read the letter several times, but was unsure as how to proceed. On the one hand, he clearly saw the need for Peter Friedrichsen to meet his grandsons and seek reconciliation with them, but on the other hand, he knew how deeply hurt the boys had been, how deeply they grieved the loss of their mother, and how often they relived the pain that she had suffered. From their conversations, he feared that the boys would have difficulty forgiving the people who had mistreated their mother during her short and pain-filled life.

Their mother, Christina, had been the constant stabilizing influence in her sons' young lives. She had raised them, provided for them and, until her untimely death, had always been there for them. Their grandfather, on the other hand, had neglected his daughter, their mother. He had marginal-ized her, referring to her as his sister rather than his daughter. The brothers believed that during her childhood and youth, at a time when she needed him most, her father, Peter Friedrichsen, had deserted her. And yet here he was, this time as Reverend Peter Friedrichsen – well known and highly venerated – who now late in life wanted to make peace with the sons of the very person he had abandoned. Yet, how could one deprive this old man of the joy of meeting and interacting with his grandsons and their children?

Heinrich felt that he could probably help guide Alex through this issue, but he was not sure how Nicholas would react. Nicholas felt things far more deeply. He was easily hurt and quickly offended. These personality traits caused him to internalize life's scrapes and bruises, and at times drive him into emotional depression from which he had difficulty escaping. Heinrich reflected upon the matter for several days, waiting for the right moment to present the situation to Alex. One night after the grandchildren were in bed and the adults were sitting around the kitchen table, he brought up the subject.

"Last month while I was in Winkler," he began, "I met a very close relative of yours – your mother's father, your grandfather." Heinrich showed Alex the letter that he had received from Peter Friedrichsen and repeated the astounding news that Alex's grandfather was alive and well, and wanted to meet his grandsons. Alex hardly reacted. He had believed his grandparents were dead and his initial reaction to the letter was to allow them to remain so.

"He would like to visit you," Heinrich softly repeated. "He says that he wants to connect with you. How do you feel about this?" Everyone remained quiet while Alex processed the information.

After a few moments, Alex replied, "I think I'd better discuss this matter with Nicholas."

"Yes, of course," replied Heinrich.

Nicholas's reaction to the letter and the news that his grandfather was alive was every bit as tepid as Alex's had been. Heinrich did not push the issue. He patiently waited for a response from the boys. Both brothers realized that Peter Friedrichsen was now an old man, looking for closure to past events in his life. From the letter, it seemed that he had changed and now wished to make things right. As he could no longer speak to their mother, he needed to meet her sons and hopefully receive their forgiveness.

Heinrich was relieved that Alex and Nicholas agreed to allow him to arrange a meeting with their grandfather. The little children were delighted at the prospect of meeting their dads' grandfather. Their concept of grandfather had been formed through their interactions with Heinrich Gerbrandt and Uri Hershberger, two of the kindest and most generous people in Harwood. In their view, grandfathers were people from whom one could extract favours, and seek refuge and understanding when parents became too strict.

A letter exchange was initiated and before the end of summer an opportunity for a visit was arranged. Peter Friedrichsen had been invited to speak at a conference in Winnipeg. From there, he and his wife, Margareta, would travel by train to Brandon where they would be met by Margareta's cousin and husband, who lived nearby in the tiny hamlet of Delia. Alex and Nicholas would pick them up from there and drive them to Harwood. The entire venture was somewhat unsettling to Margareta, their step-grand-mother. She had grown accustomed to her station in life and to the higher standard of living that accompanied it. She enjoyed her level of California comfort, and felt that the nearer she stayed to Brandon, a place she could actually find on the map, the less disruption there would be for her. The wild Canadian west scared her. Peter Friedrichsen also felt uneasy, but for entirely different reasons.

Margareta suffered from headaches that she believed were brought on by country dust or by animal smells, or even by odours that escaped from outdoor toilets. Ironically, what she feared most was what she found in her cousin's home in Delia. Willy and Lena Epp were kind, hospitable people, but they were not well off. Their house was small. In California, it would be referred to as a shack. As overnight guests, Margareta and Peter Friedrichsen were asked to sleep in a room with a narrow, sagging bed and a flimsy curtain that served as a door to separate their bedroom from the main living area. The house did not have hot water, or even running water for that matter. The toilet was outside, just beyond the reach of an angry farm dog whose chain would likely break were any guest to attempt a mid-night trip to the outhouse.

On Sunday morning, a car with Heinrich, Alex, and Nicholas drove up to the Epp farmhouse in Delia. Heinrich introduced Peter Friedrichsen and his wife, Margareta to Peter's grandsons. *They look quite respectable,* thought Margareta. *They are clean, adequately dressed and they wear good leather shoes.*

The sight of his two tall, handsome grandsons blew Peter away. And the car that they drove, a recent Ford, was far newer than what he or his friends were accustomed to driving. The boys were shy and unusually quiet, unsure of themselves, not knowing how to react or what to expect from this situation. It took about thirty miles of travel for any meaningful conversation to develop among the passengers who, although closely related, were at the same time total strangers. Margareta sat in the back seat with a damp handkerchief held tightly against her nose to protect her from dust and foul animal smells she might encounter so far removed from California civilization. The fact that an overnight rain had settled the dust on the road escaped her attention. Nicholas later remarked that the people riding in the car were probably responsible for any foul smells she feared. Heinrich took it upon himself to keep the conversation flowing.

At the farmhouse in Harwood, the guests were treated to a sumptuous chicken dinner with all the trimmings prepared by Marusia and Sarah. To ease Alex and Nicholas's apprehension and help relieve any discomfort the brothers may feel, the women decided to cook a delicious Sunday dinner, one that would help present their husbands and families in a favourable light. New potatoes and fresh vegetables from the garden floated about in delicious sauces of butter and cream. Sarah and her mother had baked Saskatoon berry pies, a western Canadian delicacy, served as desert under gobs of thick whipped cream. No one knew what to expect from these new grandparents.

Margareta was shocked and surprised at what she found. Here in the middle of the wild frontier was a well-constructed and very tastefully decorated farmhouse complete with newly painted woodwork and stylish wallpaper. The fact that indoor toilets, telephone, and electricity had reached this primitive backwater was a further revelation to her. The view from the living room window revealed a naturally manicured valley with trees, green grass, and wild flowers that gently descended toward a winding creek. Margareta was speechless. The house itself, as explained by Heinrich, had been moved to this location by Alex and rebuilt on a sturdy concrete foundation with a full basement. This place would certainly measure up to Margareta's own home, or those of her socially acceptable friends. The table in the large dining room was beautifully set on a white tablecloth with several vases of flowers along with matching dishes and cutlery. Peter and Margareta hardly knew what to say.

Peter carefully introduced himself to everyone in attendance, including each child. In public, when presenting a lecture from behind the safety of a pulpit or lectern, words came easily to him. Now he struggled to articulate the many thoughts and feelings that surged through his heart. When little Stephanie threw her arms around his neck and gave him a hug, he shed tears. She and her siblings and cousins were his great-grandchildren, his progeny, and these offspring were not what he had expected from Christina, his daughter. Whenever he looked at a child, he was sure that he was staring into the face of either Christina Friedrichsen, or her mother, Raisa Brodsky. The few pictures of Christina made him cry. This display of emotion softened his grandsons' feelings toward him. He did notice there were no pictures of Raisa Brodsky, his first wife, his first love. All he had were distant, half-forgotten memories.

During the noon meal, the conversation gradually began to relax. The children had been instructed by their parents to be on their best behaviour, eat in the kitchen, and not interrupt the adults. But the grandparents' more tolerant view of this directive carried the day. The frequent interruptions by the children helped to establish a more relaxed and noisier atmosphere. Heinrich Gerbrandt bragged about Alex and Nicholas, and along with Uri and Ruth Hershberger, missed few opportunities to put the boys at ease by teasing them. Heinrich couldn't resist describing the first few years in Harwood as two skinny, illiterate orphans took up residence in a chicken coop on his yard. "*Dumma Russe Bengels*," (stupid Russian boys) interjected Nicholas. These were probably the living arrangements that Margareta had expected to find. Now, less than twenty years later, both Alex and Nicholas had completed Manitoba high school equivalency, were able to read and write in English, German, and Russian, and were taking courses at Brandon College. They were also prosperous farmers and businessmen.

Uri agreed with Heinrich that Alex and Nicholas were the driving force behind the Gerbrandt and Hershberger farming operations.

After dinner, Heinrich gave Peter Friedrichsen a tour of the farm. In the barnyard, Dick and Tom, the two underworked and overfed geldings slowly trotted over to nuzzle Aaron, Jacob, and their cousins, Ronald and Daniel, Nicholas's sons. The young boys straddling the barnyard fence filled the old men's ears with details no one really cared to hear. Behind the men, walked Nicholas with his daughters, followed by Alex carrying little Stephanie, who interjected her views regarding every situation with additional details she thought her brothers might have missed. Peter didn't want to get his clothes all barn-smelly, so he and the entourage carefully avoided the cow stalls and totally ignored the chicken coop. The little boys wanted to show the old man the haymow where they had built forts and tunnels in the middle of the stacks of straw and hay bales. Peter decided against this idea, promising on his next visit to climb up the vertical ladder to the haymow and examine their straw forts then.

Once through the barn, the tour continued past several large granaries and two grain trucks, towards the newly constructed machine shed. Heinrich opened the huge door to display a wide range of expensive machinery. There was a new self-propelled combine, a swather, and several huge John Deere diesel tractors capable of pulling five and six furrow ploughs at speeds that work horses, even Clydesdales and Percherons, could only dream of. Near the back of the shed were discers, seeders, and grain augers, among other pieces of farm equipment that Peter Friedrichsen had never seen before. With numerous interruptions and corrections by his grandsons, Heinrich attempted to explain in general terms what each piece was designed to accomplish. In the back corner of the building was an office with comfortable chairs, a telephone, filing cabinets, and various pieces of office paraphernalia.

"Who owns this?" asked Peter

"Alex and Nicholas," replied Heinrich.

"Can they afford this?" came the astonished question.

"Let's just say they also own the local John Deere dealership," was the reply.

As the entourage returned to the house for *Faspa*, a light Sunday afternoon meal of coffee, buns and cheese, Peter was speechless. Once inside the house, his thoughts were interrupted by his wife's shrill question, "I hope your new suit doesn't smell like the barn."

"No," replied Peter. "It smells like green John Deere paint and diesel fuel – lots of it."

Peter had agreed to preach at the Sunday evening service of the Harwood Mennonite Church where one final surprise awaited him. The Friedrichsen family in Russia had always valued singing and even Peter prided himself on his strong bass voice. He was delighted to learn that his grandsons had continued this singing tradition and, together with their friends Johann and Willy Bergman, Alex and Nicholas had prepared a song for the evening. What Peter didn't realize was that the quartet had sung together for several years. They had been coached by Helena Gerbrandt and later by Mrs. Stuart, voice teacher and conductor of the Brandon Choral Society who in exchange for singing instruction, asked the four boys to sing in her Christmas and Easter choirs.

The song the quartet chose to sing at this service mirrored the theme of the entire visit, "Marvellous Grace of Our Loving Lord." The singing stopped Peter in his tracks, yet again. He had not heard his father's high tenor voice for many years, but now he heard it again, not once, but twice – first from Nicholas, and then again from Alex. Grace, the theme of the song, was also the topic of his sermon. The song so moved Peter that he tossed aside his notes and spoke from the heart. He told several stories related to the topic and asked the quartet to sing once more. Even Margareta momentarily thought she was back in California. Peter stated his belief that more truths were conveyed through song than through the spoken word, and ended his homily with an expression of heartfelt thanks for the grace and forgiveness he had experienced on this day. He ended with the reading of a verse from Isaiah 35:5: "*Then will the eyes of the blind be opened, and the ears of the deaf unstopped ...*" His certainly had been.

The ride back to Delia found everyone in a more relaxed mood. Conversation flowed freely as Peter shared stories from his childhood and memories of his daughter, their mother, and her extended family. Margareta who also had experienced an eventful day, fell asleep almost immediately as she pondered the many facts and details that had altered her attitude toward people who were not from California. Once she had fallen asleep in the back corner of the car, Peter leaned across the front seat and shared personal details of his life with Raisa Brodsky and her family that he had never shared with anyone, least of all Margareta. He asked the boys to tell him everything they could recall about their mother. The fact that Yitzhak Brodsky had become a high-ranking Bolshevik did not surprise him. Even as a little boy, Yitzhak had shown sufficient craftiness and enough stubborn ambition to succeed in most any situation.

Once the car stopped next to the Epp farmhouse, everyone got out. Peter embraced and kissed both Alex and Nicholas, telling them how much he loved them and how proud he was of them. He begged for further opportunities to visit them. This had been a time of healing for Peter, and an opportunity for reconciliation that even the boys appeared to appreciate. Before the car drove off, they all promised to visit again and to write often.

The next visit never came. Exactly three weeks after their farewell, a telegram arrived in Harwood addressed to Alex and Nicholas Friedrichsen. It read:

Peter Friedrichsen gravely ill (stop) severe stroke.

The next day, before the Harwood relatives could decide upon a course of action, a second telegram bluntly stated:

Peter Friedrichsen died this morning at 7:35 a.m.

A telephone call to Reedley, California confirmed the news that Peter Friedrichsen had suffered a massive stroke and died the following day. Alex spoke to Anne Friedrichsen, a woman his age with whom he shared a grandfather.

At the funeral, next to the coffin of the late Peter Friedrichsen stood a lovely bouquet of autumn flowers with an attached note:

In loving memory, your family from Canada:

Alexander and Marusia, Nicholas and Sarah, and great-grandchildren Suzanna, Aaron, Jacob, Stephanie, and Ronald, Thomas, Daniel, Carolyn and Jennifer.

Chapter 10

Jacob – Tsaritsyn, 1970

JACOB FRIEDRICHSEN, MARUSIA AND ALEX'S SECOND OLDEST SON, WAS A step closer toward realizing his ultimate dream of winning a federal riding and sitting as a member of parliament in the Canadian House of Commons. Some would say that Jacob's new job had simply fallen from the sky, while others claimed that he carried a horseshoe in his hip pocket. But even his harshest critics would have to admit that Jacob had prepared very well for a future in politics, and when the opportunity presented itself, he was ready to take it.

As a freethinking law student, Jacob had drifted away from the principles of free enterprise and small government to which his family members held. Much to the consternation of his father and older brother Aaron, he withdrew his allegiance from right wing political parties that held such views and moved far enough to the left to feel comfortable in the national Liberal Party. Once a Liberal, Jacob was more than just a nominal party member. He was an energetic self-starter who involved himself in various party functions, advocating for local candidates in federal elections and working long hours at fundraising endeavours. At conventions, he made his views known by raising questions from the floor and speaking to controversial policy issues in either English or French, whether or not the situation warranted it. Fortunately for him, the right people took note of this brash young lawyer who, on the one hand, irritated many of the party faithful with his outspoken opinions, but, on the other hand attracted voters by delivering his views in more than one language. And not only in English or

French, Jacob also spoke other languages and moved with reasonable ease within Ukrainian, German and Jewish circles.

James Gleason, a seasoned politician and local member of parliament, became aware of Jacob Friedrichsen, the outspoken young man who according to his advisors could be of use to their cause. Gleason was an astute and experienced politician, recently appointed to cabinet as Minister of Trade and Commerce. His Liberal colleagues, including the prime minister, considered him a valued member of government, but worried that Gleason spoke only English and did not connect well with non English voters. At social gatherings, when under the influence of a few glasses of his favourite scotch, he would annoy his advisors by proudly announcing to all within earshot that he spoke only one language – English – and that he spoke it rather badly. He also had a poor track record for supporting causes sympathetic to French Canadians and there were those in the Liberal party who took note of this.

Gleason's advisors were fully aware of their minister's public image that needed a little polishing and felt that Friedrichsen might be the right person to help Gleason accomplish this. Gleason agreed and decided to meet Jacob. He interviewed him briefly and promptly offered him a job on his staff. Jacob was delighted. He wasn't sure what his new job entailed, nor what his duties would be. He simply knew that he would be spending time in Ottawa, so he immediately began to fine-tune his knowledge of French language and culture.

There were whispers among faithful Liberals that this brash young lawyer was under-qualified for this position. Others, however, felt that a little guidance and a little more experience would enable him to do well among other advisors and lobbyists with whom he would rub shoulders. Besides, his tireless advocacy for the Liberal party had helped Gleason get elected and this service needed to be rewarded.

Jacob certainly had the necessary social skills to get along in Ottawa. Here was an entertaining extrovert who at parties and official social functions could interact with anyone, and do so in several languages. His ability to imitate the accents and eccentricities of dignitaries was also seen as an advantage. At social events, he would impersonate the voices and man-nerisms of others, bringing down the house with laughter, and at times, coming dangerously close to offending his father and grandfather who, unfortunately, had become prime material for his stand-up routines. His classmates claimed that his gregarious personality, rather than his study habits, had helped him attain passing grades. Yet, somehow he graduated with marks high enough to be accepted to the newly-named Brandon University. Here Jacob pursued his favourite activities, namely debating with his professors, arguing with most everyone, and auditioning for major roles in the drama club. Upon graduation, his professors were relieved to pass along this life-of-the-party extrovert to the University of Manitoba School of Law in hopes that he would finally learn to work hard, develop some honest study habits, and reach his full potential. In law school, it became obvious that politics was not merely one of Jacob's interests – it was his only interest. For him, there was no Plan B unless, as he once confessed to several close friends, he could become an actor or perhaps a standup comedian, both occupations totally unthinkable for a Mennonite farm boy from Harwood, Manitoba. Politics was bad enough.

Once in Ottawa, Jacob relied upon the personable qualities he had inherited from his father. "This kid is a good speaker and an adequate debater, and above all, he knows when to speak and when to keep his mouth shut," stated Gleason's chief of staff. Jacob used every opportunity to display his knowledge of languages, an ability that his boss, James Gleason could put to good use while attempting to raise his own profile and advance his own political career. Gleason, in his new position as Minister of Trade and Commerce, correctly realized, that Canada needed to expand its trade with Europe, especially with resource rich countries like Russia that were in need of new technologies to develop their gas and oil resources. Gleason was encouraged to establish personal contact with his foreign counterparts and to travel to Europe to connect with them. Jacob, who spoke Russian, German, and French quite well, was seen as a valuable assistant on such foreign trips.

***

The Friedrichsen family was proud of their son, and secretly a little relieved that the boy who broke machinery, buried tractors in mud, and generally did the wrong thing when it came to anything mechanical, would be earning his living elsewhere. Jacob, as whispered by local farmers, was definitely Heinrich Gerbrandt's grandson. The stories of grandfather and grandson's misadventures with tractors and machinery spiced up many a Harwood conversation.

As concerned parents, Alex and Marusia worried about their son. Ottawa was far enough away, but trips to other lands, especially travel to countries behind the iron curtain, were strongly discouraged. But when the opportunity to accompany Gleason on a trip to Europe presented itself, Jacob chose to ignore the explicit wishes of his parents and gladly agreed to accompany a trade mission into Warsaw Pact countries, including travelling to the USSR itself. Not only did Jacob willingly agree to go, he even suggested to the tour organizers some additional industrial centres that he felt the Minister needed to visit. Had he been aware of his son's plan to visit these Russian cities, Alex would have been deeply, deeply worried. "What if someone were to suspect a connection between Jacob and the pre-Bolshevik capitalists, or between his father and the train crew that had illegally escaped Russia in 1929?" he would reason. At times, Alex was shocked at the Brodsky chutzpah Jacob had inherited from his Jewish grandmother, but then again, the Friedrichsen side of Jacob's genetic make-up also had its own share of willingness to push boundaries.

What no one in Ottawa realized was that Volgograd, the former Stalingrad and a city that Jacob hoped to visit, was the city where his paternal great-grandfather, the first Alexander Mikhailov, had once lived. Marusia reluctantly agreed to let Jacob go. Somehow she had gained the impression that Canadian security guards – in her view an early version of American Navy Seals – would protect the Canadian delegates with tanks and guns.

Jacob prepared for the trip very thoughtfully. He spent about thirty minutes packing his suitcase, checking his passport and travel documents, and spent at least an hour or so hiding Swiss watches, ladies' jewelry, and a wad of American money in one, five, and ten dollar denominations that he intended to take with him. He also carefully studied and memorized maps of the Russian cities the delegation was planning to visit. He had successfully convinced the minister that a side trip to Volgograd, the city that had once armed the Imperial Army, would be of benefit to Canadian industrial interests. He pointed out that factories that had built tanks and guns for the czar, now produced oil and natural gas refining equipment – an interest that Canada shared with Russia. Jacob had read all he could about Volgograd, spoken to members of the Soviet embassy, and learned that the modern factories in this city again produced steel that was cast into various products, mainly automobile and airplane parts. All sensitive munitions manufacturing had been relocated elsewhere, so the Russian government would have no objection to a foreign trade delegation visiting this city.

The tour, as proposed by the Canadians and finally accepted by Soviet officials, was heavily slanted in Russia's favour. The host country, eager to portray itself in a most positive light, would not allow the tour to visit any sites that could possibly embarrass the regime. The tour, of course would include the Kremlin with Saint Basil's Cathedral in Moscow's Red Square and the Hermitage of St. Petersburg, including a brief tour of the Winter Palace that had been stormed by the Bolsheviks in 1917. They would also visit the Bolshoi Theatre in Moscow that was unveiling a new production of Tchaikovsky's opera, *Eugene Onegin*. Jacob had heard stories that his great-grandparents, Alexander and Anastasia Mikhailov, had faithfully supported this theatre and that the opera *Eugene Onegin* had helped to bring his grandparents, Alexander Mikhailov and Christina Friedrichsen together. Later, when the tour reached Moscow, during the performance at this opera, Jacob waited patiently for the "Letter Scene" to be sung. This was the piece of music that his grandmother, Christina Friedrichsen had sung to her boyfriend, Alexander Mikhailov, who became her husband. According to Jacob's father, this piece of music had made Alexander fall in love with Christina and this led to a marriage that produced a son, his father. Jacob did his best to fully appreciate the "Letter Scene" that he easily recognized, but failed to understand why Onegin had not immediately responded to Tatyana's declaration of love and married her, saving him and everyone else in the theatre from an additional hour of Tchaikovsky's music.

***

To the Russian authorities, a tour by a foreign delegation was always a carefully staged event. It was an opportunity to show the world the modern USSR, especially the huge technological advances that had been achieved under a communist government. De-escalating tension between the East and the West was part of their agenda, but Russia fully realized that a bargaining position slanted in its favour needed to be built upon strength. It was not averse to leaving the impression that its military capability was up to that of the USA.

One look at the officials assigned to host this mission, however, must have raised suspicion that Canada, and this delegation in particular, did not rate very highly in the eyes of Andrei Gromyko, the Russian foreign minister. To him, this was merely another opportunity to feed a western country another dose of propaganda, particularly a close neighbour of the United States, and help Russia at the very least boost its foreign image. The Canadians, on the other hand, who in addition to developing trade opportunities with a powerful and resource rich nation such as Russia, were also interested in establishing their own foreign policy, independent from that of the U.S.

Boris Leskow, or "Smiles," as he was quickly renamed by one of Jacob's friends, was the Russian leader assigned to travel with the Canadian delegation. He was the largest member of the group by at least a hundred pounds, and weight, possibly even age, clearly made him the boss. *He must be a faithful party member*, thought Jacob, *because he is not particularly well suited to lead an international trade delegation.*

Smiles wore a dark woolen suit that caused him to perspire heavily yet managed to successfully keep most of his body odours tightly locked up inside. He rarely removed his thick worsted jacket, even on warm days. The jacket in question concealed a white shirt with a visible sweat ring around the collar that constantly threatened to crawl out and slide up the back of his neck. *The shirt must cling to his torso like wet wallpaper,* thought Jacob. Smiles' amply endowed stomach flopped over a strained leather belt that did its best to keep his internal organs where they belonged and where they had once been. Whenever he coughed, his entire body would heave upwards, exposing the tarnished image of a bucking bronco engraved upon a sweaty metal belt buckle holding his trousers and most everything else in place. "Must be a gift from a Calgarian," quipped one of the Canadians.

A hammer and sickle logo stamped onto a red tie hung off to one side of Smiles' neck, and only partially concealed the seriously strained buttons on his shirt. His long, well-oiled hair was slicked straight back. Thick bushy eyebrows, bloodshot eyes, and a somewhat bulbous nose – the centrepiece of his facial features – drew attention away from a gold front tooth that must have cost the Russian state plenty of rubles. His bad breath always carried the room. Even at a distance, his breath reminded Jacob of the smell of fluid that oozed from the radiator of the old Fargo truck on the Friedrichsen farm. *He looks like he could be the son of Grigori Rasputin,* thought Jacob.

The junior tour guide, Viktor Ignatyev, nicknamed "Chuckles," spoke English quite well, but only when Smiles permitted him to do so. He was clearly the brighter of the two who understood most of Jacob's humour. He might even have laughed out loud, had he received permission to do so, but Smiles, his boss, kept a tight grip on the situation keeping him from showing any spontaneous emotion. Chuckles' job, as apprentice to the tour leader, was to sit in a tight seat next to Smiles, learn all he could from his mentor, and absorb the sweat and bad air that escaped from Smiles' body. The fact that the two of them shared a hotel room, and possibly a bed, brought gasps of disbelief from the Canadians. The Russian diet, rich in cabbage, borscht and beans must have created an adventure for anyone attempting to sleep next to Smiles.

Jacob cautiously, yet persistently, joked and schmoozed his way into the hearts of the Russians, mostly humourless individuals who were effectively schooled in the art of stoicism and betrayed no emotion through any facial expression. Jacob spoke with them, asking questions about their families and interests, but always received carefully rehearsed formal replies. The ice between them was only partially broken the day Jacob launched into a comedic stand-up routine of a French Canadian attempting to speak Russian. Initially his act only brought half grins to the faces of his hosts, but eventually several functionaries, especially one bus driver, broke out into laughter. Unfortunately, Jacob's humour was often lost on the Canadians, most of whom understood French almost as badly as they understood Russian.

Chuckles, the younger tour leader, had his English lines down pat. He knew what to say and when to say it, delivering his words with deadpan facial expressions. Most importantly, he knew when to shut up. Smiles frequently interrupted Chuckles in mid-sentence with additional information that Jacob was expected to translate, even though Smiles had no idea what Chuckles was attempting to say at that moment. Jacob thanked Smiles profusely for the valuable information, but took liberties when editing and translating these highly spun facts to his fellow Canadians. Jacob's Russian was very good. Fortunately for him, it was an academic Russian that betrayed little understanding of the vernacular – the street language – the kind of words used by George Zabilski whenever he pinched his finger or struck his thumb with a hammer. Therefore no one ever suspected Jacob's direct lineage to people who were Russian and who once lived here.

James Gleason agreed to Jacob's suggestion to include the city of Volgograd on the tour. Smiles allowed the request and Volgograd became their final stop. This was a major industrial centre built along the confluence of the Tsaritsyn and Volga rivers, and had been the scene of major historical events. Following the devastation of World War II, Volgograd had again risen from the ashes.

Members of the Canadian trade delegation were growing weary of eating Russian food and being regaled with unending facts about Soviet culture. At this point, they were more interested in returning home than visiting more cities, regardless of their historical significance. The entire entourage arrived in Volgograd and checked into a decent hotel. Everyone needed a little rest and relaxation after a gruelling schedule of touring factories, visiting arts and recreation facilities, and listening to an unending description of the wonderful life under Soviet communism. Even Smiles took off a few hours, probably to replenish his private supply of Russian vodka. He left the delegation in the capable hands of his younger assistant, Chuckles.

Volgograd, known as Stalingrad from 1925 to 1961, was of enormous interest to students of history. In 1942 and 1943, it had been the site of one of history's most horrific battles as German and Russian armies fought for supremacy of this city. Close to two million civilians and army personnel perished in the conflict. Although the USSR had prevailed in this vicious battle, the city suffered nearly complete destruction. Fortunately, Stalingrad had been rebuilt, renamed Volgograd, and was again developing important industries. Steel production, shipbuilding, and oil refining were thriving, and the manufacture of airplane and vehicles parts was on the rise. As in other cities, the Russian hosts had again permitted the delegation to tour several, very carefully chosen, industrial sites. But very few members of the tour knew the significance that this city held for Jacob. Few realized that Stalingrad, once known as Tsaritsyn, had been a major industrial centre before the revolution of 1917. Still fewer realized that the initial industrial base of this area had been built and presided over by Alexander Mikhailov, Sr. and, definitely no one knew that Alexander Mikhailov was Jacob's great-grandfather.

Jacob, a student of history, was well aware of the destruction that the German bombing of the Second World War had inflicted upon the city, and the carnage that had been wreaked upon its people. He sadly accepted the likelihood that nothing of the Mikhailov industrial complex would have survived. Nevertheless, he was determined to take a closer look. As the group toured several carefully selected sites, Jacob patiently continued to endure the canned and regurgitated information spewed forth by Smiles and Chuckles. "This is where the Russian people took a stand against Nazi aggression. This is where they suffered incredible losses, and this is where they held ground and broke the back of the German army. Following the city's decimation and upon the ashes of Czarist imperialism and Nazi aggression, the Russian workers rebuilt their lives and rebuilt modern industry" … and on and on.

What the tour delegation did not know, and what Jacob chose not to reveal, certainly not to the Russian tour guides, was the fact that the big push behind this city's pre-revolution industrial development came from Alexander Mikhailov, his great-grandfather. This information had been entirely omitted from Chuckles' canned commentary. Jacob would have loved to uncover old family records, visit cemeteries, or simply enter rooms where his great-grandfather may have lived and worked. There must have been schools that his grandfather attended and churches where his Mikhailov ancestors were baptized. But Jacob was enough of a realist to accept the fact that the German airplanes that mercilessly bombed this city to bits, laid waste to the vast majority of buildings and landmarks, had also destroyed all sites important to him. Besides, his great-grandparents belonged to a different era and a different generation that served Nicholas II, the czar who was assassinated by Lenin and the Bolsheviks.

Could my Mikhailov ancestors have survived the communist takeover with the draconian measures instituted by Stalin against property owners? he wondered. If so, his great-grandfather Mikhailov would likely have been kept as manager of his factories for perhaps a decade or so, at least until a new generation of industrial leaders faithful to Stalin had been trained. Once the communists had sucked all the knowledge out of Mikhailov, they would have likely disposed of him and his family, and no headstone honouring them would have been erected. Jacob also knew that following the communist takeover, grave sites of wealthy people had been disturbed with headstones removed and reused for more important purposes. Jacob was deeply pained by these thoughts. He longed to know more about his ancestors and feel their presence in some way, at least to know where they had lived, breathed and walked.

The big break in Jacob's quest to discover his ancestral roots came on the final day on a tour of yet another memorial site, as Smiles and Chuckles yet again spouted details of the bravery and competency of the Red Army and the sacrificial resilience of the Russian people in holding out against the German army. This particular site, a tiny city museum, included a sizeable pictorial display of areas of Stalingrad before the German bombing and what they looked like immediately thereafter. Although poorly organized, the museum had some interesting artifacts, as well as a number of photos that had survived the war in remarkably good condition. Jacob pored over these, hoping to find some evidence that the Mikhailov factories had existed and prove that stories passed down from his grandmother were true.

After an hour or so in the humid confines of this poorly ventilated space, after most of the delegation had wandered outside, Jacob spotted something beneath a pile of papers that stopped him dead in his tracks. It was a photo, a large photo about eight by ten inches in size, partially obscured by a frame of some sort. It showed a group of men carefully positioned, standing next to a two-storey building. In the background, Jacob recognized two tall smokestacks. The taller one carried Cyrillic lettering that spelled the name "Mikhailov" running vertically from the top of the stack to the bottom. Jacob had viewed this scene many times, perhaps from a different angle, but undeniably it was the same scene. He and his father had studied their only photo of this site many times, and together had speculated about the size and grandeur of the factories and the huge power-generating installations that required stacks of this size to be built. But the picture he now pored over also included people, perhaps a hundred or so. The photo was large enough for Jacob to make out the facial features of some the dignitaries who stood in the front row with the lengthy smokestacks appearing in the background.

This is what he was looking for. These must have been employees, workers at the Mikhailov factories. Contrary to communist propaganda that the wealthy imperialists had abused workers, these employees appeared to be suitably dressed and looked to be well fed. In the foreground, near the main entrance of what must have been the administrative building, stood a group of well-dressed men, probably managers and administrators. In the middle of this group was the imposing figure of a gentleman with a black beard, wearing a dark suit, top hat, and a rather silly pretentious-looking bow tie. The picture was large enough to make out sufficient facial detail to strongly suggest that this was the same person seen in the Mikhailov framed family photo that stood on the Friedrichsen mantelpiece in Harwood. The likeness of the two gentlemen was undeniable. This must be Alexander Mikhailov, Sr. – Jacob's great-grandfather.

Jacob approached the curator, drew his attention to this interesting photo and was flabbergasted to learn from him that these stacks were still standing. Somehow they had survived the ferocious bombing attacks by German planes. The building in front of the tall stacks, that once housed the administrative offices, had been converted into a hospital in 1942 to treat the many wounded. The curator also confirmed to Jacob that his own grandfather and uncles had once worked in this factory. As far as the curator knew, the square two-storey office building in front of the stacks had once again become the main office of a factory that now manufactured car parts. In 1945, after the war, the main powerhouse, miraculously intact, was again fired up and since that time the sturdily constructed tall stacks continued to belch out thick, power-producing smoke.

Following this tour, hopefully the last for some of the exhausted Canadians, the delegation returned to the hotel for a long afternoon nap and a free evening with no prearranged activity. The day ended even earlier for Smiles, who retreated to his quarters to nurse a stronger than usual hangover. He had proceeded to kick Chuckles out of his room and ordered him to sleep elsewhere. Jacob, of course, said nothing to Smiles, but began working on Chuckles, to try to convince him to take a little trip.

By mid-afternoon, Jacob and Chuckles were bumping along the streets of Volgograd in an old taxi, heading to the site of the former Mikhailov factories. A Swiss watch on his wrist, a few U.S. dollars in his pocket, and the absence of Smiles transformed Chuckles into a talkative and friendly fellow. The taxi driver noticed that his old taxi had never run so well. The full tank of gas and the dollars in his hip pocket helped the motor purr like a kitten.

After what seemed like a long adventurous ride through the city along streets full of deep potholes and through intersections where the stoplights had ceased to function, the old taxi approached its destination. They passed new, cheaply constructed apartments, all clones of one another. They saw boarded up houses and buildings where rich people once lived that had only partially survived the German bombing attacks. They passed piles of rubble where something of significance had once stood, now given over to cats and rodents. These were areas not normally shown to tourists. The driver and Chuckles appeared to be embarrassed by the rundown state of this section of the city – Smiles would never have allowed such a side trip.

The taxi continued along deserted alleyways, probably in search of a shortcut, and crossed one or two narrow streets before turning left onto a wider boulevard where weeds and overgrown grass now disgraced an old historic street, ironically named "*Garden Allée.*" And there in the distance they saw the two smokestacks. Jacob waited impatiently as they drove toward the office building and parked in a designated area that was almost totally deserted by cars. By now Jacob was on a first name basis with both Chuckles and the taxi driver. Once they exited the taxi, Jacob asked permission to take their picture, first in front of the taxi, and then standing next to a blooming lilac bush. He strategically positioned the poses to allow the two tall stacks to be clearly visible in the background of each picture.

The factory had lost its strategic importance, so Chuckles relaxed the security measures he was required to follow, and allowed Jacob to walk up to the former administrative building. A watchman, halfway through his mid-afternoon siesta, responded with a smile as Jacob offered him a friendly greeting and pressed a few dollars into his hand. Thereafter, the watchman chose to remain in his comfortable chair as Jacob walked through the main door.

Before Chuckles could react, Jacob trotted briskly up a short flight of stairs, through a set of doors into the general office. Chuckles quickly caught up to him, explaining to the astonished office staff that Jacob was a member of a foreign trade mission that was touring automobile manufacturing facilities in Russia. Jacob's friendly and confident demeanour convinced the office staff that he must be a person of importance. They were so impressed to meet a foreigner who spoke Russian, albeit with an interesting, unidentifiable accent that they offered him a chair. The commotion in the front office caused the director to come out of his inner office to see what all the excitement was about. The director, an amiable fellow, accepted this visit as a personal compliment and an honour he had not expected to receive, certainly not from such a high-ranking dignitary. He promptly invited Jacob and Chuckles into his private office.

Inside stood a huge oak desk, much too heavy to be stolen and carried away, several old over-stuffed leather chairs, and some large oak bookshelves and filing cabinets firmly bolted against the walls. Jacob asked to take the director's picture in his inner office, first a frontal shot and then from several different angles. At Chuckles' suggestion, Jacob was invited to sit in the director's chair. With a huge grin on his face, Jacob struck a number of comedic poses and had his photo taken from several additional angles to allow all the furnishings to be clearly seen on the pictures. Jacob felt that a few compliments to the director and his assistant, as well as a generous donation to the company's social fund would give him full run of the place. Unfortunately, the factory floor had been temporarily shut down for repairs and couldn't be toured.

So, this is where great-grandfather Mikhailov presided over his factories. This is where his wife, Anastasia, would have visited him, probably with their son, Alexander, Jr., who would have crawled across the floor and bounced on his father's knee. This also is where Christina Friedrichsen would have come and brought her baby, Alexander, Jacob's father, had the great-grandparents ever bothered to answer any of Christina's letters.

Chuckles must have sensed that this was no ordinary visit. Surely he suspected Jacob of having some connection to this place. But he said nothing, and was rewarded for his cooperation with an additional American twenty dollars to buy his wife and child something special. The taxi driver insisted they end the visit with a stop at a pub where they could all enjoy a drink. Jacob bought several rounds for the faithful patrons, and sang along heartily with at least two or three Russian songs he had learned from his father.

The next morning, a tired Canadian delegation, a rested Smiles, and slightly hungover Chuckles flew back to Moscow. The Canadians offered a few gifts to their Russian hosts, and Jacob, as a final gesture of goodwill, discreetly gave Smiles a Swiss wristwatch. Afterwards, the Canadian delegation caught the next international flight and left directly for home.

***

Within minutes of landing in Ottawa, Jacob ran to a nearby photo shop, identified himself as a member of the recently returned trade mission to Russia and offered to pay a handsome premium to have his films developed immediately. Then he phoned his brother, Aaron, who happened to be in Winnipeg on business, and asked to be picked up at the Winnipeg airport. With a stack of developed pictures in his briefcase, Jacob returned to the airport and boarded the next flight to Winnipeg.

At 2:00 a.m., Jacob and Aaron arrived at the Friedrichsen farmhouse in Harwood. Together, they barged into their parents' bedroom and began regaling both Mother and Father with incredible stories of Jacob's experiences in Russia. Aaron had already heard these stories on the car ride to Harwood, but wanted to see the pictures Jacob had taken. Aaron was again spellbound by Jacob's stories of the Mikhailov factory. Sitting next to Jacob on their parents' bed, he enjoyed hearing them all again and observing his father's reaction. For an hour or so, Alex Friedrichsen never got a word in edgewise. He reached for his glasses and meticulously examined all the pictures. Then he walked downstairs and compared the pictures of the Volgograd factory with its smokestacks to the photos that he had received from his mother. The whole family affirmed the fact that the picture Jacob had secretly taken of the man with the tall hat and black suit standing in the centre of the large photo was indeed their grandfather and great-grandfather, Alexander Mikhailov, Sr. – Christina Friedrichsen's stories had been validated.

Chapter 11
Stephanie – 1973

THE LAST FRIDAY OF APRIL, THE BUSIEST DAY OF THE MONTH AND BY far the busiest time of the year, saw the Friedrichsen household in Harwood turn into a centre of frenetic activity. The year-end tax returns now almost complete needed to be posted, and now the springtime activities for farmers and machinery dealers were beginning to gear up. At the Friedrichsen home, the telephone rang incessantly.

"So this is what life has become," muttered Marusia to herself as she abandoned her cold morning cup of coffee for the fourth or fifth time. "A person can't even enjoy a few minutes of uninterrupted peace." But she knew well the importance of jumping to the telephone whenever it rang. There were business matters that needed attention – trucks and tractors that depended upon messages for her to relay, and calls from tax accountants who seemingly never got all the details straight. The Friedrichsen business interests had grown well beyond the home telephone, but there were still calls, usually from salespeople or frustrated customers, who needed to speak directly to either Alex or Marusia.

The last call, however, was different. It came from Ottawa, long distance, from someone whose name she failed to recognize and whose voice she could not identify. A deep, officious sounding male voice she dared not ignore asked to speak to a Miss Stephanie Friedrichsen, who fortunately happened to be home for a few weeks and was still fast asleep in her bed. Marusia was relieved to hear that this call was not for her, but at the same time she felt uneasy that a voice she didn't recognize wished to speak to her daughter. *Oh dear*, thought Marusia. *Has this girl lost her passport again?*

Marusia called up the stairs for Stephanie, who stumbled out of bed and with a housecoat loosely draped across her shoulders, half tripped her way down the steps without slippers or socks as quickly as her sleepy legs would allow. Stephanie took the receiver in one hand, rubbed the sleep out of her eyes with the other, slumped into a chair and breathed a feeble "Hello" into the receiver. During the next few moments her facial expressions underwent a complete transformation as they migrated from quasi-comatose boredom, to mild surprise, and finally to wild disbelief. In a voice somewhere between a breathy whisper and a muffled scream, she politely ended the call with "Thank you, thank you very much." Now fully awake she jumped up, threw down the receiver, and let out an earsplitting operatic-like whoop, making Marusia spill her coffee and causing the little family dog to scamper for cover.

"I won! I won!" she screamed.

A day or two later, a registered letter from the cultural attaché of the Canadian Department of Foreign Affairs in Ottawa confirmed the news that had launched Stephanie into such euphoric rapture and at the same time thrown the Friedrichsen household into total disarray. It was marked 'Personal and Confidential', and clearly confirmed the news that Stephanie had won a major international music competition. As the first place winner in the vocal category, she was invited to sing on the stage of the Odessa Opera House where she would be appearing with the Leningrad National Orchestra. From Stephanie's perspective this was all she needed to know – were any other details at this time really necessary?

Marusia shared her daughter's excitement, at least initially, and let out a few whoops of her own. But quickly returned to reality once she realized that Odessa was in the USSR and Stephanie would be required to travel to a city behind the iron curtain, a place from which Marusia and her parents had fled. Stephanie would be entering the land that had claimed the lives of her mother's first husband, her paternal grandparents and many of her relatives. Moreover, it was the place from where her father and her uncle had illegally escaped.

Once Alex Friedrichsen had digested the news and managed to get out a few words of his own, he boomed out his predictable reaction loudly and clearly. "No way!" he shouted. "No one from that blood-drenched land is ever getting near my daughter."

Marusia became quiet as she realized that yet again she would need to negotiate the narrow pathway that existed between her children's ambitions and her husband's concern for safety and security. Aaron jokingly asked how many tractors Friedrichsen John Deere would need to sell to fund additional gowns, coaching fees, and travel expenses. Julie wondered if the shops of Odessa carried Italian fashions, and Jacob, who was home for a few days, insisted on travelling with Stephanie, promising his father that he would never ever again visit Volgograd.

Four weeks later, an Air Canada 747 left Toronto for Frankfurt. Onboard were Alex, Marusia, and Jacob Friedrichsen, and of course, Stephanie. The plan was to leave Alex and Marusia in the safety of a Frankfurt hotel where they would be close enough to the action to "pray intelligently" for the safety of their children without actually entering the USSR. The plan was for Stephanie and Jacob to stay in Frankfurt for several days to overcome jetlag, and then fly on to Odessa. Jacob was instructed to stay with Stephanie at all times. Facetiously, he asked if this also meant accompanying her to the bathroom. Marusia gave her son a gentle swat for that comment. Alex would not allow his wife to enter the USSR. They had both been born there and the stories of Stalin's attempt to repatriate Russian citizens were still fresh in his mind. In his overly cautious nature – paranoia according to his children – Alex believed that Russian rail authorities might still be looking for the two boys who had abandoned their train in Riga almost fifty years ago.

"That train no longer exists," insisted Jacob, "and that engineer named Uri, or whatever his name was, will by now have drunk himself into oblivion. Stephanie doesn't know a single thing about steam locomotives. Why would anyone trace her name to any Brodsky, Mikhailov, or Kotelnikov relative? Besides, why would Russia even want to keep someone like Stephanie who has never held down an honest paying job?"

***

This was Stephanie's first big break. She had previously placed third and fourth at several prestigious competitions, and on several occasions had even received personal notes of encouragement from jury members and conversations of introduction with important conductors and agents. But she had never walked away with any significant prize. Her career continued to depend on a few singing jobs that did not pay very well, and on Mom and Dad's Chargex credit card to help her stay afloat in New York and continue to hope for the big break. Her singing teacher at Juilliard had high hopes for Stephanie. She pushed her into competitions and found performing opportunities for her to advance, or as Stephanie would say, kick-start her career. When this particular competition was drawn to Stephanie's attention she thought, *Not another vocal competition. My confidence can't handle another rejection.* But to keep her singing teacher happy, Stephanie had reluctantly agreed to give it one last try.

The competition in question was sponsored by the Russian Department of Cultural Affairs to be held in conjunction with the 1973 Universiade, a multi-sport event organized by the International University Sports Federation. This year it was hosted by the USSR. These prestigious games were considered by many to be the dress rehearsal for the Olympics as they brought together the world's best student athletes for two weeks of intense competition. As host country, the USSR, always attempting to polish its international image, had decided to add a cultural component to the Universiade. Both the sporting competitions and cultural events were scheduled to be held in carefully selected cities so the USSR could showcase its artists, as well as its athletes, and of course, show off its impressive cultural halls and sports facilities.

Games and sporting activities rarely captured the interest of the Friedrichsen children. They limited their athletic endeavours to pasture baseball played on natural grass with cow pies and salt licks for bases, or pond hockey on natural ice with frozen horse buns as pucks. Upon hearing the exciting news that Stephanie had won something, Jacob immediately researched the Universiade and elatedly announced to all that this was big stuff. These were world events and the world media would be there to cover them.

The cultural component of the Universiade was planned to culminate in a festival of concerts and recitals to be held in the lovely historic and newly-renovated Odessa Opera House, the most beautiful building in Odessa. The USSR advertised these prestigious events internationally, and scheduled them to allow as many foreign dignitaries as possible to attend. In the spirit of open competition, as repeatedly stated on all publicity sent out by the USSR, the final evening was to feature the three winners of the USSR-sponsored International Music Competition for piano, strings, and voice. The winners would perform with the prestigious Leningrad National Orchestra, an internationally acclaimed orchestra. Stephanie Friedrichsen, a Canadian soprano studying at Juilliard in New York, had won first place in the vocal competition.

***

According to Stephanie's over dramatic account, getting to this place had taken her from the heights of heaven to the depths of hell and then back to heaven again. With the encouragement of her vocal coaches, she submitted an application along with a requisite recording of "vocal music from the standard classical repertoire to include four languages and four contrasting styles." Stephanie hired an excellent accompanist, an expensive and first-rate recording engineer, and submitted a very fine recording of her singing. The recording included a Handel aria, Bellini songs, some folk-song arrangements by Mussorgsky, the Schubert *Suleika Lieder*, and her favourite, the aria "Glitter and be Gay" from Leonard Bernstein's operetta, *Candide*. Stephanie was very well prepared – her language diction was good, her Russian pronunciation was excellent, and her personality, prone to the overly dramatic, added an edge of excitement to her singing. At the final competition she showed such a mature understanding of language and poetry that the Russian chairperson who addressed her in Russian was surprised to receive back a few sentences answered haltingly and spoken with a thick Harwood accent.

The requirements for the second round of the competition were more specific. The winners had three weeks to submit a second recording of "three arias or concert pieces from the standard classical repertoire representing three languages and three contrasting styles." Only one piece could be repeated from the first round. Additionally, each singer was required to include a recording of a newly commissioned unaccompanied composition by a young Russian composer that they would receive only two weeks before the application deadline. This new piece, considered a quick study, was set to a series of Russian vowels and vocal sounds – nonsense syllables, as Stephanie called them that, according to her, were totally unsingable. Stephanie's teacher sympathized with her student's frustration and advised her to, "Give it a program. Make it Russian. Make it mean something. Describe something memorable, some scene or dramatic event from your life."

Such as choking myself, thought Stephanie. The event in her life that best matched the unreasonable vocal gymnastics required by the composer was a scene from her childhood where the neighbour's raging bull charged across their yard, tearing up the flowers in its path, and frightening the dogs silly. Her dad had corralled the beast from the safety of a tractor seat. In the lyrical sections of this composition she simply imagined the bull grazing in a quiet pastoral scene, fattening those parts of his body that would find their way as juicy steaks onto someone's dinner plate.

When she later met the composer in Odessa, her eyes widened in disbelief as he complimented her on her mature interpretation and her musical insights, especially her ability to capture the essence of the piece. "Only those singers who understand the Russian soul can fully draw out all the nuances of this music."

Sounds like Russian bull to me, thought a smiling Stephanie.

The second piece that Stephanie submitted was the "Letter Scene" from Tchaikovsky's opera, *Eugene Onegin*. Including this piece in a competition at this level was a risky move and done against the counsel of her vocal coaches. Singers are always advised to stay within their present capabilities. Stephanie was still rather young to understand all the nuances of the character, and probably as yet not mature enough to sustain the entire role over a full orchestra in a large opera house.

"Never confuse a conductor or agent. Never include music beyond your Fach, (vocal category), your present ability," her coaches would warn. "This simply confuses them and presents you as a singer who hasn't yet found her place or discovered who she is." All this was true, and Stephanie was indeed too young to sing the entire role of Tatyana. But she was drawn to this character, and especially to the chosen scene. She loved the music of Tchaikovsky and had the Russian pronunciation and dramatic understanding of the character down pat.

Those who won the second round of the competition were asked to appear in person at one of several centres. The finalists from North America were invited to sing at the Recital Hall in Lincoln Center, New York. Five contestants had made it this far, and each was required to present a half-hour program. Following the New York competition, a jury of five members would travel on to several other centres in Europe and Asia. Following their last stop in Tokyo, they would announce a winner, a runner-up, and a second runner-up.

Stephanie didn't trust the vocal jury. She believed that they were there to frustrate and intimidate the singers. The chairperson, a vocal coach from the Bolshoi in Moscow who addressed Stephanie in Russian, was very professional, as well as kind. He listened attentively. A short fat jury member, probably an Italian tenor, appeared to mouth the words of the Italian arias and conduct certain phrases with his hand, possibly the only music he recognized. A third member of the jury, a tall smartly dressed gentleman stared straight ahead without moving a muscle, with a deadpan expression on his face. Yet, he applauded politely at all the appropriate places. *He is definitely German*, thought Stephanie. Then there was the retired, dramatic, overbearing soprano, who hung baubles, jangles, and pieces of glittering jewelry from various parts of her body. She freely flaunted her opinions in what sounded like Texan English. This woman did not relax into her chair, but sat as close to the table as her ample bosom would allow. A sturdy arm hoisted up on the table supported her double chin. She was the animated one, the one who loudly grabbed a pencil to write a few words of reflective wisdom whenever she detected a mistake. She snorted loudly to remind everyone that only she and the singer knew how large a breath was required to complete the next demanding phrase. Her perfume choked the room. Then there was the final jurist, no doubt a laid-back contralto, sitting all by herself. She felt so comfortable and relaxed that she stifled yawns and appeared to be reading either a magazine or her most recent newspaper reviews. Either she knew the repertoire cold, or didn't have a clue what was going on.

Stephanie began her program with the aria, "Tornami a vagheggiar" from Handel's *Alcina,* a piece she had sung many times. Knowing the aria well boosted her confidence and allowed her to fly through the coloratura passages, ornamenting the vocal lines at will and showing off those high notes that captured everyone's attention. Stephanie felt well rested, properly warmed up, and was prepared to blow away the jury and the audience. The accompanist however, assigned to the contestants was a rugged individualist who claimed to know everything, sight-read anything, and transpose any piece of music into any key. Stephanie thought his tempi, all sixteen of them, were highly interesting, but nowhere near the tempo that they nor Handel, the dead composer, had initially agreed upon. In his piano playing, the man dragged the tempo when she needed forward motion to finish a long line, and rushed when she needed time to control the florid passages she was attempting to ornament.

The next pieces were fine, but she didn't sing as well as she had hoped. Stephanie was still a little rattled by the first aria. By the time "Clair de lune," the second piece from *Quatre Chansons de Jeunesse* by Debussy came up, she had calmed down sufficiently to spin out lovely legato lines with effortless and exquisitely beautiful high notes. The "Allerseelen" and "Zueignung"

Lieder from the next group of songs also went well, but again the tempi chosen by the accompanist completely changed the character that Richard Strauss, the composer, Stephanie Friedrichsen, and God had intended.

At this point Stephanie was angry. Really angry! She felt happy to challenge the conventional wisdom of her coaches and defiant toward those who advised her against singing Tatyana's "Letter Scene." She dug into the first bars with more passion than either Tchaikovsky, the composer, or Pushkin, whose novel the opera was based on, had ever envisioned. The emotion was real. She was frustrated and angry, not with Onegin, the antagonist to her character, but to the studio accompanist who was attempting to pass himself off as a professional. This piece was still a little heavy for her, but the frustration building within her gave her more than enough passion and vocal strength to convincingly perform the piece.

Stephanie sang to the end, offered her most elegant operatic bow, and acknowledged the accompanist with a rather flippant condescending gesture of her hand. The applause and curtain calls that the audience awarded her came as a complete surprise. Angrily, she marched back to the green room and hurled a book entitled, "Italian Arias to Calm the Soul" against the wall. Then she went out for a beer with several friends, something she rarely did.

She returned home a few days later and cried on her dad's shoulder. She ate her mother's home cooking, and contemplated a bleak, uncertain future. Stephanie was discouraged, convinced that her prospects for a career had withered on the vine. Perhaps she should move back to Harwood, learn to drive trucks, sell tractors, and castrate calves ... or perhaps castrate annoying accompanists. Several days later, the telephone rang.

Chapter 12
Return to Odessa – 1973

AN EDITORIAL IN THE TORONTO STAR BRAZENLY INSINUATED THAT Canadian athletes sent to the 1973 World Student Games had embarrassed their country. "Our athletes came home with only one gold, five silver, and a handful of bronze medals … far fewer than countries with smaller populations and poorer training facilities." From Vancouver to Halifax, and all places in between, people were quick to ask, "Were these really Canada's best athletes? Was the coaching up to international standards? Was enough money set aside to send young athletes to world-class events to allow them to sharpen their skills?" To make matters worse, the federal and provincial governments were again disagreeing over who should fund proper athletic training facilities at Canadian universities.

Eugene Lynch, the Canadian Minister of Sports and Recreation, was caught in the middle. On the one hand, he needed to answer the hard questions posed by journalists as to why Canadian athletes had not performed up to expectations. Then on the other hand, he had to defend the athletes and coaches, underpaid practitioners of their passion who had done their best with the limited resources his department had allowed for them. "Why not send Guy LaFleur, Larry Robinson, or a few Maple Leaf hockey stars over there to show those pink commies what sport is all about," he facetiously muttered to his advisors. Escaping his notice was the fact that these were summer games that didn't include ice hockey.

Eugene Lynch was a political appointee, another faithful Ontario Liberal recently rewarded with a cabinet position for some service he had done for the party. His main attribute, according to *The Globe and Mail*, was "his ability to get elected." In many circles, his commitment to sport and recreation, his supposed area of expertise, was called into question by the large belt he needed to keep his beer gut in place. His ample girth simply did not convince anyone that he was dedicated to the task of helping Canadians improve their physical fitness. Someone had even drawn attention to the fact that the words "Lynch" and "lunch" differed by only one letter. Perhaps this is why Eugene felt so drawn to both.

Lynch's commitment to culture, classical music in particular, was even lower on his priority scale than his commitment to sports and recreation. *Why did Canada choose this girl, Stephanie Friedrichsen, as its representative?* he kept asking himself. He had on one or two occasions heard the type of music she sang and was firmly convinced that her style of singing did not represent the musical tastes of the voters in his riding. Personally, he preferred country and western. He had grown up listening to Hank Snow and Willie Nelson. He thought Patsy Cline's songs were about as far as his interests in classical music were prepared to go. Lynch knew what he liked, or perhaps he liked what he knew, and unfortunately that was very little. He also failed to comprehend the fact that Stephanie's appearance at this event was based on her winning first place at an international competition, and not on some arbitrary decision made by some governing body.

The entire trip to Russia made him uncomfortable. Eugene Lynch lived in a world of blue-collar factory workers, autoworkers, and steel workers. These were people with a proper work ethic who paid taxes and made up the backbone of this country. Athletes and artists, however, contributed nothing to society. But here he was in Odessa, mingling with Red Communists and foreign dignitaries whose languages he did not understand, with athletes whose physical pursuits he understood even less, and with classical musicians whose music he didn't understand at all.

***

Jacob Friedrichsen knew how to travel. The card he flashed to Russian customs officials identified him as a Member of the Canadian House of Commons. This totally impressed the authorities who afforded him better treatment than they gave Stephanie, the first place winner of the vocal competition. The diplomatic deference shown to Jacob kept questions from officials to a minimum, and no one asked how much American money he and Stephanie were carrying.

Within hours of landing in Odessa, Stephanie and Jacob were checked into a lovely hotel, among the best Odessa had to offer. Stephanie needed time to acclimatize to the coastal sea air and continue to get over jet lag. The hotel provided her with a spacious studio to practice her regimen of vocal exercises and allow her to sing through the music she had come to perform. Jacob was certainly here to support his little sister. But he had also come to Odessa for another reason, and this reason received his immediate attention. Like other children, he had grown up with stories of his ancestors, grandparents, and great-grandparents. In his case, however, he knew most of these people by name only, and had never met his paternal grandparents. There were pictures, a few letters, but no documents to support these stories and this fact left him feeling rather unsettled. Jacob had grown up with his Gerbrandt grandparents on his mother's side, and an aunt and cousins who lived in Winnipeg. This gave him some sense of knowing who he was. But on his father's side there was a big void. He wasn't even sure whether he should call himself Friedrichsen or Mikhailov.

His father and Uncle Nicholas spoke little of their childhood, rarely mentioning events from their past. Clearly, they were attempting to put certain memories behind them. But in rare moments when the past did come up, one name always surfaced – that of Raisa Brodsky, also known as Christina Friedrichsen, and later as Christina Kotelnikov. This was their mother. When Alex and Nicholas spoke of her, their demeanour would change and interesting details would begin to flow. Their mother, clearly a saint, had left a legacy for her sons to follow that helped them know who they were. Jacob repeatedly heard that at a time when religious practice was being forbidden, Christina firmly stood behind her convictions. Her

Christian faith, her courage, her tenacity to fight for what was right, and for her sons in particular, had not only given them life, but had also instilled in them values whereby to live. This had helped them to endure a difficult childhood and survive a youth filled with fear, insecurity, and danger.

But not knowing what happened to their mother after her death troubled Alex and Nicholas deeply. They had two old letters to go by, as well as the account by Walter Friesen whom they had met in the Moscow train station. They accepted the fact that their mother was dead, but the absence of details regarding events following her death filled them with misgiving. Had her Uncle Yitzak Brodsky indeed claimed her body, as one letter had stated? Had he moved her to Odessa, as presumed, and buried her in some old ancestral plot, or had her remains simply been disposed of in a shallow grave and thereafter violated by vandals or even dogs? This was their fear. In the late 1920s, at the time of her death, Rosenthal was still in the grips of chaos brought on by the Bolshevik revolution. The interment of a poor, penniless widow would not have been very important. If their mother were indeed buried in Odessa, would a proper headstone have marked the location of her grave? Furthermore, would that headstone have survived the events of the 1930s and the tumultuous disruptions of World War ii, or was the account of her burial based on some unverifiable family legend that had evolved over time?

These thoughts plagued Jacob. He knew that the city of Odessa had been spared the ravages of war that Stalingrad had endured, so perhaps there was hope that her grave could be found, if it even existed. Finding it would satisfy Jacob's obsession to bring the final part of her story to a conclusion and allow Alex and Nicholas Friedrichsen to finally experience a sense of closure.

***

On his second day in Odessa, Jacob, with his knowledge of the Russian language, a city map, a cooperative taxi driver whom he had hired for the day, and a wad of American dollars in his hip pocket, set out to search for the grave of Raisa Brodsky. He reasoned that her Uncle Yitzhak Brodsky would have buried his niece under the name of Raisa Brodsky, rather than Christina Friedrichsen, the Christian name given to her by her Christian grandparents. Jacob patiently travelled from office to office, asking many questions. He dealt with bureaucrat after bureaucrat, pored over maps and documents shown to him, and always flashed the card that identified him as a member of the Canadian House of Commons. He skillfully schmoozed his way from one person to the next. By the second day, after walking up and down hundreds of flights of stairs and covering a distance of many kilometres, he succeeded in finding someone who appeared to be interested in his cause.

This official impressed Jacob as being both competent and honest, and his promise to search through old records to see if such a grave even existed gave Jacob a little hope. He felt encouraged and excited. As the day wore on, however, his newfound optimism was overtaken by a sense of reality as he began to mistrust his initial gut reaction. Perhaps this accommodating individual, who was pleasant enough, was more interested in the American dollars left on his desk than he was in helping Jacob. Why should anyone be interested in finding the grave of his grandmother? Perhaps no useful information would be forthcoming because quite possibly there was none.

By mid-afternoon, a confused and somewhat dejected Jacob returned to his hotel room, and sat down and stared at the telephone. He felt he had done all he could. If he did not hear back from this official, he would have to accept the grim reality that no grave marker existed, and worse yet, perhaps the remains of Raisa Brodsky would never be found. At least he could still look forward to Stephanie's performance. By late afternoon, Jacob's patience had reached an end. His hope had run dry. If this official was honest and trustworthy and if he had found something, he would certainly have contacted him by now. In his heart, Jacob felt his quest had reached its end.

It was 5:30 p.m. and all offices were now closed. Jacob decided to head to the restaurant for something to eat and then sleep on the matter. As he opened the door to leave his room, the telephone rang. He quickly rushed back and picked up the receiver to hear a voice say, "I've found something that may be of interest to you. I'm free tonight. If you wish I'll meet you at your hotel in one hour." Was this true? Jacob could hardly breathe. Had he found another history buff, a sleuth like himself who enjoyed solving old family mysteries, or did this person, like Jacob, also have Jewish ancestors that must not be forgotten?

An old beat-up Lada pulled up in front of the hotel main entrance. Jacob got in and was fully prepared to part with a few more American twenty dollar bills. Instead the driver said, "There is a grave of a woman named Raisa, whose last name has been partially erased from the file that I located. She died around 1929 and could be buried most anywhere. But I know of an old cemetery next to a synagogue that my grandparents once attended. Perhaps it's worth a look." Jacob totally agreed.

The Lada bumped along Odessa streets toward an abandoned Jewish cemetery located in an older part of the city, a few blocks from the Opera House where Stephanie would be singing. The bureaucrat, now turned ally, was clearly a history buff. Perhaps he was hoping to reconnect with his own ancestral Jewish roots. Perhaps he was motivated by the biblical imperative known as *zakhor*, the ethical duty to remember. One would need to be Jewish to fully appreciate the strength of this exhortation. The car bumped along streets toward the area where the cemetery was thought to be located. Little did Jacob realize that as they passed the city park, they drove over the exact spot where Alexander Mikhailov, Jr., Jacob's grandfather had lost his life some sixty years before.

The driver parked the car and together they followed an old city map that led them along partially overgrown paths, through abandoned alleys, and along narrow neglected streets. Finally, after a difficult twenty-minute walk they approached a large, old, well-constructed building. Beside it stood a sturdy ancient stonewall. According to his new friend, Jacob learned that at the beginning of the century this old brick structure had been an important synagogue in the city. Jacob walked up to the adjoining old wall, felt along the solid surface and found a protruding stone still securely imbedded in the deteriorating mortar. He cautiously stepped up and leaned over the top. From here, he looked down upon a scene that made his heart sink.

It was indeed a cemetery, but it was woefully overgrown with weeds, tall grass, and bushes, littered with garbage that had been thoughtlessly tossed over the wall. Impressive old headstones in various states of disrepair, yet far too heavy to be pushed over, proudly held their heads above the overgrowth defying attempts to desecrate them. These stones identified the cemetery as a place where rich and influential people had once been buried. But now it was occupied by rodents that fed sumptuously on the thick vegetation and rotting debris that defiled the place. Jacob viewed the sight of a well-fed cat with guarded reassurance.

The two men located the cemetery's main entrance, cut through a chain with a bolt cutter they had brought along, forced open the rusty gate and walked through. To their relief, the light from the setting sun still illuminated the names on many of the old headstones, but on some, they had to brush away fungus and moss in order to read the engraved lettering that weather and vandals had further obscured. They stumbled along over the abandoned terrain through the rubble, moving slowly from stone to stone, stopping only long enough to scrape away enough dirt and moss to read the name. Their pant legs had become wet and dirty and their shoes were caked with filth.

As they neared the back of the cemetery the fear of finding nothing was beginning to take hold. Exhausted and discouraged, and now prepared to give up, the two men made one last push toward the corner farthest away from the front gate before ending this futile exercise. One final glance along the darkening horizon brought Jacob's heartbeat to an almost complete stop. From out of nowhere, a gravestone appeared before him. It was not nearly the largest nor most grandiose, yet it was a stone, a visible and undeniable reminder that Raisa Brodsky, 1894–1929, had once lived on this earth and was buried here. The stone leaned precariously to one side, undermined by the unstable earth that had settled throughout the years creating an ugly hole once the coffin lid had collapsed upon the remains of Raisa Brodsky. Jacob, totally overcome with emotion, walked blindly toward the stone. As he drew near, the slippery mud and grass that stuck to his feet caused him to lose his footing and he slipped and fell into the ugly sinkhole.

With the seat of his pants he landed on a pile of rusty cans and broken glass jars. A nest of rodents who had taken refuge in the hole immediately scampered away in fear. A vandal's tool had chipped away a corner of the headstone, and ugly, green filth along with several decades of bird droppings further desecrated the stone. From his vantage point in the sunken hole Jacob could clearly see the name "Raisa Brodsky." He gasped with emotion, awestruck and dumbfounded at the sight before him, yet at the same time grateful that his dad and Uncle Nicholas weren't here to see the condition of their mother's grave.

The next day, Jacob found the custodian – the person charged with the responsibility of caring for old graveyards. Jacob negotiated a generous financial arrangement with this person. He gave him several hundred rubles and told him that this amount would be doubled if the cemetery were cleaned up within a week, before his return flight to Canada. Jacob specifically requested that the grave of Raisa Brodsky be restored. He asked that the headstone be straightened, cleaned and polished, and the ugly hole filled in. He asked for new sod to be laid around the grave. Whether it was the rubles, or the suspicion that other dignitaries attending the Universiade could also seek their ancestors' graves, is not clear, but the custodian immediately set about to earn the generous fee that Jacob had promised him.

***

On their second day in Odessa, while Jacob was searching for their grandmother's grave, Stephanie attended her first rehearsal with the Leningrad National Orchestra at the Odessa Opera House. She felt uneasy. Communication with the orchestra administration had been minimal and it was difficult to know what anyone expected of her. The conductor, whoever he was, had not even scheduled a piano rehearsal, only one session with the orchestra to be followed by the dress rehearsal and then the performance. Whether he considered Stephanie a seasoned professional who needed little rehearsal time, or saw her as an insignificant student whose singing needn't be taken seriously, is not clear. "Is it below the Leningrad Orchestra's dignity to appear on stage with a student?" she defensively asked herself, "Even one who has won an international competition?"

Stephanie arrived early by taxi, and was shown to a spacious dressing room outfitted with extravagantly puffed up leather furniture and a Persian carpet she was hesitant to walk upon. The room had an ornately decorated high ceiling, as well as a wall with tall mirrors framed by bright lights. She also had her own private washroom. Stephanie immediately began exploring the room to examine the signed photographs of internationally recognized musicians, dancers, and actors who had also dressed here. She calmed her initial feelings of insignificance by singing through her regimen of warm-up exercises, then wandered about and waited.

Ten minutes before her call time, the director of the festival knocked at her door, introduced himself and congratulated her on winning the competition. He then escorted her onto the main stage of the Odessa Opera House. Stephanie was too intimidated to be impressed. With flowery language and grand gestures, the festival director introduced her to Valery Simonov, the conductor, who in turn introduced her to the Leningrad National Orchestra whose members responded with stiff, somewhat disinterested, applause. The size of the orchestra, the large brass and woodwind sections and the sheer number of percussion pieces, confirmed Stephanie's view of her own insignificance. She welcomed the conductor's suggestion to face the orchestra during the rehearsal. *It's probably their only opportunity to hear me*, she thought.

The orchestra, caught up in its own world, tuned quickly and began to play the first piece. Stephanie had only seen a piano arrangement of the score and didn't know what tonal combinations the large orchestra would throw at her. The young maiden described in the first Mussorgsky folksong of her program *Must have been a seven foot, 200 pound Russian peasant girl who might have played linebacker for the Winnipeg Blue Bombers*, she thought. No one asked her opinion regarding tempo, dynamic, or interpretation. The orchestra simply launched into the lengthy introduction with no regard for the singer, who was expected to follow the score and enter at the right time. Stephanie's initial feeling of intimidation was growing into annoyance, but she masked her insecurity and indignation with an outward display of over-confidence. She boldly sang her first entry with full rich tone and continued to meticulously observe all the tempo and dynamic markings indicated in the score.

This was actually the premier performance of this group of songs, at least in this arrangement, and no one was sure what to expect. The conductor had selected and orchestrated four Russian folksongs from a collection by Modest Mussorgsky, and even he appeared to be surprised at what he was hearing. During the first song, Stephanie noticed from the corner of her eye that the director of the festival quietly left his seat and walked toward the lip of the stage. Once the orchestra had finished playing the postlude, he and the conductor made friendly eye contact. They appeared to be happy, perhaps relieved, that the vocal competition had chosen well. The somewhat pompous conductor took note of Stephanie's careful preparation and made mention of her beautiful Russian pronunciation. This compliment was affirmed by the orchestral players with gentle tapping of violin bows on their music stands. The other three pieces also went well. The conductor's suggestions were mainly directed to the orchestra. Stephanie sensed by their expressions that the orchestra members had warmed to her. She was gaining some respect.

The "Letter Scene" from *Eugene Onegin* created some tension. The orchestra had played this opera many times under various conductors and an interpretation, possibly dating back to Tchaikovsky himself, had become ingrained in their playing. Simonov, with less experience in opera, had some of his own ideas regarding Tchaikovsky's style and insisted on introducing these against the orchestra's resistance. His instructions, partially ignored by the orchestra, grew into frustration on his part that overflowed into anger as he abandoned his broken English in favour of more expressive and crude Russian remarks. His cutting directives toward the string section developed into rather patronizing comments toward the singer.

At some point, Stephanie innocently requested clarification on some musical detail and politely articulated her question in good, although not perfect Russian, yet nevertheless vastly better than the English spoken by the conductor. She asked additional questions regarding the psychological mindset of the character Tatyana in this particular scene, and what bearing, if any, this might have upon the tempo. These were questions that the conductor, and probably most orchestral members, had never considered. By the end of the rehearsal, the conductor and the orchestra were on her side.

Gone were the patronizing comments from the conductor and the cynical sideways glances by the orchestra members. Here was a singer, a young woman from North America, who had studied the score thoughtfully, had arrived at an interpretation she was willing to defend, and this deserved respect. Following the initial session with the orchestra, the conductor requested a piano rehearsal with Stephanie to solidify some of the musical details that had been discussed.

The day of the final concert arrived. That morning, Jacob and Stephanie took a taxi to the gravesite where Raisa Brodsky lay buried. They had come to give their grandmother the memorial service she probably never had. The grave had been restored to Jacob's wishes. He and Stephanie lovingly placed a large bouquet of beautiful summer flowers into an elegant vase, placing it next her headstone. They sang the hymn, "Gott ist die Liebe" (God is love), a song their grandmother would have known and likely would have sung to them had she been with them during their childhood. Next they read passages of scripture from the Psalms and offered prayers. They then took pictures of the gravesite and walked away. Stephanie returned to her hotel room to begin preparations for her performance that evening.

The concert, the final event of the Universiade, was scheduled to begin at 8:00 p.m. The closing ceremonies for all sporting competitions had drawn to a close, and all cultural events associated with the Universiade had now taken place. This concert, the encore for the Universiade, was the final event. The Russian authorities, as reported in the press, were pleased with the results of the Universiade. Their athletes had performed well and the USSR had successfully showcased those parts of their country they wanted foreigners to see. Russia's international reputation for excellence in the arts, especially ballet, had yet again been established. Now at this concert, they wished to demonstrate to foreign dignitaries the largesse of the USSR, which had not only sponsored an international music competition, but also allowed three student winners – all foreigners – to perform on the stage of the Odessa Opera House with their internationally acclaimed Leningrad National Orchestra. In the first half of the program, the audience would hear a violinist from Germany, followed by a pianist from Tokyo. And in the second half, they would hear Stephanie Friedrichsen, a soprano from Harwood, Manitoba.

It was a beautiful evening and Eugene Lynch, ever the good politician, arrived early with interpreters Andy Chernikov and Alfred Friesen in tow. The three presented themselves in proper concert attire – tuxedo suits, ruffled shirts, and black bow ties – all paid for by Canadian taxpayers. Lynch and his entourage of two established their presence by confidently parading up and down the beautifully decorated promenade before making their entrance into the Opera House, past the main doors and through the elegant foyer that had once so intimidated Christina Friedrichsen. Lynch continued to dish out a series of well-rehearsed compliments to Soviet officials, foreign dignitaries, and most everyone who looked important.

The officious demeanour of Eugene Lynch was in stark contrast to the foul humour he successfully hid from view. He felt coerced to attend this final musical event that he considered to be a total waste of his valuable time. A further contributing factor to his bad mood was the seat to which he had been assigned. He, a Canadian of rank, was expected to sit near the back of the main floor and off to the side while the rows ahead of him were occupied by the elite, the people of high society, whose hands he was expected to shake and whose egos he was expected to kiss up to. These were Soviet dignitaries, foreign government representatives, sports celebrities, and even Americans, while he, the leader of the Canadian delegation, was asked to sit near the back squeezed between his two aides. He knew that Jacob Friedrichsen had managed to trade main floor tickets for front row balcony seats that he in turn had distributed to other Canadians. Why had he not been included in Jacob's inner circle? Perhaps Lynch hadn't yet comprehended the fact that Stephanie Friedrichsen was Jacob's sister.

During the first half of the concert, Lynch sat quietly and applauded at all the correct places. During intermission, he continued his practice of glad-handing his way from one end of the foyer to the other, fearing that the pasted smile on his face could become permanent. While he was conducting his official duties, a brilliant plan began to take shape in his crafty little mind. When the bells summoned the concertgoers back to their seats to begin the second half, he pulled it off perfectly. With the audience moving in one direction toward their seats, this sneaky old buzzard struck out in the opposite direction, walking slowly toward the washroom, then just as the last few people were settling into their seats, he discreetly slipped out the side door.

The aides, who were instructed to stay at his side at all times and follow a step or two behind, were suddenly surprised to find themselves outside the Opera House. *Free at last!* thought Lynch. He complained that the close air in the concert hall was adversely affecting his breathing, a condition he had only very recently discovered. He reasoned that all three of them had more than adequately fulfilled their obligation to Canada, to the Russian hosts, and especially to classical music.

A gentle knock at the dressing room door let Stephanie know that the people were returning to their seats and the second half of the concert was about to begin. Stephanie had completed her regimen of physical and vocal warm-up exercises, had checked and double-checked the zippers, hooks and eyes of her gown, and had straightened her pearls and earrings for the hundredth time. She confidently walked out of her dressing room, perspiring on the inside, but exuding calmness and complete control on the outside. The conductor, Valery Simonov, greeted her most warmly and reassured her she would sing very well. The patronizing grin he had displayed upon their first meeting had disappeared, wiped off his face by the quality of Stephanie's talent, or perhaps by the common experience shared by seasoned musicians who, before a performance, frequently experience an "us against them, we'd better stick together" feeling. Simonov offered her his arm and told Stephanie how lovely she looked. Then at the precise moment the orchestra finished tuning, he led her onto the main stage of the world famous Odessa Opera House.

"Practice what you know," Stephanie told herself. "Inhale slowly and deeply as you take four steps – one, two three, four – then exhale slowly during the next four." This was her trick for remaining calm, keeping her heart from racing, and above all, maintaining control of her breath. She reached centre stage and politely acknowledged the applause with the smile she had inherited from her grandmother, Raisa. The applause appeared to be louder from the orchestra behind her than from the audience. *The musicians are on my side*, she thought. She established eye contact with the conductor and nodded as if to say, "Let's go."

Stephanie looked lovely. Her hair was done in an up-do held in place by jewelled combs. Her floor-length royal blue gown of flowing chiffon was a last minute purchase found in Winnipeg and refitted for this occasion. Her sister-in-law, Julie, loved the gown, though her mother, Marusia, felt that the neckline plunged too low. But after a series of practice bows, Stephanie convinced her mother that everything would be securely held in place and from a distance nothing would be revealed to anyone. Alex had gulped at the cost of the gown, but no one had yet told him how much the elegant string of pearls that completed the ensemble had cost. He spoiled his youngest daughter and reasoned that the sale of one or two more John Deere tractors would cover the cost of this entire adventure.

Outside the concert hall, a lovely warm spring evening with a gentle breeze off the Black Sea graced the visitors who had come to Odessa. Coats and umbrellas were entirely unnecessary. Lynch half-apologized to his aides and again reassured them that their official obligations to Canadian taxpayers had been fully met. He advised them that a walk in the fresh air would help digest the rich food they'd eaten earlier at the sumptuous banquet spread for the foreigners by their Soviet hosts. Lynch thought he could get a review of the concert from some of his American counterparts, just enough information to convince Jacob Friedrichsen, whom he described as a puffed up peacock, that he had really enjoyed his sister's singing.

Stephanie began the second half of the program with a group of Mussorgsky folk songs orchestrated by the conductor, Valery Simonv. These were pieces most Russians knew very well. The first song entitled, "The Mockingbird Sang No More," is a strophic tune sung by a peasant girl who falls in love with a young officer, the son of a wealthy father, but is forced to give him up when he is tragically killed. The piece went quite well. Stephanie kept her voice positioned high and forward, knowing where to place the Russian vowels, and managed to maintain secure breath support on those "stupid low notes" that Russian composers love so well. The forte phrases were probably a little pushed. "Stay within yourself, don't try to knock out the back wall. Make the orchestra adjust to you," she mentally repeated to herself. This oft-stated advice had been drilled into her head by her vocal coaches. She allowed the high note to soar effortlessly above the audience and heard a few snorts from the conductor that she interpreted as compliments.

Following the first song, some idiot from the balcony broke into applause before the entire group of songs had been performed. Fortunately this graceless interruption died just as quickly as it began, as neither Stephanie nor the conductor responded. *Silly Jacob ... should have left him at home,* thought Stephanie, smiling to herself. Jacob was sure that he had detected a little dryness in his sister's voice and had decided to give her a moment to bite her tongue, or rearrange the piece of apple in her cheek, or whatever she needed to keep her saliva flowing. He was the one who had started the applause.

The other three pieces in the group were not as vocally taxing as the first and these also went well. The orchestra was a delight. The ensemble playing was very tight, the balance was perfect, and the conductor knew exactly how to meld the various colours into a beautifully homogenous sound that carefully supported yet never overpowered Stephanie's singing. The audience was very reassuring. Those who understood Russian and were familiar with the songs generously expressed their appreciation of her impeccable pronunciation and also her high notes, which when she was on, were incredibly beautiful. Tonight she was on.

***

Lynch and his aides were relieved to notice how well the music carried outdoors in the cool evening air. The Opera House was not air-conditioned and the temperature during the first half of the program rose steadily as the poor performers and audience members were contending with heat generated by the bodies of the well-fed dignitaries. During intermission, the windows and doors of the Opera House had been flung open and left that way. The police were instructed to keep noisy traffic far away. This suited Lynch and his aides perfectly well. They found they could walk a distance from the Opera House and still hear the music. This encouraged them to slowly make their way around the back of the Opera House, and then stroll along a quiet alley for a block or so. The fact that they could still hear the music allowed them to walk still farther. Lynch was confident that he could hurry back and mingle with the appreciative audience once the final applause had ended.

The alley along which they walked, squeezed into a narrow path that led directly to a rusty iron gate partially concealed by overgrown bushes. This back gate had recently been repaired and left unlocked. With a hefty push, it creaked open once again and the inquisitive visitors invited themselves in to look around. This suited Andy Chernikov, a student of history, very well. Once past the gate, they made their way to the far corner of an old cemetery where large, impressive head stones told the story that important people had once lived in this area. The cemetery had been neglected, yet very recent attempts had been made to clean up the place as grass had been mowed and weeds trimmed. Some stones were damaged with corners chipped off, and others had been defaced and vandalized. All were seriously weathered.

They noticed that some recent attempt at restoration had been made. Someone had tried to remove paint and graffiti from the stones and had taken pains to straighten them into their rightful positions. As Lynch and his aides turned to leave, the last light of the setting sun reflected brightly off the face of a shiny, recently buffed stone that looked like it didn't belong here. This caught the attention of Andy Chernikov. "Let's have a closer look," he said.

Lynch felt he had to accede to Andy's wish. After all, he had pulled his young aide from a concert that he, no doubt, would have enjoyed. The men could still faintly hear the second piece on the program, the overture to Beethoven's opera *Fidelio*. This orchestral overture was a tribute to non-Russian music allowed by Soviet cultural authorities. The opera's heroic theme tells the story of Leonora, disguised as a prison guard named Fidelio, rescues her husband Florestan, a political prisoner, from death. The theme of love and courage conquering political oppression fit in well with the communist credo. State authorities had allowed this composition to become a favourite of the Leningrad National Orchestra.

The headstone that caught the attention of Lynch and his aides had been hewn out of dark gray granite neatly cut on all sides with a name and dates in Cyrillic lettering engraved on the front surface. "Raisa Brodsky," read Andy Chernikov, "1894–1929." The stone had been recently polished, the gravesite tidied, and the grass around the stone neatly manicured. Leaning against the stone was a beautiful vase with a lovely bouquet of freshly-cut flowers.

"Looks like someone's relatives finally got around to paying their last respects," quipped Lynch. "Maybe they should have done more while this person was alive."

There were no other markings on the stone – no icon linking the person to any denomination. There was no cross, no star of David, nothing to indicate the person's religion or racial origin. Yet, the stone stood out from the rest. But what caught the attention of the guests was the size and beauty of the stone. "Who in 1929, at a time when Russia was still in turmoil, could afford something like this?" asked Andy Chernikov, a student of Russian history. "Her family must have been high ranking members of the Communist Party."

Alfred Friesen, a member of the Canadian delegation, asked Andy Chernikov to read the name again. Upon hearing it read aloud for the second time, he reflected for a moment as though he had known or at least heard of a person by this name. Slowly memories began to return to his mind as he recalled hearing his father tell the story of a girl by this name who had once lived next door to his late father's family in Rosenthal, a village near Zaporozhe. "My parents talked about a girl named Raisa Brodsky, who also went by the name Christina Friedrichsen." As he began to piece together his recollection of interesting details, further information flooded back to him. "Something about her, or perhaps the circumstances that followed her, were details that bothered my dad his entire life. 'We sinned against this girl,' my father once said. 'We drove her out of Rosenthal. We caused her to run away from home, and after that her life spiralled downward.'" Andy Chernikov and Eugene Lynch began listening with interest.

"According to my father, there was some family scandal with her older brother that somehow reflected back upon her. As a young teenager, Raisa, or Christina as she was also known, left home and somehow ended up in Odessa. A year or so later she returned with a baby in her arms, claiming that she had married an army officer who had been killed. Of course, no one believed her story, least of all the part that her late husband's family was well off and that they would soon be sending for her. The war had not even yet begun. People had pity on her and gave her menial jobs, paying her a pittance so she could care for her baby and her aging grandparents. But the malicious gossip continued. A year or so later when it became obvious that no rich family would ever send for her, she moved in with a Russian school teacher whom she claimed to have married and soon after had a second baby." Lynch was engrossed by the details of Friesen's story and, together with Chernikov, began asking questions.

"According to my father, she lived with this schoolteacher together with her two boys. Later, they heard that the schoolteacher had been fired from his position and died shortly afterwards. The young widow was again plunged into poverty. People helped her, but never accepted her socially, and the gossip about her was merciless. Although my father did not know her well, he felt guilty about the treatment he had allowed his younger sister and cousins to show this girl."

The others were now fully captured by Friesen's story. "What happened to her?"

"My father never said," replied Friesen. "Apparently, when her boys became teenagers, they were seen riding with Nestor Makhno, and his army of anarchists."

"Bad mistake," interjected Chernikov. "Very few of Makhno's men survived. Many died of typhus brought on by filth and malnutrition, or were killed. The Red Army under Trotsky finally defeated them, I believe, and probably forced the survivors to join their army. Makhno escaped to Paris and died of natural causes. But many members of his gang did not fare as well."

Alfred continued, "Even at the end of his life, my father wondered what would have happened to Raisa had the people treated her with kindness and respect and accepted her? Would her boys have survived? Would they have needed to be swept up and consumed by the anarchy of the time?"

***

Stephanie left her dressing room, this time to sing the aria by Tchaikovsky, considered by the conductor to be the centrepiece of the program. It was the "Letter Scene" from *Eugene Onegin*, a lengthy dramatic outpouring of emotion by a teenage girl who wrestles with her feelings of love for the character, Eugene Onegin. As she walked toward the stage, she passed a staircase that led to an outside door. Little did she realize that her grandmother Raisa and grandfather Alexander had many years before pressed their ears against this door to hear the very piece she was about to sing. Stephanie looked the part, and like her grandmother Raisa, she could sing the part. Now she walked out to generous applause from both the audience and also from the orchestra. This boosted her confidence.

The orchestra began the introduction to set the stage for the scene. Stephanie needed to trust the conductor, whom she had won over to her side, to hold the orchestra from playing too loudly and overpowering her.

For her part, she was determined to be heard. *They may not like me,* she thought, *but they will not forget me.*

Stephanie loved the role of Tatyana and had studied the score extensively. She had written a music history paper about this scene and felt she understood the character and situation very well. But Tatyana had feelings that Stephanie at her tender age had probably not experienced, certainly not as deeply as the feelings her grandmother Raisa would have shown when she sang this piece to her lover, Alexander Mikhailov. Stephanie threw caution to the wind, and determined to allow her confidence to mirror the recklessness of the character, Tatyana, who as a young girl was breaking all rules of propriety by declaring her love to Onegin, a pompous, self-absorbed egotist. Her voice was warmed up and it was time to rely on her vocal technique. She knew her high notes, and her ability to reflect drama and emotion through her rich tone were her strongest assets. "Dance with the one who brung you," was advice from her vocal coach that kept playing in her mind.

At the beginning of the piece, Stephanie feared she was giving too much. She didn't want to tire too quickly and needed to save her best for the final A-flat waiting at the end of this fourteen-minute scene. The low notes were of greater concern than the high notes. Too much push or insecure breath support could result in weak, thin sounds. The drama was there. The audience, especially those who understood every word of her perfectly sung Russian, saw the character Tatyana wrestle with her feelings while writing a letter, then tearing it up, and finally committing to paper exactly what she felt. The climax was sung with a dramatic flourish that contained every ounce of intensity Stephanie was capable of producing. The passion in her singing mirrored the passion in her grandmother's singing, as well as the passion that the character Tatyana felt as she finally convinced herself to cross all lines of propriety and pour out her feelings of love to the pompous Onegin who went on to reject her. The audience was sure that at least several worthless louts, like the character Onegin, had broken the heart of this poor vulnerable girl. Stephanie finished the aria breathing as heavily as any athlete who had just completed a marathon, and perspiring just as heavily into her lovely gown. The audience sat perfectly still, enraptured in silence for what seemed like minutes until the conductor lowered his stick. Then they erupted into thunderous applause. In one great gesture they rose to their feet and shouted "Brava!" in any number of languages and accents. Some, mainly Americans, even dared to whistle – something considered rude by the Europeans.

In the quiet distance, the three Canadians still in the cemetery also heard Stephanie pour everything she had into the climax of the aria. In the stillness of the evening air, her voice projected beautifully, as did the sound of tumultuous applause that followed. Alfred Friesen quit talking and listened. *Perhaps somewhere in the great beyond, Raisa Brodsky, also known as Christina Friedrichsen, whose body lies buried here, is also listening,* he thought.

Sitting on his haunches, Andy Chernikov reflectively ran his fingers along the perfect lettering of the name "Raisa Brodsky" cut into the polished headstone. *Why is a name so obviously Jewish written in Cyrillic rather than Hebrew lettering?* he wondered.

"Let's get back," Lynch suggested.

"Take your time," assured Friesen. "There will be at least one encore. There always is."

"Do you think that the person buried here could be the same Raisa you told us about?" asked Lynch.

"It's possible," answered Friesen. "The dates match, and she did have contact with people in Odessa."

The conductor immediately silenced the applause as he escorted Stephanie back onto the stage for an encore. They strained to hear Valery Simanov announce that she would be singing the "Vocalise" (song without words) by Sergei Rachmaninoff. Simanov failed to mention the fact that Stephanie had not rehearsed the piece with the orchestra. At their first meeting, Stephanie had suggested this "Vocalise" as an encore, but both conductor and concertmaster thought it was too long and too grandiose and rejected her suggestion. Besides, an encore after such a lengthy program likely would not be necessary. But this was decided before they had heard Stephanie sing the Tchaikovsky "Letter Scene." Following the first rehearsal, the conductor began to question the wisdom of this earlier decision, and certainly after the dress rehearsal he knew that there could be a change in plan. He requested the librarian to have the orchestra parts of the Rachmaninoff on hand. Tonight, Stephanie's rendition of the "Letter Scene" had so impressed him that once they were off stage, he hugged her and whispered into her ear that they should do the Rachmaninoff piece. Stephanie agreed. They quickly discussed tempi and repeated sections and then walked back on stage.

The orchestra began the introduction. Stephanie was happy with the tempo. She loved the piece, having sung it several times before. With beautiful tone, she delivered a pure and honest performance. She allowed her musical instincts to shape the phrases and never called unnecessary attention to her singing by interjecting tempo or dynamic changes not called for by the score. The conductor decided to help Stephanie by pushing the tempo through the climax, the ascending line that led to a high C-sharp. But this was entirely unnecessary. Stephanie held a steady tempo with perfect breath control as her voice floated smoothly through this difficult passage. The retard at the height of the phrase was given its full due and her exquisitely beautiful high C-sharp soared effortlessly through the Opera House, through the open doors and windows to the place where Lynch and his aides were patiently waiting to re-enter the foyer. Alfred Friesen and Andy Chernikov were trying their best to listen.

The applause was tumultuous.

Lynch continued to reflect upon the life of Raisa Brodsky. He was engrossed by Friesen's story and was still asking questions. "Surely, the woman in the grave we visited is not the same person whom you told us about?"

"Who knows?" answered Friesen.

"So if it is indeed the same Raisa as you have suggested, what would have happened to her sons, the ones who got mixed up with the gangs of anarchists?" he asked.

"They would have perished," replied Andy Chernikov.

239

"They simply never had a chance," affirmed Alfred Friesen.

About the Author

HAROLD WIENS IS A SINGER AND PROFESSOR EMERITUS WHO RECENTLY
retired from the Department of Music, University of Alberta, where
he held a teaching position for thirty-five years. A graduate of Wilfrid
Laurier University, Harold spent five years studying and performing in
Germany, and graduated from the Nordwestdeutsche Musik-Akademie
with honours. He has appeared as recitalist and soloist with orchestras and
choral societies in a number of countries throughout Europe. Also, he has
performed across Canada and the U.S.A. Radio and television recordings
include appearances on the national CBC networks and recordings for
Radio-Canada International. He has published his research on the role of
voice training/development in managing stress and also its healing effect
upon Parkinson's Disease.

Harold and his wife Diana are empty-nesters who live in Edmonton,
Alberta. Their daughter Juliana is in Halifax and their son Michael, wife
Brooke and grandchildren Braxton and Alexa live in Burlington, Ontario.

The fictional events in this book were inspired by the experiences
of Harold's parents, Nikolai and Anna Wiens. In 1925, as Russian
Mennonites, they immigrated to Hepburn, Saskatchewan from Tschongrav,
Crimea. Two years later, they relocated to Manitoba where they survived
the Great Depression on farms in Holmfield and in the Killarney and
Dauphin areas.